White Rebels in Black

Social History, Popular Culture, and Politics in Germany
Kathleen Canning, Series Editor

For a complete list of titles, please see www.press.umich.edu

White Rebels in Black

German Appropriation
of Black Popular Culture

PRISCILLA LAYNE

UNIVERSITY OF MICHIGAN PRESS
Ann Arbor

Published in the United States of America by the
University of Michigan Press
Manufactured in the United States of America
⊛ Printed on acid-free paper

2021   2020   2019   2018   4   3   2   1

A CIP catalog record for this book is available from the British Library.

Library of Congress Cataloging-in-Publication Data

Names: Layne, Priscilla, author.
Title: White rebels in Black : German appropriation of Black popular culture / Priscilla Layne.
    Description: Ann Arbor : University of Michigan Press, [2018] | Series: Social history, popular culture, and politics in Germany | Includes filmography. | Includes bibliographical references and index. | Identifiers: LCCN 2017053881 (print) | LCCN 2018004612 (ebook) | ISBN 9780472123834 (e-book) | ISBN 9780472130801 (hardcover : alk. paper)
Subjects: LCSH: German literature—20th century—History and criticism. | German literature—Black authors—History and criticism. | Blacks in literature. | Masculinity in literature. | Blacks in popular culture—Germany—History—20th century. | Motion pictures—Germany—History—20th century. | Blacks in motion pictures. | Masculinity in motion pictures. | Blacks—Race identity—Germany. | Whites—Race identity—Germany.
Classification: LCC PT149.B55 (ebook) | LCC PT149.B55 L39 2018 (print) | DDC 830.9/896—dc23
LC record available at https://lccn.loc.gov/2017053881

This book is dedicated to my son, Liam Herbert Layne-Kopf, and to my late maternal grandparents, Gloria Williams and Livingston Phillips.

Acknowledgments

It takes a village to raise a child. It also takes a village to transform a student into a scholar and bring a book from concept to publication. This book would not have been possible without a wealth of people who have supported me both professionally and personally.

First and foremost, I'd like to acknowledge the two people for whom I have my existence to thank: my mother, Diana Lucinda Layne, and my father, Bancroft Earl Levy. My parents immigrated to the United States from Barbados and Jamaica respectively. If it weren't for their own drive for success and their value of education, I wouldn't be where I am today. And they have continued to support me through adulthood, sometimes with financial support, often with emotional support or childcare. I experienced a lot of ups and downs during these past seven years, and if it were not for my parents' love and support, this journey would have been a lot more difficult.

Second, I'd like to thank my academic mother or *Doktormutter*, Deniz Göktürk. Deniz has been a mentor to me since my first days of graduate school at the University of California at Berkeley. She was often a tough critic, but that is exactly what I valued in our relationship. I knew she would not accept anything mediocre. And though it sometimes felt her suggestions sent me down a rabbit hole of references, in the end her recommendations were always valuable and I'm glad I went down that rabbit hole. Deniz is definitely the person whose academic endeavors have been most influential in my professional life. And on a personal level, she is a cherished friend with whom I look forward to keeping in touch for many years to come. There were several other professors at Berkeley who were also influential, helpful, and supportive, especially the other two members of my dissertation committee: Tony Kaes and Jocelyne Guilbault. Also special thanks to another professor in the UC system, whom I was lucky to meet during her stay in North Carolina, Jane Newman. Finally, a special thanks to several people who made graduate school a lovelier experience: Kristin Dickinson, Robin Ellis, and my fellow cohort member and dear friend Melissa Etzler, who actually volunteered to proofread my dissertation free of charge so many years ago. Thanks also to Paul Dobryden for telling me about the film *Ich küsse ihre Hand, Madame.*

I am blessed to have not only been mentored by professors at my home institutions, but also by many people in the fields of German studies and African diaspora studies who luckily were willing to give me advice on my work and career. Several of those people are members of Women in German Studies, like Sara Lennox, Faye Stewart, and Hester Baer. Some of the mentors outside of German studies are Tina Campt and fellow Mellon Mays Fellows Michelle Wright and Kimberly Juanita Brown. And of course there are colleagues abroad who have been helpful as well, especially Sabine Broeck, Frauke Berndt, Lily Tonger-Erk, and Franziska Bergmann.

Since joining the faculty at the University of North Carolina at Chapel Hill, my group of friends and family has grown to include many wonderful colleagues. Some of the people in German studies in North Carolina who have aided me with career advice, feedback on my writing, and general life coaching are Inga Pollmann, Gabriel Trop, Ruth von Bernuth, Richard Langston, Jonathan Hess, Clayton Koelb, Ewa Wampuszyc, and Jakob Norberg. There are also many colleagues across campus in other departments who have been equally supportive, like Ariana Vigil, Michael Palm, Karla Slocum, Kia Caldwell, and Patricia Parker. And a special thanks to my fellow scholars of Black German studies, who have included me in their panels, shared book titles with me, given me emotional support and feedback on my work, and inspired me with their own awesome endeavors: Fatima El-Tayeb, Peggy Piesche, Michelle Eley, Jamele Watkins, Kira Thurman, Sonja Donaldson, Tiffany Florvil, Karina Griffith, Rosemarie Pena, and Vanessa Plumly.

Regarding this book in particular, a few years ago, several scholars attended a book manuscript workshop, for which they read an earlier draft of this book and generously gave me their time and feedback. Those people are Leslie Adelson, Katrin Sieg, Jonathan Wipplinger, Fitzhugh Brundage, Ann Marie Rassmussen, Adriane Lenz-Smith, and Jonathan Hess. Furthermore, this book would be nowhere as good as it is if not for the extensive feedback provided by Sara Lennox and Michelle Wright, whose suggestions for improvement were priceless, as well as the generous help of Sohini Sengupta at the Center for Faculty Excellence at UNC and Sonam Singh, my absolute favorite copy editor. I would also like to thank the staff at the University of Michigan Press, in particular LeAnn Fields, Christopher Dreyer, and series editor Dr. Kathleen

Canning. And a special thanks to Philipp Khabo Köpsell, who is the one artist discussed in this book with whom I've had personal contact. Philipp has been supportive of my work, both by agreeing to an interview several years ago and by giving me a free copy of the book *Afro-shop*. I am eternally grateful and I recognize how indebted I am to black German artists who are willing to take the time to speak with me. I hope this book brings well-deserved attention to the black German community, including its wealth of talented artists.

I want to thank all of the faculty and staff whom I've met over the years, who are associated with the Mellon Mays Undergraduate Fellowship and the Moore Undergraduate Research Apprenticeship, including Elise LaRose, Josephine Moreno, Rosa Perelmutter, Charlene Regester, Kennetta Hammond Perry, Sandy Darity, and countless others whom I have not named individually. Programs like MMUF and MURAP help support young scholars of color like myself, who otherwise would feel totally lost and alienated in this world of academia. As you can see, I received a lot of help in my endeavors, and words really cannot express the gratitude I feel for all of these people and many more whom I could not name individually. I hope to give back to the academic community, my local community, and a global community of activists and scholars as a show of gratitude to all of these people who have made this book possible.

Finally, I would like to thank the artist Marc Brandenburg for generously providing the image for the cover from his performance "Full Circle" and Juergen Heinrichs for helping me get in touch with him. And thank you to Cambridge Scholars Publishing for printing an earlier draft of chapter 2 as "Waiting for My Band: Music, Legacy and Identity in Peter Zadek's *Ich bin ein Elefant, Madame*," in *Rebellion and Revolution: Defiance in German Language, History and Art*, edited by Melissa Etzler and Priscilla Layne (Cambridge: Cambridge Scholars Publishing, 2010), 204–23.

Contents

Introduction

White Rebels in Black: German Appropriation of Black Popular Culture is an investigation of how blackness functions as an ontology in postwar Germany as it is represented in literature and film by white Germans, black Germans, and African Americans. Since the emergence of critical race theory in the 1970s, scholars have argued that, rather than a biological fact, race is a social construct strategically mobilized to include or exclude people.[1] From the standpoint of a white "we," the first blacks whom white Germans encountered in their territories came to symbolize all that was "other" or "not us." As historian Peter Martin states in *Schwarze Teufel, edle Mohren*, a history of how blackness has been conceived by white Germans over centuries, the "image of blacks created by them [white Germans] always hid their own image of a desired social order."[2] For centuries, indigenous white Germans have perceived white skin as the norm and, therefore, the presence of black bodies (whether African, Caribbean, or African American) immediately signified social change.[3] Whether or not that change was perceived as positive or negative depends on the historical context, the place within Germany (urban vs. rural, coastal vs. inland, East vs. West) as well as the national origin of the black individual. As Martin observes, white Germans' opinions of blacks have not remained static but have changed. For example, while white Germans of the early modern period might have admired the cultivated "Oriental" Ethiopian servants present at royal courts (such as the minor character depicted in the Nazi propaganda film *Jud Süss*, 1940), the advent of transatlantic slavery changed white Germans' opinions of blacks. In order to justify slavery and profit from the slave trade without moral conflict, it was necessary for white Germans to assume that all blacks are primitive and barely human.[4]

White Rebels in Black is concerned with what blackness symbolizes in East and West Germany from the end of World War II until the present. In particular, I argue that, since the war, black popular culture has been mobilized to signify rebellion and a positive escape and a point of solidarity for white German males rebelling against the legacy of Nazi Germany, represented by authoritarianism and racism and found in hegemonic masculinity. In postwar German novels and films, black popular culture is consistently portrayed as something modern and liberating that can free male white German rebels from the social constraints of convention.

The first three chapters look at a selective history of white German artists—novelists, poets, and filmmakers—in postwar Nazi Germany whose rebellious white male protagonists use black popular culture as a vehicle to allow them to step out of their (white) shells and behave in a manner that mainstream society considered oppositional to conventional German cultural practices. Reversing the gaze, the fourth and fifth chapters concern works by African American and black German artists who take issue with white Germans' fantasies about blackness. The chapters in the book are linked by the following key threads: cultural appropriation of black culture, the significance of black popular music, and the male protagonists' proximity to hegemonic masculinity. I seek to tell a specific narrative that brings together these threads, asking how, following World War II, black popular culture is depicted as being especially of interest to male characters who are oppressed by hegemonic German masculinity. Admittedly, my interest in popular music has a personal connection. From an early age, music has been for me a "technology of the self" that shaped my experience of the world, helped me navigate my relationships with others, and functioned as a tool with which I constructed different identities.[5] From listening to my mother's Jackson 5 albums at the age of five, to discovering punk and new wave on MTV, associating with various subcultures as a teen, DJing at college, and now continuing to collect vinyl as an adult, I have always been particularly interested in music's role in socialization and in self-fashioning. For the characters discussed in this book, music is the gateway that introduces them to black popular culture. My critique of this association between white German male rebels and black culture is that blackness is posited as always already outside of German culture and in opposition to German culture, foreclosing the possibility of being both black and German.

White Rebels in Black intervenes in the largely positive discussion of the white German valorization of black popular culture by insisting that the postwar white German interest in black popular culture should be read not only as an act of empathy or solidarity with the Other, but at times as a selfish attempt to resolve postwar guilt over the Holocaust. By focusing on the limits of cross-racial identification, this book is heavily indebted to Katrin Sieg's work in *Ethnic Drag*, where she considered "how to navigate the pitfalls of cross-racial attraction and material appropriation, and how to challenge the internal logic that connects the symbolic revelation and adoration of racial others with their economic social, and political disempowerment."[6] The main difference between my study and Sieg's is that, while she explores a multitude of cross-racial identifications in Germany—for example, identification with Jews, Native Americans, blacks, Asians, and Turks—I solely focus on white German identification with black culture and how this identification changes over time.

Two more texts on which my work builds are Uta Poiger's *Jazz, Rock, Rebels* and Timothy Schroer's *Recasting Race after World War II: Germans and African Americans in American-Occupied Germany*, both of which investigate race relations, gender, and black music in the years immediately following the war. Poiger's claims about how race, masculinity, and rebellion intersected in public discourse are priceless for my own argument. In her discussion of the arrival of rock and roll in East and West Germany and the *Halbstarken* phenomenon in the 1950s, Poiger claims that both East and West Germany "emphasized connections between male unruliness and African American culture."[7] Poiger's discussion of this period is also helpful because not only does she find journalistic reviews of rock and roll culture that have racist undertones, but at the same time reviewers criticized American racism and depicted white Germans as "better" antiracists who had learned their lesson from World War II.

Schroer's work is especially pertinent because he brings the issue of whiteness to the forefront in his discussion of postwar Germany.[8] This is important because, while the concept of race was rejected in both East and West Germany following the war, that does not mean that an understanding of whiteness did not persist. Schroer argues that due to American influence, white West Germans traded in the concept of an Aryan identity for whiteness. Schroer sees the U.S. military as having played a large role in this shift:

> American policy makers consistently sought to persuade the Germans that they were not Aryans; they were white. The effort to convince Germans that they were white, not Aryan, served to bridge the purported racial division between Germans and other whites while simultaneously reinforcing the division between Germans and blacks.[9]

In this book, I pick up on Poiger's constellation of race, masculinity, and rebellion and Schroer's argument that the battle around German identity following World War II depended on blackness. However, while Poiger's and Schoer's monographs are largely historical accounts and more concerned with defining whiteness in postwar Germany, the present study explores how blackness was defined vis-à-vis whiteness by looking at examples of cultural appropriation in aesthetic texts by white Germans, as well as responses to this appropriation from African Americans and black Germans.

Another key scholar who has written about German appropriation of blackness is the German historian Detlef Siegfried. In his investigation of the "white negro" in 1950s and 1960s West Germany, Siegfried found that, while the appropriation of black culture began as a "countercultural practice . . . , it was eventually integrated into the 'cultural industrial' cycles of value and contributed to the enthomogenization of lifestyles and a 'diversification of a spectrum of norms.'"[10] But even if appropriating black culture has led to new norms in Germany and to a de-homogenization of lifestyles, this has not solved the problem of antiblack racism in Germany. As Moritz Ege states in *Schwarz werden*, his monograph on the appropriation of black culture in the 1960s and 1970s, white Germans who appropriated black culture "often *failed to see* the individuality of black people and the differences between them . . . in many cases [white Germans] contributed to solidifying the nexus of skin color and culture and—mostly as *unintended consequences*—contributed to the process of racialization."[11]

Ege points out that, despite good intentions on the part of the actors, white German appropriation of black culture can have several negative effects. In fact, white German appropriation of black culture is often an egocentric, fetishizing undertaking that, especially during the postwar period, reflects a feeling of guilt rather than an honest desire to fight racism *and* rescind white privilege. But this observation is not new; it has been explored by scholars like Ege, Poiger, and Yara-Collette Lemke Muniz de Faria.[12] In *Schwarz werden*, Moritz Ege comments that the white fans of black culture probably did not believe they knew what it was like to be black, but that this does not take away from the cultural importance of their actions.[13] Ege suggests we understand white German appropriation of blackness as simply a way of engaging with the world, "part of a general rhetoric."[14] What *White Rebels in Black* adds to this conversation is insisting that accepting appropriation of blackness as a rhetorical act does not get to the core of the problem, which is that using blackness as a symbol of Otherness not only traps both black and white actors in a binary, but more specifically limits the possibilities of black subjectivity. By bringing African Americans and black Germans into this conversation, I offer a more extensive exploration of the ramifications of white German appropriation of blackness.[15] This book builds on the important work done by the aforementioned historians by focusing on literary and visual analysis of fictional texts to look at how black popular culture is represented in Germany, why white German artists associate their characters with black popular culture, and how white

Germans, black Germans, and African Americans imagine themselves and each other.

Cultural Appropriation

When I informed people, while working on this project, that I was writing a book about white German cultural appropriation of black culture, a frequent response was skepticism about the phenomenon. People often asked, what do I mean by cultural appropriation in German culture? Is it cultural appropriation when a white character in a German novel plays jazz? Is it cultural appropriation for a white German author to create an African American character in a novel? What about a white German director who uses blues as background music in a film? Don't popular genres rooted in the African American experience like hip-hop eventually become a part of a global culture? And if so, when does this happen? Is cultural appropriation always negative? And what differentiates "cultural appropriation" from more positively loaded terms for different types of cross-cultural "borrowing," like Dick Hebdige's punk as "bricolage" in *Subculture: The Meaning of Style* or Ella Shohat and Robert Stam's "cultural syncretism" in *Unthinking Eurocentrism*?[16]

James O. Young defines cultural appropriation as "appropriation that occurs across the boundaries of cultures. Members of one culture (I will call them *outsiders*) take for their own, or for their own use, items produced by a member or members of another culture (call them *insiders*)."[17] Young applies the concept of cultural appropriation "to any use of something developed in one cultural context by someone who belongs to another culture,"[18] identifying several categories of such appropriation: of objects, content, style, motifs, and subjects. For my purposes, style and subject are most relevant. Style appropriation is when "artists produce works with stylistic elements in common with the works of another culture."[19] Quoting the Canada Council, Young describes subject appropriation as "'the depiction of . . . cultures other than one's own, either in fiction or non-fiction.'"[20] In subject appropriation, nothing is actually taken, however:

> Indeed, subject appropriation is controversial precisely because outsiders draw upon their own experiences of other cultures. Since outsiders do not have access to the experience of insiders, one might argue, outsiders are bound to misrepresent the culture of insiders. Since the works of outsiders distort the insiders' culture, they may be thought to have

aesthetic flaws. Since artists could misrepresent the culture of others in a harmful or offensive manner, subject appropriation could also be morally objectionable.[21]

Subject appropriation is the most applicable term for the texts I will be discussing in the first half of this book. The first three chapters of this book address texts that one might not think of as appropriating black culture. In fact, on more than one occasion, German scholars have reproached me with the question, "What does *The Tin Drum* have to do with blackness?" And it is precisely because the references to blackness in *The Tin Drum* and the subsequent German novels and films discussed in these chapters often go unnoticed that I have *chosen* these texts. As an ethnically Caribbean, African American scholar of German studies, I have been particularly aware of and intrigued by the ways in which blackness has been invoked on the margins of narratives by white German artists. Having spent several years living in Germany, including three years as a student and a summer as a visiting assistant professor, I am acutely aware of what blackness can signify in Germany based on the images and assumptions people projected onto me.

Yet unpacking blackness as a signifier in German texts is not the responsibility of people of color alone, and white scholars have also contributed intellectual labor to this work.[22] The fact that most audiences have either ignored references to blackness, taken them for granted, or discounted their possible cultural significance shows that audiences may assume a natural connection between white Germans and African American culture without challenging the politics of appropriation. But there is something inherently political at play when a white, male German artist uses African American culture or an African American character in his art. And the failure to look into these references strips African American culture of its historical significance in the construction of white German cultural norms and resigns African American culture to a nice backdrop consisting of familiar props, like jazz, hip-hop, or the blues, whose presence can be explained by the global consumption of popular culture. A postcolonial theoretical line of thinking suggests we instead take a look at texts with peripheral black characters or peripheral black tropes to question why they are there and what they say about the white protagonist. It is important to ask what knowledge about blackness is being conveyed in each case. On what assumptions is the knowledge based? How might this knowledge really convey nothing about black people, but rather something about white Germans?[23]

By examining literary texts that are precisely *not* known for an engagement with blackness, *White Rebels in Black* shows how prevalent white German interest in black culture was. The intervention I make into this discourse considers this question: If white Germans' appropriation of blackness as a means of rebelling against cultural norms does not necessarily aid antiracist efforts or allow white Germans to become "minor" in a Deleuzian sense, what position should they take instead? To answer this question, one has to look to texts written by black authors, which is why chapter 4 and 5 are concerned with works by African American and black German authors.

The political nature of cultural appropriation becomes evident when one considers aboriginal Canadian filmmaker Loretta Todd's definition of the word. Todd first defines its opposite, cultural autonomy:

> Cultural autonomy signifies a right to cultural specificity, a right to one's origins and histories as told from within the culture and not mediated from without. Appropriation occurs when someone else becomes the expert on your experience and is deemed more knowledgeable about who you are than yourself . . . appropriation is so obviously an agent of colonialism and patriarchy.[24]

According to Todd, when Europeans first encountered Native peoples, they "perceived the land, the resources the land held and the means by which others expressed their relationship to the land, as their property, to be conquered or subdued and finally possessed."[25] This cultural chauvinism was evident during the colonial period, when white German researchers traveled to Africa to study "primitive" peoples, as exemplified by a book like Eugen Fisher's *The Rehoboth Bastards and the Problem of Miscegenation among Humans* (1913). In addition to these allegedly scientific texts, white Germans' presence in Africa also inspired colonial literature like Gustav Frenssen's *Peter Moors Fahrt nach Südwest* (1906), a piece of propaganda aimed at teaching German children their right to adventure and exploration in the "Dark Continent."[26]

The focus of my first chapter is the portrayal of blackness in Günter Grass's novel *The Tin Drum* (1959). While Frenssen's Peter Moor is entirely ignorant about Africa and travels to the colonies to kill blacks and defend white German culture from them, Grass's protagonist, Oskar Mazerath, presents himself as a kind of an expert on black culture who is sympathetic to blacks and literally attuned to their culture. If Grass's protagonist praises black culture rather than deriding it, does that mean Grass is off the hook for misrepresentation or cultural chauvinism?

According to Todd, in today's art world "appropriation is performed in the guise of multiculturalism, so-called cultural understanding and good old-fashioned artistic license."[27] Thus, one could argue that the black cultural tropes in *The Tin Drum* are simply a reflection of global culture in the twentieth century and that Grass is permitted to draw on this global culture for his novel without responsibility for why and how he chooses to portray black culture. However, Todd warns against this trend, arguing:

> If there is to be a "new, global post-modern village culture," one organized around the recognition of difference and the acceptance of its "opaqueness," it cannot include appropriation. The artist must be aware of the specificity of culture or the artist will give way to the Benetton myth, of recording in "his language while pretending to speak through mine."[28]

While I do not agree with Todd that art must be free of *any* appropriation, we as critics must always interrogate the appropriation we encounter in art. Thus, when we read *The Tin Drum* or any number of postwar German novels by white authors featuring aspects of black culture, it is important to acknowledge that we are often reading a white German's fantasy about blackness and not a testament to what actually is black culture. Building on Todd's observations, I argue that when a construction of blackness is received without any reflection on or interrogation of its origins, this obscures the genealogy of the representation, which can potentially have devastating consequences. As May Ayim pointed out in her master's thesis, part of which was published in the seminal work *Showing Our Colors* (1992), German literary history is full of degrading and narrow images of blacks. While not all of the black figures in these books are villains or present for comic relief, they often share negative characteristics that have been associated with blacks since the invention of the primitive, backward "Neger" during the sixteenth century.[29] For centuries, these negative characteristics found throughout German literature and film contributed to forming an image of blacks that, until recently, went largely unchallenged. When one does not take cultural appropriation seriously, one potentially denies a group cultural autonomy. Thus, my goal is not only to interrogate how blackness has been constructed in German texts since 1945 but also to consider how blacks (particularly African Americans and black Germans) have sought to define themselves and where these competing representations come into conflict.

What Is Black Popular Culture?

My understanding of "race" and my use of the terms "blacks" and "whites" in this book reflect an attempt to take neither an essentialist nor a purely constructivist approach to race. While I do subscribe to the social constructionist view that "there is no biological or genetic basis for dividing the world's population into distinct racial groups,"[30] I still use the terms "blacks" and "whites," because I acknowledge that "the socially constructed nature of race *doesn't* mean that our understanding of race and racial categories isn't somehow real or that it doesn't have real effects."[31] As philosopher Charles W. Mills argues in *Blackness Visible*:

> Room can be made for race as both real and unreal: that race can be ontological without being biological, metaphysical without being physical, existential without being essential, shaping one's being without being in one's shape. . . . So the task of those working on race is to put race in quotes, "race," while still insisting that *nevertheless, it exists* (and moves people).[32]

While black popular music is my major focus, the texts I discuss often comment on a wider range of black popular culture. Thus, throughout this book, I use the broader term "black popular culture" to refer to a sphere of acts, performances, and identifications originating in the African diaspora. My definition of black popular culture is based on Stuart Hall's arguments in his essay "What is This 'Black' in Black Popular Culture?" Hall stresses that black popular culture is a product of the specific experience of the African diaspora and that it is characterized by an overdetermination. This overdetermination corresponds to the fact that, during transatlantic slavery, because the descendants of Africans were excluded from the cultural mainstream, few performative spaces were left to them.[33] Thus, the culture produced in the African diaspora was affected by the social and economic circumstances and limitations under which blacks suffered. Furthermore, black popular culture is a hybrid; it exists at the intersection of what slaves inherited from Africa and the intermingling cultures found in the New World. Working off of Cornel West, Hall defines black popular culture:

> Selective appropriation, incorporation, and rearticulation of European ideologies, cultures, and institutions, alongside an African heritage . . . led to linguistic innovations in rhetorical stylization of the body, forms of oc-

cupying an alien social space, heightened expressions, hairstyles, ways of walking, standing and talking, and a means of constituting and sustaining camaraderie.[34]

Regarding the question of why black popular culture is often considered rebellious among whites—a question pursued throughout this book—I find African American writer and New York Times book critic Anatole Broyard's thoughts on the inaccessibility of black cultural production useful.[35] Broyard's comments come from a 1948 essay on "hipsters"—a term that designated a black subcultural figure in the 1940s and a white subcultural figure in the 1950s (which I address further in chapter 2), and has since resurfaced to designate a certain postmodern aesthetic, deeply embedded in cultural appropriation and the politics of gentrification.[36] As read by Mark Greif, Broyard

> insisted that black people in America were subject to decisions made about their lives by conspiracies of power which held a monopoly on information and knowledge that they *could never* possibly know. The "hip" reaction was to insist, purely symbolically on forms of knowledge which you, the black knower, possessed before anyone else, and in fact before the creation of positive knowledge—*a priori*.[37]

Thus, according to Broyard, black Americans circumvented their exclusion from the ownership of positive knowledge by creating their *own* form of *a priori* knowledge, inaccessible to whites. This could be considered the origin of how black culture comes to signify coolness and symbolic rebellion in mythical understandings of blackness.

Though Broyard discusses black *American* cultural production, his thoughts can easily be applied to the cultural production of black peoples around the world. On every continent where black people have been subjected to a society dominated by white supremacy, they have developed "ways of walking, standing and talking" to symbolically oppose those in power. Thus, I use the term "black popular culture," as opposed to "African American culture," in order to emphasize the diversity of the African diaspora. If we return to the example of music, although genres like jazz and hip-hop are thought of as African American, they draw on a variety of cultures that include African, Caribbean, and Afro-European influences. As Paul Gilroy suggests in *The Black Atlantic*, if one does not consider the exchange that takes place *within* the African diaspora and neglects to interrogate African Americans' dominance in black popular culture, African Americans may seem the essential black community from which all "authentic" black popular culture originates. Stuart Hall argues that thinking about black popular culture in this manner "naturalizes and dehistoricizes difference, mistaking what is historical and cultural for what is natural, biological, and genetic."[38]

Although this book focuses on practices and sensibilities associated with African Americans, I do not assume that the terms "black" or "blackness" can be equated with African American culture. Rather, I focus on African American culture because of the prominent role it has had in Germany for centuries. Since the nineteenth century, American culture has been attractive to white Germans because they perceived it as not only foreign but modern. However, African American culture was not merely valued because it was *American*. As the descendants of Africans who had been ripped from their homelands and forced into contact with European styles, American blacks were seen as primitive *yet* modern, oppressed *yet* also producers of different, liberating styles.[39] In contrast to Africa, which has historically been thought of as backward, dark, uncanny, and more frightening,[40] African American culture was seen as cutting edge and innovative. And white Germans' interest in the African American experience was reinforced with the presence of African American soldiers who participated in the occupation of Germany following World War II.

Finally, I've chosen the term "black popular culture" because, despite the prominent role African Americans have in Germany, a clear picture of black popular culture in postwar Germany requires a discussion of other politically black subjects, such as Africans and black Germans.[41] German stereotypes about African Americans and stereotypes about Africans often overlap. And, in turn, these stereotypes are often projected onto black Germans.[42] Using the term "black popular culture" helps situate African Americans in conversation with these other groups. This complex network of associations reminds us that African American culture does not develop, and is not received, in isolation from the rest of the African diaspora. White Germans' focus on the black *American* experience just demonstrates the imbalance of power within the African diaspora, which most often prefers African American culture.[43] The term black popular culture allows me to counteract this dominance by stressing the diversity of the category and establishing pertinent interconnections, even as I examine specific subjects who are informed by them.

Germans and Black Popular Music

African American influence on German musical culture might be most familiar from the jazz age of the 1920s, an era prompted by the exchange of records between Americans and Germans following World War I.[44] Nevertheless, jazz aficionados were not the only fans of black popular culture at this time. The avant-garde Dadaists were also fascinated by the opposing "primitivism" and modernity of black culture. Consuming black culture was certainly inhibited in the 1930s when the Nazis seized power and condemned jazz as degenerate art. However, even under the repressive and watchful eye of the Nazi regime, Germans still managed to maintain a jazz culture. And following World War II, jazz clubs served as a space of rebellion for Germans who did not fit into mainstream culture.

As this book is an investigation into how blackness is used to define the parameters of white German cultural norms, it is important to consider one of the first and most significant German encounters with black popular culture. Fittingly, this is a musical example, coming from the Fisk Jubilee Singers' tour of Germany between November 1877 and July 1878, only a few years after the founding of the Second German Empire.[45] In a diary entry, Ella Shepphard, one of the Singers, wrote about her experience during a reception, when a white German countess was astonished both by her ability to speak English and by her modern dress. Sheppard asked the Countess, "'What did you expect me to have on?' She replied, 'Oh, Africani, Africani.' I suppose she suspected us to have on only five yards of calico wrapped about *à l'Africaine*."[46] This is an excellent example of the ambivalent nature of white Germans' reception of black popular culture and their confusion about how to interpret African American performers. As Kira Thurman points out, the German press varied between calling the Singers "Negroes from Africa" and "Negroes from America."[47] The fact that either phrase could be used to describe the group shows that, for the white German press, "all blacks shared many commonalities, regardless of their geographical location."[48]

While the first white Germans to encounter black popular culture were tempted to expect "primitive customs" from African Americans, they were pleasantly surprised by their modernity and were happy to herald them "missionaries . . . not only among the colored race of America and Africa but also among us civilized Europeans" and they hoped these black missionaries would teach "something to German culture, whose foundations '[were] beginning to decay.'"[49] And the reason why blacks could reinvigorate German music was not because black popular culture was seen as cultured, but because it was seen as "naturally" different. Thurman notes that the Fisk Jubilee Singers' performances were often described in reviews with adjectives like "natural" and "pure," reinforcing the idea that black people are more primitive and closer to nature. Thus, fans of black popular culture were not looking to learn something *from* African Americans, but to appropriate from them—take some of their "natural" spark and infuse it into German music in order to revive the decaying culture of the "old world."[50]

Music is of particular importance for this book, because in each chapter, playing, singing, or listening to music functions as a gateway to black popular culture or a way of expressing solidarity with African Americans. Most literary depictions of African Americans in the postwar period by white German authors have something to do with music. This is because white German engagement with African American culture is intimately intertwined with music consumption. During the postwar period, music became important for shaping identities, and, since the postwar period, African American musical innovations have dominated trends around the world. From the arrival of rock and roll in 1955, to the emergence of soul, R & B, funk, and now hip-hop, most white German fantasies about African Americans and black popular culture are linked to music. White German characters in novels, plays, and films speak of consuming black music, mention specific black artists, or frequent spaces where black music is played. I read music as an auditory "contact zone" through which people can experience cultural encounters despite their own immobility.

One of the reasons why music has played such an important role in "black cultural traffic" to Germany is that many of the first African Americans who traveled to Germany were musicians.[51] And for white Germans who had never been to the United States or encountered African Americans face to face, in the nineteenth and early twentieth centuries, black popular culture came packaged as Negro spirituals and jazz tunes. In *Small Acts*, Paul Gilroy offers the following Bakhtinian explanation for why black music[52] has been so appealing:

> It is so often argued that the spontaneity of black musical forms, their performance aesthetic and commitment to improvisation have made them into something of a magnet for other social groups. Certainly the centrality that issues of sexuality, eroticism and gender conflict enjoy within black folk cultures has given them a wide constituency. Their Rabelaisian power to carnivalize and disperse the dominant order through an intimate yet public discourse on sexuality and the body has drawn many outsiders into a dense complex network of black cultural symbols.[53]

Regarding the importance of improvisation in black music, James Snead argues that, while white European culture tends to avoid repetition due to an impulse toward progress, it is precisely the repetition in black culture and music that allows for innovative improvisation: "Repetition in black culture finds its most characteristic shape in performance: rhythm in music and dance and language. . . . Repetitive words and rhythms have long been recognized as a focal constituent of African music and its American descendants—slave-songs, blues, spirituals, and jazz."[54] In addition to black popular music's distinct repetition and improvisation, Gilroy and German ethnomusicologist Peter Wicke also acknowledge the unique appeal that black popular music has through its dialectic of uniting the subjective and the objective—the performer with the audience.[55]

Race and Hegemonic German Masculinities

In addition to race and music, masculinity is another major thread in this book, because the artists and protagonists I discuss are male. The study of masculinity began in the 1970s, in the midst of second-wave feminism, when researchers began examining masculinity within the realm of standpoint theory and roles.[56] In Germany, two of the texts published during the initial phase of men's studies are Klaus Theweleit's two-volume investigation of masculinity and fascism, *Männerphantasien* (1977) and the edited volume *Männersachen: Verständigungstexte* (1979) by Hans-Ulrich Müller-Schwefe. These books were published during the era of "new subjectivity," when in contrast to the more political engagement with the world during the 1960s, German men turned their gaze inward and examined their familial relationships, especially father-son relationships. Theweleit's text is considered a foundational one for masculinity studies. And though it is nearly forty years old and Theweleit has since moved on to other fields, he is still a leading voice in the field.[57] Nonetheless, especially in the last twenty-five years, there has been an increase in publications on masculinity in Germany; with emphasis placed on the Middle Ages, the emerging bourgeois masculinity in the eighteenth century, the family man of the nineteenth century, the crisis of modern masculinity at the turn of the twentieth century, and the gender upheavals of Weimar and the 1960s.[58]

For my purposes, an important turn in masculinity studies is the introduction of the term "hegemonic masculinity," coined by Australian sociologist R. W. Connell. In the seminal text *Masculinities* (1995), Connell defines it as follows:

> At any given time, one form of masculinity rather than others is culturally exalted. Hegemonic masculinity can be defined as the configuration of gender practice which embodies the currently accepted answer to the problem of the legitimacy of patriarchy, which guarantees (or is taken to

guarantee) the dominant position of men and the subordination of women. This is not to say that the most visible bearers of hegemonic masculinity are always the most powerful people. . . . Nevertheless, hegemony is likely to be established only if there is some correspondence between cultural ideal and institutional power, collective if not individual.[59]

For a scholar interested in the intersection of gender and race, the significance of Connell's term is that it asks one to move beyond simple binaries of white versus black and male versus female. In the context of postwar Germany, white men have had more power and are generally seen as the norm compared to men of color. Nevertheless, hegemonic masculinity asks us to look within the broad category of white German men and consider that some may actually be marginalized because they do not correspond to hegemonic masculine norms. Throughout *Masculinities*, Connell reminds us that hegemonic masculinity in a given culture is an ideal that relatively few men actually meet. How a man is viewed by society all depends on how he relates to hegemonic masculinity, to what extent he fits this ideal. According to Connell, men can either try hard to meet hegemonic standards, try to "reformulate the definition of masculinity, bringing it closer to what is now possible," or "reject masculinity as a package— criticizing the physical stereotypes, and moving towards a countersexist politics. . . . The one thing none of these men can do is ignore it."[60] All the male protagonists who are the focus of this book are at odds with German hegemonic masculinity.

Though Connell doesn't spend a significant amount of time discussing race, since her subjects are white Australian men, she does indicate that the association between hegemonic masculinity and rationality has important implications for the ways in which race and masculinities intersect.[61] Connell states:

Science and technology, seen by the dominant ideology as the motors of progress, are culturally defined as a masculine realm. Hegemonic masculinity establishes its hegemony partly by its claim to embody the power of reason, and thus represent the interests of the whole society; it is a mistake to identify hegemonic masculinity purely with physical aggression.[62]

This link between hegemonic masculinity and reason, and the notion that hegemonic masculinity is not necessarily physically aggressive, both have important ramifications for *White Rebels in Black*. If hegemonic masculinity is on the side of reason, then men of color, who for centuries have been considered *irrational*, are automatically not included.[63] One sees this reflected in

Theweleit's *Male Fantasies*. Examining texts written by white German men in the fascist *Freikorps*, Theweleit assessed that masculinity was constructed first and foremost as a protection against femininity—a fear stemming from the childhood relationship with the mother. In the binary these men created between masculinity and femininity, femininity not only represented irrationality, but was often racialized and associated with the Other, such as foreign political groups like the Bolshevists. By focusing on the way that masculinity was constructed in the *Freikorps*, Theweleit's work offers a look into the emergence of a notion of a German masculinity dependent on whiteness and anxious about purity.

Examining Masculinity in Literature

Literature professor Isabel Karremann argues that literature is an especially promising medium in which to study masculinity because "literary texts reflect and scrutinize images of masculinity and create new fictions of masculinity."[64] Toni Tholen, another important scholar in German masculinity studies, presents a similar argument, stating that it is productive "if one does not view male literary figures as only individuals, representatives, ideals, set roles, or even fantasy figures, but instead as always constructed, modeled, fantasized, and staged—*male* figures are first and foremost marked."[65] What is important about Tholen's move, from male literary figures as representatives or fantasy, to *constructed* and *fantasized* figures are the questions it evokes. Who is doing the constructing and fantasizing, and what are these constructions and fantasies based on? Thus, investigating how a male literary figure's masculinity is constructed allows a look into the hegemonic masculinity of the time and whether the figure adheres to or breaks from this norm, which leads one to ask why the author made this decision for the character.

Masculinity plays a central role here because the cultural appropriation on which I focus is entangled with the white German protagonists' fears and anxieties about their own masculinity. All of the protagonists, authors and directors in the study are males, either German, African American, or black German. The German and black German men feel uneasy with German cultural norms, and part of their unease has to do with their discomfort with hegemonic German masculinity. Each chapter considers the hegemonic German masculinity of the time, its deviations, and how these masculinities related to whiteness, black popular culture, and the competing feelings of desire, envy, sympathy, and fear that black popular culture can evoke. As one might expect, in each chapter the hegemonic masculinity changes because "when conditions for the defence of patriarchy change, the bases for the dominance of a particular masculinity are eroded. New groups may challenge old solutions and construct a new hegemony."[66] Connell argues that during "crisis tendencies in power relations" that hegemonic masculinity is directly threatened and that at these times one finds "demands for the reconstruction of masculinity."[67] In the first chapter of this book, the outbreak of World War II creates the crisis in power relations; in chapter 2, that crisis is driven by the subsequent revolt of postwar youth against authority figures during the *Halbstarken* riots of the 1950s and the student movement of the late 1960s; and in chapter 3, the social crisis is caused by the growing dissatisfaction with the German Democratic Republic (GDR) in the 1970s and the economic depression in the former East following reunification.

Taking literary scholar Klaus Bogdal's history of German masculinity into consideration, I suggest that the male rebels in this book can be understood in terms of how they relate to postwar hegemonic German masculinity.[68] According to Bogdal, the bourgeois demands of being producer, protector, and provider are at the center of this masculinity. Three of the white German protagonists I discuss, Oskar Mazerath in *The Tin Drum*, Edgar Wibeau in *The New Sufferings of Young W*, and Schultze in *Schultze Gets the Blues*, suffer from the failure to fulfill these requirements. Each character desires more freedom than society allows. Oskar does not want to grow (physically) and be forced into the responsibilities that go along with being a fully participating adult in Nazi Germany. Edgar also would prefer to stay young—his affinity for nature and art make him seek company with women and children rather than adult men. Schultze desires freedom of mobility across physical spaces but also acoustical freedom to consume and play new kinds of music. As a result of their unusual personality, lifestyle, and life choices, none of these figures succeeds in having a family—for reasons that I will explore in greater detail in each chapter.

While the white male characters suffer from weak masculinity or hypomasculinity, in contrast, the black males suffer from a hypermasculinity (often expressed as hypersexuality) that makes it impossible for them to conform to bourgeois norms. In chapter 4, the African American protagonists Ferguson and "Youth" come to Germany in part because they believe the country can offer sexual experiences free of the Puritan norms confining them in America. Both men eventually realize that a stay in Berlin's countercultural jungle will not help them escape normative heterosexual relationships and the responsibilities that go along with them. Chapter 5 discusses poems by black German artist Philipp Khabo Köpsell, in which the lyric persona thematizes how the myth of hypersexuality has been a burden to black men and is an important part of how black men are racialized and criminalized in Germany. Finally, there is one anomaly: Jochen Rull, the protagonist discussed in chapter 2, who suffers neither from hypo- nor hypermasculinity. Rather, a quintessential figure for the '68 student movement, Rull rejects becoming a "real" man altogether and the narrative's ending leaves us with no inkling as to whether or not he accepts responsibility for his future and will be integrated into society.

My focus on how race and masculinity intersect does not, however, suggest that femininity was never discussed in relation to race in postwar Germany. There are certainly examples of encounters between white German women and black popular culture or black men, encounters that have been documented in literature and film both by Germans and by Americans, as well as discussed in historical texts.[69] There are also instances of white German men interacting with black femininity. These instances, however, seem to be generally underrepresented, both in German cultural productions like literature and film and in investigations thereof.[70] Eric Lott notes that black-white cultural exchanges have commonly been between men.[71] A possible explanation for this bias is that female-male encounters are especially undesired, for fear of miscegenation.[72] Females are capable of producing children, and this creates the possibility of modifying whiteness in a more physical or permanent way that is not implied by male-to-male encounters. Interestingly, citing a study by Werner J. Cahnman from the 1960s, Detlef Siegfried states that, while white German women showed no preference for different minority groups (whether Jews, Israelis, blacks, or Italians), 87% of white German men polled expressed interest in having a black friend. But both groups were skeptical about so-called *Mischehen* (mixed marriages).[73]

I believe white Germans' engagement with black masculinity during the postwar period actually forms a kind of dialectic: black masculinity is perceived as both safe and threatening. It is safe because male-to-male encounters produce no children and pose no biological threat to the nation. Yet any homosexual desire in such an encounter would deviate from hegemonic masculinity. Furthermore, black masculinity is also threatening because of the racist myth of the black man as hypersexual perpetrator. The proliferation of white German representations of black masculinity in the postwar period could be a symptomatic response to the greater presence of black men in occupied Germany and the resulting fear of black male sexuality. In this case, representing black masculinity in German literature and films by white artists could serve to contain the fear of the Other through performativity, by precluding intercultural

dialogue, because in Katrin Sieg's words "the diffuse blankness of the foreigner's subjectivity . . . allows the German authors to construct a monolithic
notion of oppression. They ventriloquize this ostensibly speechless, subaltern
subject in order to further their underlying political agendas."[74]

Chapter Overview

Because this book spans six decades and, in a sense, three different Germanies,
I always consider how each rebel positions himself in relation to his respective
time and place. The book is chronologically structured and divided into five
chapters, beginning in the 1950s and ending in the 2000s. For each decade, I
look at East or West Germany and finally a reunified Federal Republic of Germany through a particular cultural artifact. In each chapter, I examine how the
rebel defines black popular culture, and investigate whether his appropriation
of black popular culture implies something primitive and one-sided, or whether
he embraces the many contradictions, nuances, and differences found in black
popular culture. In the first three chapters, the texts portray white German rebels associated with black culture. In contrast, chapters 4 and 5 are meant to
deconstruct these postwar notions of blackness and propose a way of understanding black culture and black identity that breaks away from the inside/
outside, black/white, and center/margins perspectives. I conclude with some
reflections on how appropriation of black culture relates to *Vergangenheitsbewältigung*—the German coming to grips with its Nazi past—and why Germans have long been so preoccupied with *American* black bodies and why
blackness continues to be linked to rebellion, despite the increasingly normalized presence of black Germans and the popularity of a black U.S. president,
for eight years, who was the most powerful man in the world, as such, imple-
menter of policies that were far from rebellious.

In chapter 1, taking Günter Grass's *Tin Drum* and his autobiography as
my focus, I revisit the white modernist interest in black popular culture and
jazz and consider how this fascination with black music continues into the
postwar period. I question how Oskar's association with black popular
culture—his penchant for speaking through rhythm with the tin drum, his adult
career as a jazz musician, and his fear of the mythical female "black cook"
from children's nursery rhymes—might represent his white German shame
and desire to come to terms with its persecution of Others in the colonies and
under the Nazi regime.

Chapter Two discusses Thomas Valentin's novel *Die Unberatenen* (*The*

Unadvised, 1963) and its film adaptation, Peter Zadek's, *Ich bin ein Elefant, Madame* (1968). Valentin's novel takes place in 1963, on the verge of the German student movement when young Germans rebelled against the social and political conservatism of the 1950s. The student protagonist, Jochen Rull, is considered a rebel because he resists the state's rhetoric about its socialist neighbor, East Germany, questions how "democratic" his teachers really are, and wonders whether some fascist ideology still lingers among West Germany's civil servants. Zadek places the narrative in 1968, at the high point of the student movement. In this chapter I question Valentin's purpose for associating Rull with black popular culture, in particular Louis Armstrong, and how Zadek's critique of postwar Germany might change when he replaces *black* popular music with the rock music of the white American group Velvet Underground.

Chapter 3 looks at the encounter with black popular culture in two texts, one set in the GDR and the second in Germany after reunification: Ulrich Plenzdorf's *The New Sufferings of Young W* (1972) and Michael Schorr's *Schultze Gets the Blues* (2003), respectively. While the majority of this work focuses on texts from the Federal Republic of Germany that equate black popular culture with rebellion and the effect of this equivalence on white German masculinity from the 1950s until reunification, the same argument can be made for East Germany. Thus, I look at two texts that show us how blackness was discussed in the GDR and how these attitudes changed or persisted after reunification. Despite a gap of more than thirty years between the texts, and their existence in disparaging political contexts, both address the issue of developing a romantic idea of black popular culture as liberating in constrictive spaces where there is little access to this culture.

Chapter 4, "Two Black Boys Look at the White Boy," does exactly what its title proclaims: It reverses the gaze to examine how white German expectations of an essential black subject come into conflict with the perspectives of African American characters in Germany in two aesthetic works by African American men, Paul Beatty's novel *Slumberland* (2008), and Mark Stewart's musical *Passing Strange* (2009). Both texts portray the journey of young, middle-class African American men to Berlin during the 1970s and 1980s—a tumultuous period for the city during which it had a vibrant counterculture. My analysis considers what these African American characters are seeking in Germany, how they react to white Germans' attitudes toward black culture, and how Beatty and Stewart challenge essential notions of blackness.

Chapter 5 introduces black German perspectives on the intersection of race and gender in Germany. First, I consider how black German men have related to hegemonic masculinity since Nazi Germany, looking at four autobiographies by black German men: Hans Jürgen Massaquoi's *Destined to Witness* (1999), Theodor Michael's *Deutsch sein und schwarz dazu: Erinnerungen eines Afro-Deutschen* (2013), Günther Kaufmann's *Der Weisse Neger vom Hasenbergl* (2005), and Charly Graf's *Kämpfe für dein Leben* (2011). I then turn to the work of black German poet Philipp Khabo Köpsell, in order to discuss how his texts engage with the topics of black masculinity, German norms, and the influence of African American culture, especially hip-hop and Afrofuturism. Köpsell's engagement with Afrofuturism indicates a break between how his generation and older generations of black Germans view identity, and I question what Afrofuturism contributes to black German discussions about race, nation, and identity.

In the conclusion chapter, I ask to what extent white German males' engagement with African American history—a history of Others for whose suffering they are not responsible—is an attempt to right the wrongs of the Nazi past or to refuse to recognize these wrongs. If a German author associates his protagonist with black culture without positioning the character vis-à-vis the Nazi past, is this a sign of normalization? A sign of the natural "cosmopolitical memory" emerging in our age of globalization? A sign of ignoring white privilege, of historical revisionism, or an attempt to downplay the trauma caused by this past? And how have notions of black popular culture in Germany been affected by globalization, and by the historical election of America's first black president?

CHAPTER I

Who's Afraid of the Black Cook?

Whenever I mention that this chapter begins with an analysis of Günter Grass's three-part novel *The Tin Drum*, the most common reaction is surprise. What does Grass's epic novel have to do with blackness? In fact, Oskar Mazerath, the protagonist, has several unusual connections and engagements with black culture.

Blackness is most clearly present in the novel in the form of the *schwarze Köchin* (Black Cook), whose significance has been debated by many scholars.[1] The Black Cook first makes her appearance as the figure of a nursery rhyme that the neighborhood children sing when Oskar is a child. However, throughout the course of Oskar's narrative, as Oskar grows older, the Black Cook comes to take on a mythological presence. She appears to be invoked during his moments of intense fear, such as when he witnesses the neighborhood grocer Greff's body hanging in the cellar of his shop, or at the end of the book, when Oskar is on the run from the police and he envisions the Black Cook waiting along with police to capture him.

Most scholars interpret the Black Cook as representing either fear, specifically Oskar's fear of femininity, or some kind of guilt, whether it is Oskar's individual guilt or the collective guilt of white Germans (Brodsky, Krimmer, Kónya-Jobs). Barbara Becker-Cantarino argues against reading the "black" of the Black Cook as a racial marker.[2] However, that is precisely the line of argument I wish to pursue. *What if the Black Cook is meant to be a racial signifier?*

In this chapter, I look more closely at several unusual connections and engagements Oskar has with black culture. Some of them are framed positively, such as his talent for drumming and his stint as a jazz musician in the third part of novel. However, his fear of the Black Cook is certainly a negative engagement, and it is significant that the novel closes with this figure.

Oskar uses black popular culture to rebel against hegemonic German masculinity, first as a child and then as an adult. As a child, this means refusing to speak and, instead, using his drum to communicate. For this reason, he is deemed mentally challenged by the state and is excused from taking part in society—he is excluded from formal schooling and all of the other social institutions he would have otherwise been involved in, including gendered and militarized institutions like the Hitler Youth. Oskar makes it clear throughout that he has no desire to become an adult or participate in the adult world and, therefore, stunts his growth. His figurative return to the womb to escape the outside world is associated with his interest in blackness, primitivism, and innocence.

However, once the war is over and the danger of fascism is gone, Oskar decides to grow again. As an adult, Oskar's rebellion through black culture is manifested in his participation in a jazz band. In doing so, he rejects the hegemonic masculinity prevailing during the postwar period that would expect a man to participate in the economic wonder of capitalism as a business owner or a worker. Moreover, he plays music not for money but to help white Germans deal with their fascist past.

The final part of my argument is that Oskar's fear of the Black Cook represents his white German guilt. Though others have made this argument (Brodsky, Krimmer, Kónya-Jobs), I push the notion of Oskar's guilt further than they, arguing that Oskar carries the burden, not just of World War II, but of German racism and exploitation of minorities, as during the colonial past. The specter of the colonial can be found in Oskar's rejection of his parents' business—a colonial wares shop. The Black Cook's pursuit of him until the very end of the novel insists that, despite Oskar's attempts to identify himself with minorities and fashion himself as a victim, he is still implicated in Germany's racist crimes. Though Oskar was never a Nazi soldier because of his perceived disability, he did work for the Ministry of Propaganda as a performer and is therefore implicated in the regime. Thus, he may try to align himself with minorities via black culture, but he is still complicit in the regime. That is why the Black Cook haunts him.

Interwoven in my discussion are references to Grass's autobiography, *Peeling the Onion*. I reference it to demonstrate Grass's feelings of guilt about his participation in fascist society and his awareness of and interest in black popular culture.[3] I also examine several scenes from Völker Schlöndorff's film adaptation of *The Tin Drum*, from 1979, to show that its interpretation of themes from the novel—black music, the Black Cook, and Oskar's fear of femininity—supports my own.

A Synopsis of *The Tin Drum*

The Tin Drum caused quite a controversy when it was first published in 1959. Part of the uproar stemmed from the novel's unusual protagonist, Oskar Mazerath. Oskar's childlike appearance and innocence in combination with his strangely sophisticated mental capacity—he claims to have been born with fully matured intelligence and awareness—results in an unusual take on Nazi Germany and the early postwar years.[4] The narrative style of the novel is such that it is difficult to consider Oskar a reliable narrator, and to know how much agency to attribute to him.

Oskar's reliability as a narrator is called into question by his positionality. The novel begins with Oskar as an adult, roughly thirty years old and a patient in a mental institution. His narration is complicated by the fact that it is based on his highly subjective memory. Some of his "memory" includes telling the story of his mother's conception, based on hearsay. For a brief moment, Oskar even passes on the task of doing the writing to his caretaker Bruno, to whom he narrates the story. The novel's multiple layers of narration, competing perspectives, and reflection on the act of narration itself make it difficult for the reader to know the extent to which the story is reliable. This problem is exemplified by the novel's opening, "Granted: I'm an inmate of a mental hospital."[5] The first word, "granted," is a speech act that qualifies whatever follows. Oskar admits that he is not speaking from a position of authority, but we should listen to him anyway. But why can't Oskar speak with authority? Is it because he has a mental illness and his testimony is therefore detached from a normative perception of reality? Or is it because, for his entire life, society has viewed him as not belonging to its hegemony? The questions raised in the novel's first word, and the admission that he is in a mental hospital, immediately make the reader skeptical toward Oskar's story and his motivations for telling this story.

After years of avoiding adult responsibilities by hiding behind a childlike persona, following his legal father's death, Oskar claims that he decides to grow because he must now take on the responsibility of providing for the family. However, at the moment he makes this decision, his little brother—and alleged son—Kurt strikes him on the head with a stone, and he falls into his father's grave. This scene mirrors an earlier one at his third birthday party, when Oskar first decides to stop growing. Oskar masks his decision with a staged fall down the basement steps. As a result, the adults believe his short stature is caused by a blow to his head during the fall. When he decides to grow again, the witnesses believe he has been miraculously healed when a rock thrown by his brother knocks him into his father's grave. In both cases, the presence of a psychological and plausible material cause for his physicality maintains a doubt that lends to the novel's postmodern aesthetic of unreliable narrative and lack of an authoritative voice.

The novel's unusual narrative style contributes to Grass's project of posing many contended questions pertaining to the roots of German fascism and white German guilt during and after World War II. Part of the reason Oskar is such an uncomfortable character is he seems to qualify as both perpetrator and victim of Nazism. This makes him an excellent character to begin with, since I seek to examine attempts in postwar literary texts to distance younger generations of white Germans from older generations more directly implicated in fascism. While Oskar continues to mature mentally after his third birthday, he maintains the stature of a child, and he communicates primarily through the beating of a toy drum. Since he has an unusual appearance and what others view as limited mental capacities, he is excused from participating in traditional forms of socialization. He does not attend school because on his first day of class, he refused to hand his drum over to his teacher. Instead, either defensively or aggressively, he shrieks—one of his many unusual talents—which causes his teacher's glasses to shatter. As a result, he is excused from school, and in lieu of formal schooling, he learns to read from a neighbor who reads to him from *Rasputin and the Women* and Goethe's *Elective Affinities*. Oskar's lack of formal education only further pushes him to the margins of society. As his peers grow up, get jobs, and join the war effort, Oskar remains at home, accompanying his mother through the town or, after her death, seeking refuge with a series of adult caretakers, who view him as a child despite his real age.

Though Oskar is occasionally victimized because of his marginal status, such as when he is bullied by neighborhood kids, at the same time he revels in being an outsider. *The Tin Drum* begins with an adult Oskar speaking from the bed of an insane asylum, where Oskar feels safe and protected. Oskar's revelry in an outsider status begins with his stories of his grandfather, Joseph Koljaicek. Oskar tells of how Koljaicek first met Oskar's Kashubian grandmother, how his mother, Agnes, was conceived, and how she met and married his father, Alfred Mazerath. Oskar claims his grandfather was not only a Polish nationalist living in Germany, but an arsonist who was sought by the police. Besides being the grandson of a criminal, what further contributes to Oskar's subversive lineage is that during his mother's marriage, she had an ongoing affair with her cousin Jan, a Pole. Thus, Oskar is not only an outsider figure because of his self-inflicted affliction and his disengagement with society, but also because his unclear lineage designates him as Kashubian, Polish, and perhaps not even German, if in fact Alfred is not really his father.

As I will elaborate in a later section, Oskar's desire to stop growing is part of a more general rejection of adulthood and more specifically his refusal to inherit the faults of his parents. It is only when all of his (suspected) parents are dead that he decides to grow again and look more like an adult. At this point, the novel moves from Danzig to West Germany, where Oskar, his mother-in-law Maria, and his brother and alleged son Kurt attempt to start over following the devastation brought by war. Back in Danzig, the family business is turned over to Fajngold, a Polish Jew newly liberated from a concentration camp. The family leaves Danzig because Maria fears that the many Poles moving into the city will not be accepting of Germans after the atrocities they faced at the hands of the Nazis. But even when Oskar decides to grow again, he does not seek out a conventional lifestyle. Instead of following a more practical trade, Oskar finds refuge in the art world: drumming for a jazz trio and eventually modeling for painters. In the following sections, I look more closely at Oskar's invocation of black culture and consider what his proximity to blackness has to do with the novel's more general themes of *Vergangenheitsbewältigung* (the struggle to overcome the negative past) and guilt.

Masculinities during Weimar and Nazi Germany

From my synopsis it is already clear that Oskar claims to be capable of feats that are impossible in real life and incapable of being reconciled with reality. Nevertheless, whether one ascribes Oskar's supernatural abilities to his abnormalities or something medical, or one concludes that his tall tales are mere fantasy, it is still productive to consider what is conveyed about Oskar's masculinity in this depiction. How does Grass position his narrator in opposition to contemporary hegemonic masculinity, and what is the purpose of this positioning?

In order to better grasp what kinds of masculinities were promoted during Hitler's rise to power and under the Nazis, it is useful to first consider what hegemonic masculinity preceded the Nazis, since they positioned themselves as critical of and fighting against Weimar trends.[6] Theweleit's *Male Fantasies* is the most comprehensive and well-known investigation of the fascist masculinity cultivated during the 1920s–1930s. Additional texts that have attempted to better understand the construction of a national, conservative masculinity during the Nazis' rise to power turn to the writing of famed German soldier Ernst Jünger.[7] Recalling the assertions made by Theweleit in *Male Fantasies*, Horst Nitschack claims that, in Jünger's texts, the male body is faced by the threat of sensuality as well as death. The threat of sensuality recalls past stereotypes of the alleged split between male/female, rational/corporeal, and white/black. Therefore, once again sensuality and feeling are associated with femininity and a lack of control, which recalls the flood, masses, and the foreign Other Theweleit discusses. In contrast, masculinity is meant to be controlled, rational, and white. The conservative males' fear of the foreign reinforces the idea that men who at the time embraced foreign culture, such as jazz fans, would have been viewed as counter to hegemonic masculinity.

Yet, Nitschack's point that white, conservative, nationalist German masculinity did not imply traditional views on gender and sexuality connects to several insights historian Dagmar Herzog makes in her seminal study *Sex after Fascism*. Herzog uncovers that, while West German students of the late 1960s believed the conservative society they were rebelling against was a product of Nazi Germany, in fact, the Nazis often promoted more liberal and occasionally contradictory messages about sex. Nazis sought to have their followers associate their party with pleasure, and therefore they were actually quite critical of Christian views of virginity and chastity.

Perhaps, when it comes to masculinity, Weimar and Nazi Germany are linked by sexual prowess. As David James Pritckett argues, the men of Weimar Germany found themselves in a new era ruled by speed, where *das Verhältnis* (an affair) was the new norm: "'The affair' became a fleeting, momentary alternative to stable marital relationships."[8] And as Herzog demonstrates, this climate of constantly changing sexual partners did not cease during the Third Reich and perhaps increased further during the postwar years, which witnessed a great deal of promiscuous sexual behavior.[9] So where can one situate Oskar in this climate of masculinity defined on the one hand by militarism and by sexual liberation on the other?

Oskar's access to hegemonic masculinity during his formative teen years, which take place during World War II, are blocked largely by his appearance. Whether one considers Oskar to merely appear childlike or to have a disability, his appearance does not make him a desirable sexual partner. His first sexual experiences are with the grocer's wife, a woman who yearns for intimacy after years of neglect from a husband, who is more interested in and attracted to his young male scouts. Oskar's second sexual partner is his neighbor, Maria, a girl slightly older than he. The narrative is unclear about whether Maria actually consents to sex with him. However, when given the choice, she clearly chooses a relationship with his father, Alfred, not Oskar—even after Alfred's death, Maria will not entertain a sexual relationship with Oskar. Furthermore, Oskar's pursuit of women following the war ends miserably with a disastrous date with a nurse and an accusation that he murdered a female neighbor—another nurse, whom he stalked. So Oskar has quite a few sexual encounters despite his stature. At the same time, Oskar's stature denies him access to hegemonic masculinity because it makes him an undesirable partner in a climate where sexual activity and masculinity are closely linked. But Oskar is not remorseful over this fact, for his ultimate goal is to become Other, become minor, exist on the margins, from where he can condemn others. And he is able to enhance this marginalization through his strategic appropriation of blackness.

Black Culture as Resistance

To understand Oskar's dialectical attraction to and repulsion from blackness, the novel's tropes of black popular culture need to be considered: Germany's ambivalent reception of jazz culture, Grass's stance toward German history and memory, and the novel's racialized iterations of black femininity. These tropes articulate a white German association between black culture and rebellion/resistance, but also a shame and desire to come to terms with the persecution of racial minorities in Germany's former colonies and under the Nazi regime.

Rhythm as Resistance

At the start of the novel, as he narrates from his institutional bed as an adult, Oskar claims his affinity for music was first revealed on the night of his birth when he observed a moth "drumming" its wings. Reflecting on the moth, thirty-year-old Oskar associates an inherent talent for drumming with Africa:

> Perhaps there are Negroes in darkest Africa and others in America who have not yet forgotten Africa, who with their innate sense of rhythm might manage, in imitation of my moth, or of African moths—which as everyone knows are larger and more splendid than those of Eastern Europe—to drum in a similar fashion: with discipline, yet freed of all restraint; I hold to my Eastern European standards, cling to that medium-sized powdery-brown moth of the hour of my birth; declare him Oskar's master. (*TD* 36)

Oskar's use of the superlative *dunkelsten* (darkest), as well as his hesitation to attribute the same rhythmic talents of Africans to African Americans, suggests he believes that rhythm is something inherently sub-Saharan, for it is not enough to be of African descent. Only those African Americans who have kept something of their "innate sense of rhythm" can drum well. In German, Oskar's use of the conjunctive "vielleicht mag es . . . . gegeben sein"[10] when he proposes that, during his birth, Africans or African Americans were simultaneously having the same experience, reveals some doubt on his part. This connection to black culture is an imagined one. Furthermore, even if Oskar expresses that he shares something with black culture, a gift for rhythm, he immediately qualifies this similarity by suggesting that he can only drum as well as an Eastern European moth. Nonetheless, his insistence that African moths are "larger and more splendid" hints of both envy and racist stereotypes of blacks' abnormal physicality and large size.[11] Thus, according to Oskar, both African moths and African men are superior drummers, and he has to be content with his limits in his drumming capabilities.

Finally, it is significant that the Africans' and African Americans' drumming is described as "with discipline, yet freed of all restraint," which presents a curious, seemingly contradicting image. In this case, discipline implies practice, focus, and mastery. However, it is unclear whether the black drummers lack restraint because they inhabit a freer society or because they do not place restraints on themselves. Either way, this juxtaposition of Oskar the European drummer with black drummers establishes one of the core associations with blackness that continues throughout the narrative: blackness as an embodiment of freedom or rebellion.

One critic, Stacey Olster, sees Oskar's identification with drumming and rhythm as a resistance to order. Olster suggests that, while one might view a tin drum as a symbol of militarism, the fact that Oskar often uses his drum to disrupt society shows that Grass is in fact working *against* the norm.[12] Furthermore, she argues that Oskar's penchant for jazz, a genre that has a relatively free form and embraces improvisation, is a further indication of his resistance to order. While I agree that Oskar's drumming should not be read as a symbol of militarism, Oskar is not set against *any* order. Rather, Oskar rejects the Western order of linear time and instead embraces the order provided by rhythm. Oskar expresses his distaste for the concept of time in the following passage:

> But grownups have a strange and childish relationship to their clocks, childish in the sense in which I was never a child. Yet the clock may well be the grownups' greatest achievement. . . . But the clock remains nothing without the grownup. He winds it, sets it forward or back, takes it to the clockmaker to be checked, cleaned, and if necessary repaired. Like the cry of the cuckoo that fades too soon, like overturned saltcellars, spiders in the morning, black cats from the left, the uncle's portrait that falls from the wall when the hook pulls from the plaster, just as with mirrors, grownups see more behind and in clocks than clocks can possibly signify. (*TD* 55–66)

This passage offers insight into not only Oskar's critique of time and how it organizes our lives but also how this relates to his rejection of the adult world. In this passage, Oskar clearly criticizes adults for their dependence on time. He finds it silly that they allow such a construction to determine their lives. For Oskar, the clock symbolizes adults' enslavement to societal order. Nevertheless, rather than rejecting order altogether, Oskar simply seeks order through rhythm. That is why he denounces his schoolmates for their lack of rhythm on the first day of school.

A good example of how Oskar's rhythmic order competes with the dominant order in society is the incident when he disrupts a local Nazi rally on the festival grounds. By drumming in a jazz style while hiding beneath the grandstand, Oskar incites the crowd to dance. When Oskar first arrives at the rally, he senses the impending fascism in the grandstand's symmetry—a forced sameness that eliminates all divergence: "The longer I scrutinized the grandstand from the front, the more suspicious I became of that symmetry which had been insufficiently relieved by Löbsack's hump" (*TD* 106). Oskar's keen awareness of the symmetry and conformity of the rally follows an earlier comment made to him by the circus clown Bebra—a dwarf who, like Oskar, claims to have stopped growing by sheer will. Prior to attending the Nazi rally, Oskar attends a circus performance with his parents where he first meets Bebra. When Bebra cannot convince Oskar to join his troupe, Bebra warns Oskar:

> They're coming! They will take over the festival grounds. They will stage torchlight parades. They will build grandstands, they will fill grandstands, they will preach our destruction from grandstands. Watch closely, my young friend, what happens on those grandstands. Always try to be sitting on the grandstands, and never standing in front of them. (*TD* 102)

As Oskar approaches the grandstand at the Nazi rally, he seems to recall Bebra's warning, and instead of attempting to participate in the action, he hides beneath the spectators. His disappointment that the District Indoctrination Head Löbsack's hump did not offer any resistance to the symmetry shows how Oskar equates difference, in this case physical difference, with possible resistance to the fascist regime.

Although Oskar does disrupt the rally, rather than initiating anarchy, the spectators' dancing "displays a strict adherence to rhythm, both in the three-four waltz time with which Oskar begins drumming and the quicker Charleston tempo into which he later moves."[13] Below the grandstand, Oskar plays "Jimmy the Tiger," a jazz tune recorded by the Original Dixieland Jazz Band in New

York and London in 1918 and 1919, respectively. The recording was not available in Germany until 1923, where it set the model for many German jazz musicians.[14] "Jimmy the Tiger" is also the song that Bebra routinely plays on bottles as part of his circus act. By appropriating Bebra's performance, Oskar heeds his advice to play the crowd before they can play him. This reference to "Jimmy the Tiger" resurfaces after the war when Oskar drums at a dance club and the patrons refer to him as Jimmy.[15] Aside from enticing the attendees of the rally to dance to "degenerate music," Oskar rebels by orchestrating a massive display of public dancing during the day—an activity that was actually banned under the Nazis.[16]

In Volker Schlöndorff's film adaptation of *The Tin Drum* (1979), the scene under the grandstand emphasizes Oskar's connection to jazz. As it begins, we see Oskar from behind as the camera follows him to the grandstand. On the way, he passes by a little girl who is urinating in a pot and to whom Oskar gives a concerned glance, indicating a displeasure with female sexuality. While in the novel Oskar initially describes his drumming in this scene as a waltz, in the film, it is clearly jazz-influenced and with a much faster tempo. Only after Oskar's drumming has disturbed the rally do some of the Hitler Youth begin playing the "Blue Danube," and those spectators who had been giving the Hitler salute begin to sway with the music and eventually dance. Crosscutting between a close-up of Oskar's drumming and the drumming of the Hitler Youth, Schlöndorff conveys the effect Oskar has on the order of the rally. Although in the novel Oskar only mentions the Nazi officials' frustration about the disorderly crowd, Schlöndorff visually portrays their inability to resist Oskar's rhythm despite their stern appearance. While a military march can still be heard, right before the musicians' playing becomes more anarchic, we get a close-up of a Nazi official's feet as his marching is interrupted by a quick step back, then forward again, as he unconsciously dances to the beat.

Drumming as Resistance to Work

In addition to reading Oskar's drumming as a resistance to order, Olster sees his rejection to working in the grocery store in the same light.[17] As an explanation for stunting his growth, Oskar offers the following reason:

> I remained the three-year-old, the gnome . . . all to bypass distinctions like big and little catechisms, to flee the clutches of a man who, while shaving at the mirror, called himself my father, to avoid, as a so-called grownup of five foot eight, being bound to a business, a grocery story

that Mazerath hoped would become the grown-up world for Oskar at twenty-one. (*TD* 48–49)

In this quote, Oskar equates recognition as an adult with the burden of taking over his father's business. In fact, Oskar has always doubted that he is really Alfred Mazerath's son. When Oskar is born, Alfred immediately gives him the burden of being both the reason for his parents' existence and the one who is supposed to inherit their business. Oskar recalls the following scene at his birth: "'It's a boy,' this Herr Mazerath said, who presumed he was my father. 'He'll take over the business someday. At last we know why we've been working our fingers to the bone'" (*TD* 35).

Alfred Mazerath owns a *Kolonialwarengeschäft* (literally, colonial goods store), a store that was struggling when he bought it.[18] According to Paul Kretschmer, *Kaufmänner* (salesmen) in northern Germany often referred to themselves as *Kolonialwarenhändler* (dealers in colonial goods). Kretschmer describes such a merchant as the equivalent of a *Kaufmann*—someone who sells "goods that are needed for the household, like sugar, salt, spices, rum, vinegar, coffee, tea, eggs."[19] In *Magic Lantern Empire*, John Phillip Short discusses how exotic products from the colonies changed German consumption in the nineteenth century:

> Most of the tropical commodities imported before 1914 flowed freely from Central and South America or from other European colonies, not from German Africa or the Pacific. These included the sundry articles of mass consumption like coffee, tea, and chocolate that Germans tellingly called *Kolonialwaren*, "colonial wares,"—a category that overlapped with *Genußmittel*, "means of enjoyment." The ubiquitous products furnished the most direct quotidian commodity link between consumers and the European overseas empires.[20]

Since Oskar's father does not acquire the store until after World War I and Germany's loss of its colonies, it's possible that the store once sold goods imported from abroad and now only the name "colonial goods store" remains.[21] Alfred Mazerath's ownership of a *Kolonialwarengeschäft* is a reminder of Germany's defeat in the war and the loss of its colonies, the majority of which were in Africa.[22] His *Kolonialwarengeschäft* also shows a desire to hold on to the past and the continued economic exploitation of the Other. According to Short, during the period of German empire, the government had promoted the

consumption of "colonial wares" in an effort to make the common man feel he
had more at stake in colonialism:

> Imperial tribute belonged to everyone. From the mid-nineteenth century,
> both the diversity and the volume of German food consumption had in-
> creased dramatically, eventuating a revolution in the way most Germans
> ate and drank. The consumption of *Genußmittel*—most significantly alco-
> hol but also colonial goods like coffee, tea, cocoa, sugar, and spices—was
> an important element of the new patterns.[23]

In his autobiography, Grass demonstrates his awareness of the German colonial legacy, not only by discussing his collection of foreign stamps but also
revealing that his family actually owned a *Kolonialwarengeschäft*.

As for Oskar's animosity toward his father and rejection of his legacy,
Grass does not indicate that Oskar has a problem with order or work as such,
but rather with following in his alleged father's footsteps. The only activity
Oskar seems willing to do is drumming, which he actually refers to as work.
Throughout the novel, Grass associates (child's) play with acts of destruction;
the few encounters Oskar has with other children result in their torture of him
and taking advantage of his small size. In child's play as Grass conceives it,
children practice for adult life. According to Walter Benjamin, child's play is
how children mimic their environment; it is how they learn to become adults.[24]
When the children in Oskar's courtyard play, they engage in behavior they see
in adults from the banal everyday—cooking and doctor visits—to the more
sinister torture and taking advantage of the weak, such as when his peers corner him in the courtyard and force him to drink urine. In contrast to this kind
of play, Grass constructs Oskar's playing music and playing the drums as work
and singing as his means of defense. Oskar states, "Only someone at play will-
fully destroys. I never played. I worked on my drum, as far as my voice was
concerned, it was used, at least initially, only in self-defense" (*TD* 53). Oskar's
differentiation between work and play also suggests that the character does not
equate *all* work with adults, and it is not *all* work that Oskar wishes to avoid.
There are several other musicians in the novel who happen to be adults and
who serve as possible models for Oskar: Bebra the circus performer and Oskar's fellow band members in The Rhine River Three. Readers can see Oskar's
philosophy concerning the difference between work and play in Grass's depiction of Meyn. Meyn, previously an alcoholic who played music for fun, gets
sober and joins the SS, after which music becomes his duty. Grass suggests

Meyn's music can be free and pleasurable only when he is drunk, and his music is not determined by others. Meyn's association with the Nazis transforms him from a drunken artist to a person capable of several inhumane acts, from murdering his once beloved cats to participating in *Kristallnacht*.

In addition to displaying a talent for rhythm, by beating his drum Oskar *does work* by acting as a historiographer. By setting music to his everyday observations—observations that include such historical moments as *Kristallnacht*, a Nazi rally in Danzig, and the battle at the Polish Post Office—he simultaneously makes note of these incidents. There are several similarities between the goals of Oskar's drumming and the goals of music in African American history, including expressing individual/subjective pain while telling the collective's story, to unite the individual and the collective, and to oppose oppression by those in power. Nevertheless, one cannot equate Oskar's drumming with African American performance. Unlike the tradition in the African diaspora of indirect confrontation through music, Oskar's musical confrontation (his drumming and screaming) is very combative, and Oskar has the privilege of being openly confrontational because he is shielded by his whiteness and his apparent youth and innocence.

The Onion Cellar: Music and Mourning

Following the war, and on the heels of his father's shooting death by Soviet soldiers, Oskar, his stepmother, Maria, and his half-brother / alleged son, Kurt, move to West Germany, where he plays in a jazz trio called The Rhine River Three. In the postwar period, older forms of jazz continued to be popular. This is demonstrated in Grass's autobiography, where during the years immediately following the war, he tells of frequenting jazz dance clubs and forming a jazz trio that played Dixieland and blues. As part of democratization, starting in 1946, the U.S. government opened up *Amerikahäuser* (America houses) throughout Germany to educate Germans about democratic and American "high" culture. According to Uta Poiger, this still, however, did not include jazz, for its old stigma of being low or popular culture (associated with black music) continued after the war.[25] By the 1950s, American and West German entertainment industries had become more important for cultural exchange than direct fraternization with GIs, and both East and West German parents became increasingly concerned about the influence of American culture on German youth.

Around 1945–1946, jazz "hot clubs," like the real one frequented by

Grass and the fictional one frequented by Oskar, were created by fans. The first of the postwar jazz fests was in Frankfurt am Main in 1953.[26] Not surprisingly, "Critics of jazz employed vocabulary drawn directly from the Weimar and Nazi years."[27] Uta Poiger points out that one critic's assertion that a West Berlin jazz club satisfied the *Urwaldinstikte* (rain forest instincts) of the audience simply "reiterated the link between jazz that dated from the 1920s and the African jungle."[28] Influenced by the moral concerns of the church, German critics of jazz worried it would make women hypersexual and men effeminate— opinions that stem from racist stereotypes about blacks. This is an example of the racist thinking cloaked in culturalist arguments that was typical of postwar Germany after the term "race" was no longer acceptable for discussion.[29] In its defense, jazz fans attempted to redeem the genre's value by stressing the European influence on African American music, an argument that nevertheless reaffirmed the superiority of European classical music. Additionally, Detlef Siegfried comments on the self-serving nature of these postwar jazz fans, "who believed they could be revolutionary, by sitting in jazz cellars and wearing their hair like [German poet Hans Magnus] Enzensberger."[30]

Oskar's jazz band performs in the Onion Cellar, a fancy bar frequented by intellectuals who pay for onions to peel to bring them to tears. Oskar describes the postwar period as a time when even those with full hearts were unable to cry, and therefore, it "will be known to posterity as the tearless century" (*TD* 525). Thus, while most Germans were unable to deal with the emotions of the past, those who could afford to went to the Onion Cellar to cry. "At last they were able to cry again. To cry properly, without restraint, to cry like mad" (*TD* 525).

It is significant that a jazz band is needed in *The Tin Drum* to help white Germans work through the emotions of the past. As I mentioned briefly in the introduction, the dialectic of communal catharsis and assertion of the individual has a long history in black popular music. According to Ben Sidran, the most common denominator of black tradition is "the striving for personal freedom through complete collective catharsis,"[31] something German philosopher Theodor Adorno would have called the "objectivity of subjectivity."[32] This communal catharsis is demonstrated when Oskar tells of a young man and woman at the Onion Cellar, who, lacking money,

> tried to save the six marks forty by experimenting with a cheap onion in her room, but it wasn't the same as in the Onion Cellar. You needed an audience. It was easier to cry in company. A true community formed when, to your left and right, fellow students from all fields, even artists and schoolboys, were weeping with you. (*TD* 506)

The association between black or foreign music and this kind of catharsis is so strong that, when the bar owner fires Oskar's band, he replaces them with a violinist "who, if you squinted a little, might have been taken for a gypsy" (*TD* 512). It appears that foreign music, especially "black" music, is necessary to induce white German mourning.[33]

During their stint in the Onion Cellar, Oskar and his bandmates only start playing after the guests are finished crying. Ironically, instead of reproducing the stereotype that jazz invokes shameless behavior, Oskar claims the bar's crowd of intellectuals engaged in a variety of "deviant" behavior—ranging from orgies to cross-dressing—as a result of their excessive crying. Meanwhile Oskar claims his music helps *restore* order, which further contradicts Stacey Olster's claims that Oskar hates order. But according to Oskar, he does not really play jazz in the Onion Cellar. Oskar, the historiographer, plays the past set to a jazz beat: "I drummed up and down former paths, showed the world as a three-year-old sees it" (*TD* 510). Here is an example of a character whose appropriation of black popular culture is a means to not just confront but *change* hegemonic German culture, something white Germans feared in the 1940s, when, as Timothy Schroer argues, jazz was considered a more dangerous form than even Negro spirituals because "Jazz uniquely threatened to undermine cultural boundaries as performers 'jazzed up' classical works and popular tunes."[34]

Oskar plays several German children's rhymes, among them "Is the Black Cook there?" that summon her whom he describes as "monstrous, coal-black" (*TD* 510). Aside from the song of the Black Cook, Oskar plays several other nursery rhymes that reduce the crowd to a childlike state; they wet themselves and wreak havoc in town, unable to find their ways home. It is this juvenile state that leads Elisabeth Krimmer to argue that "the telling name, 'Zwiebelkeller,' provides an emotional outlet for feelings of shame and guilt. In encouraging mass infantilization rather than reflection and remembrance, [Oskar's] drumming prevents true mourning or remorse."[35] Contrary to Krimmer's point, however, Oskar does the opposite. As a historiographer of the German people, drumming up the past, Oskar's playing can recall the past events the patrons of the Onion Cellar suppressed, forcing them to remember. Besides providing a kind of historiography, Oskar's drumming is also aimed at redeeming white Germans.

Moreover, in contrast to the guests of the Onion Cellar, Oskar does not need onions to mourn because the music alone helps him express his pain. Interestingly, when Oskar discusses his mourning process during these postwar years, he conveys it in the third person: "But Oskar belonged to the fortunate few who could still cry without onions. [His] drum helped [him]. Just a few specific drumbeats and Oskar was in tears, no better or worse than the expensive tears of the Onion Cellar" (*TD* 507). Relaying this information in the third person creates a distancing effect. Either Oskar must separate himself from this difficult time because it is too traumatic, or this distancing indicates that these remarks are possibly false. Presumably, the German clients of the Onion Cellar need onions to mourn because they have become emotionally numb, perhaps because the experience of war was so traumatic, or because the guilt of participating in fascist society and the recognition of the Nazis' crimes leaves no room for white Germans to mourn.[36] By claiming that he didn't need onions to mourn, Oskar marks himself off from ordinary white Germans. Thus, he suggests that he is either unaffected by his war experience or that he does not share in their guilt. This indicates one of the many parts in the novel where Oskar's narration is contradictory; for when the Black Cook makes her appearance in this third book, it becomes quite clear that Oskar is plagued with guilty feelings.

The fact that Oskar claims playing jazz—appropriating black popular culture—is enough for him to express his own subjectivity signifies another moment when the narrator attempts to establish solidarity between himself and black culture in a manner that sets him apart from his countrymen. Oskar has a hard time fitting into the West German economic miracle, not only because of his physical deformity, but also because of his status as a refugee from the East. His economic struggles offer yet another connection to the African American experience. After slavery was abolished in 1865 with the Thirteenth Amendment, and African Americans made the transition from the paternal institution of slavery to a labor market, black men had a harder time finding employment than did black women, who could more frequently do domestic work. Black men felt especially alienated. As Ben Sidran states, "It was necessary for the black ego to express itself in economic terms, particularly in an industrial, urban economy. 'In a capitalistic society, economic wealth is inextricably interwoven with manhood.'"[37] For some black men, becoming a musician was an alternative means of earning money outside of the industrial workforce.

Likewise, playing in the jazz band is Oskar's way of making money outside of bourgeois society and a means for him to rehabilitate his manhood, which has been harmed by his deformity and Maria's and Kurt's rejection of him. His outsider status makes him feel some solidarity with the African American experience, just as Grass, who, although he had been seduced by Nazi ideology, sympathized with the African American GIs discriminated against by their white peers. In his autobiography, *Peeling the Onion*, Grass recalls that white German POWs and Jews—displaced persons who had been liberated from the concentration camps and were working at the POW camp—were united over their shared condemnation of American racism: "When we argued with our Jewish coevals, they shouted 'Nazis! You Nazis!' We responded, 'Get out of here! Go to your Palestine!' But then we would laugh together over the crazy Americans, especially the education officer, whom we embarrassed with questions about his country's contemptible treatment of the 'niggers.'"[38] Grass's anecdote suggests that American racism is more appalling than German anti-Semitism.[39] Like Grass's use of the third person in his autobiography, this moment serves as a further qualifier to redeem him from his involvement in Nazism, as if to say that white German soldiers still argued and discussed issues with Jews like human beings, as opposed to white American soldiers who mistreated blacks and would not even speak to them.[40] In Grass's statements, German racism is shrouded in a more sophisticated light than crude American racism.

The location of the Onion Cellar bar in *The Tin Drum* is based on a real-life experience Grass had playing in a jazz trio in Düsseldorf. Aside from Grass, who played the washboard, the trio consisted of the flautist Horst Geldmacher and Günter Scholl, who played the guitar and banjo. Grass joined the band out of his longtime love for ragtime and blues. They frequently performed in a bar called the Czikos that had a Hungarian flare. When Grass's band was not playing, another regular performer was a "gypsy" cimbalom player, with his son on double bass. In *Peeling the Onion*, Grass comments on why the music patrons of the Onion Cellar cut onions and weep. These tools "were well suited to poke a few holes in what later came to be known as postwar society's 'inability to mourn'"[41] (*PTO* 330). Most remarkable in Grass's account of this time is his claim that jazz great Louis Armstrong once visited the bar to play with flautist Geldmacher, who "had a knack for turning German folk songs into restless emigrants and transplanting them to Alabama" (*PTO* 332). In this sense, Geldmacher's playing may have inspired Grass's fictional account of Oskar's postwar performances—both real and fictional musicians appropriated black popular culture as a means of *changing* German tradition at a time when German tradition was viewed as having led to the horrors of fascism.

The Black Cook

The final trope of black popular culture in *The Tin Drum* is the image of the *schwarze Köchin*, or Black Cook mentioned in the nursery rhyme *Ist die schwarze Köchin da?* (Is the Black Cook There?), which is a children's circle game that possibly stems from as far back as the fifteenth century. It is one of many nursery rhymes sung by the neighborhood children in the novel. Oskar grows to associate this song and the figure of the Black Cook with several traumatic experiences in his life. The song also appears several times in Schlöndorff's film adaptation. In the form of the Black Cook, black popular culture appears to Oskar as something uncanny, like a mirror onto the dark sides of his soul that haunt him. For all of the symbolism the tin drum embodies of Oskar's resistance of hegemonic Germany in the form of jazz, the negative image of the Black Cook and what it represents throughout the novel is a reminder that Oskar is deeply conflicted and still associated with Germany's racist past.

We first encounter the Black Cook as one of the nursery rhymes the children in Oskar's building sing. This is conveyed in Schlöndorff's film in a scene where Oskar, drumming away, leads a group of children who sing the rhyme as they parade through the streets. Although Oskar has already decided to stop growing at this point in the film, his peers are still relatively young and therefore his size does not yet stand out. While the children march, a small Nazi parade enters the frame from the left—a sign of the impending change in the political climate. As the Nazi parade marches from the left to the right of the frame, Oskar and the children march diagonally across the frame, cutting them off. The visual conflict of this scene might suggest that the children still symbolize hope against the emerging fascism. However, since the children get lost in this crowd of adults while they are singing the potentially racist lyrics of the "Black Cook" nursery rhyme, this scene might also foreshadow that Oskar's peers will inevitably become a part of the regime.

Oskar's compulsion to repeat this nursery rhyme and relive the trauma it invokes has to do with a specific childhood experience and a resulting fear of, and feeling of disgust for, female sexuality. In the film, Schlöndorff suggests a link between the traumatic experience of being force-fed "soup" made of urine and Oskar's fear of the Black Cook.[42] In the scene leading up to the soup incident, Oskar is seen drumming in the courtyard. Here his drumming has become jazzier than his initial, more military rhythm. In the courtyard, Oskar's peers sing the song of the Black Cook as they mix their disgusting soup. When they reach the line "Da ist sie ja" (There she is), they point at Oskar. The line "there she is" feminizes him. As opposed to the time when the children and Oskar marched and sang this song together, now that the other children have grown and Oskar has remained the same size, he has become the Other, which is reflected in his feminization. Schlöndorff's *Tin Drum* is a filmic adaptation of the novel and inevitably includes images that are not present in the text, but these changes seek to further translate the themes in the novel.[43] Thus, I offer this brief analysis of how the Black Cook is invoked in the film, to bring Schlön-dorff's interpretation of this trope into conversation with mine.

The Black Cook makes another appearance on the day that Oskar discovers the grocer Greff's body hanging in the basement. It makes sense that Oskar would sing the song of the Black Cook while viewing the corpse. Otto Kampmüller says of the rhyme:

> The game "The Black Cook" originated from the idea of the demon that haunts and snatches people. The game is supposed to help people cope with their fear of the dark unknown while they are still children. [Hans] Scheuerl quotes Sigmund Freud: "Thus an unconscious compulsive repetition drives one to confront the undesirable bit by bit in the game until one has completely overcome it and the soul is at peace again. Therefore, as a 'motor-driven hallucination,' the game can be labeled a quasi-neurotic appearance and can be equated with certain dreams and spurious actions."[44]

Oskar is clearly fearful during this scene; therefore he uses the song of the Black Cook to induce fear, using repetition compulsion to deal with the trauma and to drive the fear away. But what is Oskar afraid of? He is alone with Greff's corpse; the presence of death could be what frightens him. However, it is not just fear of the dead but a combination of that fear and a feeling of guilt that makes him avoid the cemetery in Saspe where Jan, his uncle and alleged father, is buried—a death for which Oskar feels responsible. Prior to Greff's suicide, Oskar claims to have had an affair with the grocer's wife. Therefore it could be his guilt about the affair that makes him fearful of Greff's corpse. Oskar's decision to sing the song of the Black Cook in order to chase away death's demons suggests an equivalence between blackness and death. The location of the body in the cellar also brings forth images of hell. Oskar fights his fear of death, hell, and (black) femininity by evoking the Black Cook—as white Americans use blackface to deal with anxieties about blackness.

A further mention of the Black Cook is made when Oskar evades being punished for his participation in the Stäuber Gang—a group of boys who, toward the end of the war, terrorize Hitler Youth patrols, set fires, and steal weapons and rations. While all of the members of the gang are sentenced to death by hanging, Oskar avoids this punishment because his young appearance convinces authorities that he is merely an innocent child under bad influence rather than the actual ringleader. When the other boys are sentenced to death, Oskar imagines them jumping from a diving board into nothingness while being coaxed off the edge by the only girl in the gang, Luzie Rennwand.

Because Oskar gets away without punishment, he fears Luzie will eventually come for him. "My fear is this: Luzie Rennwand has come back as a scary Black Cook to urge you to jump one last minute" (*TD* 368). Here, the evil nature of the Black Cook is associated solely with femininity and not race. Whenever Oskar mentions Luzie, he refers to her triangular face, which one can read as a reference to her vagina and therefore another confirmation of Oskar's fear of female sexuality.

In the film, the rhyme of the Black Cook is also sung by Bebra's circus troupe. For example, when the troupe visits a bunker on the coast of France, they sing a version of the song that refers to the Black Cook as being from America, instead of singing the Platters' "The Great Pretender," which is the song anachronistically included in the novel. This scene establishes a parallel with the earlier scene when Oskar and a few neighborhood children sing the song and march through the streets. Atop the bunker on the coast of France, Oskar and the dwarves are playing and amusing themselves like children, seemingly oblivious to the gravity of the war. It is during their visit to the coast, in both the novel and the film, that a corporal who is giving them a tour of the bunkers is forced by a superior to gun down a group of nuns gathering seafood. Though Corporal Lankes is certain the nuns are harmless, his superior, Lieutenant Herzog, insists they be executed in case they are actually British spies. In book 3 of the novel, Corporal Lankes will be haunted by this inhumane crime, for he feels the impulse to travel to that same coast and paint a never-ending series of dancing nuns.

The final time the song of the Black Cook is heard in the film is during Bebra's troupe's last performance for Nazi officers. As Bebra rides a unicycle through a row of swastika flags, the rest of the troupe sing the rhyme, and eventually all of the Nazis in the audience stand up, dance, and sing along. This singing is both a tribute to their youth—an attempt to recapture a simpler time before the war—and a means to chase away their fears, for ironically, as they sing about the scary Black Cook from America, the lights go out and bombs explode, signaling the American invasion.

Origin of the Black Cook Rhyme

The oldest record of the Black Cook rhyme in the *Deutsches Volksliedarchiv* (German Archive of Folk Songs) is from 1856. The version to which I refer was played in Berlin and Saxony-Anhalt. The objective of the game is to grant or deny the participants belonging to the group, and this circle game is generally only played among girls. The rules of the game are as follows:

> Before the game, the "Black Cook" is decided by counting. The children
> give each other their hands and close the circle around the "Black
> Cook" and sing the following song:
> "Is the Black Cook there?
> No, no, no!
> You have to march around three times
> The fourth time, stir the pot
> The fifth time, come with"
> When the Black Cook says "come with," she gives the child whom she
> touches on the back with these words her hand, and then the rest of
> the children continue the song.[45]

So each time the children sing "come with," the Black Cook chooses a child
and in effect brings that child out of the circle, outside of the community and
into the Black Cook's space of alienation. Thus, whoever is associated with the
Black Cook is cast out of the community as well. The Black Cook continues to
walk around the circle of children, choosing a new child each time. However,
when everyone has joined the Black Cook and only one child remains, the
object of the game is reversed. Rather than the Black Cook and her associates
being on the outside, they now form the majority and the remaining child becomes the new outsider, the new Black Cook:

> She now sings the same strophe while the circle of children continues to
> go around and on the fifth turn she takes another child with her. When
> only one child is left, all of the children walk around the last child and
> sing:
> "Is the Black Cook there?
> Yes, yes, yes!
> There she is, there she is
> The old witch from Africa"
> During the last two lines everyone stands still and points at the last
> remaining child, who often puts its hands before her eyes and hunkers
> down putting her arms in front of her face.

Although the *Deutsches Volksliedarchiv* has a version of the song stemming from 1856, according to Franz Magnus Böhme in *Deutsches Kinderlied
und Kinderspiel*, the song was first written down in Dresden in 1887 and then
in Kassel in 1896. Böhme prints a version of the song that mentions the "Black
Cook from America." If this reference appeared in the late 1880s, thirty years

after the first documentation of the song, this Black Cook from America could very well refer to the image of the black mammy in American culture. During the heyday of minstrelsy in the late nineteenth century, white American men often dressed in drag and blackface in order to perform the black mammy, and as Rainer Lotz points out, minstrelsy was also popular in Germany at this time.[46] Eric Lott links what he calls "blackface transvestitism" to both a homosexual desire for the black man and a misogynist fear of the black woman. According to Lott, such "transvestite minstrel acts" were meant to demonstrate "the profane and murderous power of women"[47]—the same power that seems to frighten Oskar. One description of the "black wench" is that she "had 'a hair trigger sort of voice' and an 'unholy laugh' capable of hurrying 'little innocent children . . . into premature graves' and convincing wicked unbelievers that 'there must, at least, be a hell.'"[48] Given that blackface troupes performed in Germany in the late nineteenth century—for example, Sam Hague's Troupe of Georgia Minstrels in 1870—perhaps Germans were familiar with the image of the mammy, and this produced a new version of the nursery rhyme about the Black Cook.[49]

The Black Cook as Fear of Female Sexuality

When *The Tin Drum* was first published, it caused outrage among some critics, who charged Grass with pornography, and the book does contain sexualized scenes that appear subversive because of its unusual narrator. Despite Oskar's abnormal behavior, however, the novel actually "preserve[s] patriarchal sexual morality."[50] Women are often merely the objects at which Oskar's desire and simultaneous disgust are directed. Oskar seems to both admire and detest powerful women. While en route from Danzig to West Germany in a train, he witnesses a young girl who, traveling with her uncle, does not shy away from fighting over his last bits of clothing after he is killed and his corpse is stripped. Her determination to survive makes her willing to wear the clothes of her dead uncle to shield her against the cold. Oskar appears both attracted to and disgusted by her, which exemplifies his uncomfortable relationship to powerful women. It is this disgust of and fear of femininity and female sexuality that determines Oskar's experiences with women where he suppresses their agency and tries to manipulate them, performing sexual acts without the other's clear consent.

Most significantly, Oskar's disgust with / fear of female sexuality is best represented by the Black Cook. It is not surprising that Oskar would project his fear of powerful women onto a black figure. In his investigation of historical

notions of blacks among eighteenth- and nineteenth-century German philoso-
phers, Sander Gilman found that "the murder and rape of the male by the female is a classic example of the disruption of divine order in the world of the
black."[51] Aside from representing powerful femininity, the black female is also
a reflection of the white man's darkest desires. Richard Dyer points out that

> white men are seen as divided, with more powerful sex drives [than white
> women] but also a greater will power. The sexual dramas of white men
> have to do with not being able to resist the drives or with struggling to
> master them. The drives are typically characterised as dark . . . the white-
> ness of white men resides in the tragic quality of their giving way to dark-
> ness and the heroism of their channeling or resisting it.[52]

Thus, for Oskar, the appearance of the Black Cook suggests he is giving in to
his darker side.

Barbara Becker-Cantarino links the figure of the Black Cook to witch
hunts in the sixteenth and seventeenth centuries.[53] She states that "Schwarze
Köchin was a circumlocution for *witch* during the witch hunts of the sixteenth
to eighteenth century to avoid being hexed by the real witch."[54] Because of the
song's link to the witch trials, Becker-Cantarino does not believe there are any
racial connotations in Grass's use of this nursery rhyme: "That the novel closes
with a ditty using the word 'black' prominently should not be read as a racial
slur or even comment. Grass plays with several symbolic—all derogative, if
not politically problematic—meanings of 'black' in German."[55] Some examples Becker-Cantarino offers are *schwarze Währung* (black or illegal currency),
schwarzer Markt (black market), *schwarz* as the color of the Christian Democratic Party, and the connection between *schwarz* and the devil.

However, we cannot assume that there are no racial connotations behind Grass's use of the German word *schwarz*. Jana Husmann-Kastein
traces the historical associations with the colors white and black in Western
Europe from the Middle Ages through the eighteenth century.[56] During the
Crusades, the white European crusaders were associated with Christ's light
and the Muslim Moors, in contrast, with the devil and were therefore referred to as the *Söhne der Finsternis* (sons of darkness).[57] Chima Oji, author of *Unter die Deutschen gefallen: Erfahrung eines Afrikaner* (*Fallen
among the Germans: The Experience of an African*), draws attention to the
hidden racism in German sayings and children's rhymes. He suggests that
these children's games plant the seeds for racist behavior in adult life. He
remarks, "Whoever as a child ran away from the 'black man' in a game is

still afraid of him today; and whoever plays the 'Black Peter game' or the game of the Black Cook or learned the children song about busy craftsmen has systematically learned to discriminate. In case of an emergency, he can only apply what he learned."[58]

When Oskar "summons" the Black Cook during his drum performance in the Onion Cellar, he describes the Black Cook as *kohlenschwarz* (coal black). If the label "Black Cook" only referred to a witch, this description of her dark physiognomy seems unnecessary. Yes, the cook's black skin could come from working with coal. Peter Unbehauen suggests that the rhyme of the Black Cook is "a song from long ago, when rust-covered cooks with wooden spoons chased off begging children in fear" and that these cooks wore black uniforms.[59] However, this explanation does not account for versions of the song in which the Black Cook is from Africa or America. This reference suggests the cook is an African or African American[60] not just a witch. It seems especially productive to consider how Grass's use of this rhyme might invoke race, considering the many other tropes of blackness in the novel.

Seeking Redemption

As I indicated at the start of this chapter, critics have conflicting opinions about how to read the Black Cook. While no other critics suggest reading the Black Cook as racially black, most agree that she is a symbol of fear, guilt, or possibly both. One critic who has argued otherwise is Antoinette T. Delaney. In *Metaphors in Grass' "Die Blechtrommel,"* Delaney notes the frequency of the most prevalent metaphors in the novel, among them the Black Cook. Rather than reading the Black Cook as a symbol for Oskar's guilt, Delaney, drawing from Schopenhauer's philosophy of *Will*, interprets the figure as a metaphor for the "cruel, chaotic world" Oskar is subject to and against which he must exercise some agency. Toward the end of the novel

> Oskar reflects upon all the suffering that he, family members, and friends experienced in their lives, and likewise, the pain they inflicted on others. He realizes that the Black Cook, the nature of the world and of human life, instigated all of them. *Luzie Rennwand* is a tensive symbol signifying the Will because of her powerful presence, and her malicious, destructive nature. She is the persistent seductive temptress with her triangular shaped face symbolizing the sexual urge, which haunts Oskar throughout the narrative.[61] (119)

I take issue with several of Delaney's claims. First of all, attributing blame for all of the negative events in Oskar's life to the Black Cook, she robs him of any agency and disregards the narrative style of the novel, which begs readers to question the truth of everything Oskar says. Second, she finds nothing wrong with the idea of attributing all that is bad in the world of the novel to female characters in order to buffer the male narrator from guilt.

In contrast, Elisabeth Krimmer reads Oskar's act of blaming the Black Cook for his misery as an indication that, by the end of the novel, "though Oskar has become older and taller, he did not grow up at all."[62] I would like to push Krimmer's argument a step further. His concluding condemnation of the Black Cook indicates, not only that Oskar has not grown up, but that all of his attempts throughout the narrative to distance himself from the adults' corrupt, racist world and to align himself with minorities, including through appropriating black culture, have not absolved him from the guilt shared by all white Germans following the war. Oskar's fear of the mythical Black Cook from children's nursery rhymes, along with his refusal to inherit his father's *Kolonialwarengeschäft*, his penchant for speaking through rhythm,[63] and his adult career as a jazz musician, articulate a white German shame and desire to come to terms with Germany's persecution of Others in the colonies and under the Nazi regime. The Black Cook represents Germany's racist past and white Germans' essentializing understanding of black popular culture that persists despite Oskar's / white Germans' attempt to identify with blacks and other marginalized people.

Krimmer believes that throughout the novel, Oskar makes himself out to be a victim.[64]

Alternating between first- and third-person singular casts Oskar [and Grass in his autobiography] as both the subject and object of his story. As a child, Oskar is abused and maltreated by the children in the neighborhood. As an adolescent, he is persecuted by the Stäuber gang, a group of delinquent young men. As a physically deformed individual, he is also a potential victim of Nazi eugenics. Hence, it is hardly surprising that Oskar, frequently victimized himself, would associate with other victims of the Nazi regime. He befriends the Jewish toy merchant Marcus, who commits suicide during *Reichskristallnacht*, and proclaims solidarity with his cousin Stephan, who is beaten up by his classmates because he is a Pole. In many ways, Oskar is among those who are particularly vulnerable to Nazi violence. At the same time, however, he also works to further the

Nazi cause. . . . Oskar is guilty not because he acts but because he fails to act when action is required.[65]

A failure to act is also something of which Grass feels guilty. In order to right Grass's wrongs—escape implication in Nazi Germany's crimes—his fictional alter ego Oskar needed not only to avoid taking part in the banal everyday life of fascism by stunting his growth but also to take on the responsibility of being the people's conscience through his drumming. It is this rebellious drumming that turns Oskar into a historiographer, constantly reminding the people of their history, helping them mourn, and reconciling the individual with the collective. Oskar's appropriation of black popular culture is reflected in these actions. But neither Grass nor Oskar remained uninvolved in the Nazi dictatorship. In their late teen years, both become implicated in the regime: Grass joined the Waffen-SS and Oskar joined a circus troupe that performs at the front for purposes of propaganda. The fact that Oskar is haunted by the Black Cook might underline his failure to truly break with Germany's crimes. The Black Cook is a mammy figure, the white man's construction of black femininity come back to haunt white men with their fears and repressed desires.

Eric Lott stresses that the fear of the black female is only one side of blackface transvestitism. The image of the minstrel mammy also allowed white men to remember the time they spent with their black caregivers as infants. The minstrel mammy evoked "the forgotten liberties of infancy—the belly and the sucking of breasts, a wallowing in shit."[66] This dialectic of desire toward / repulsion from blackness in American culture is typically embodied solely by the black mammy. Laurence A. Rickels also suggests that the Black Cook serves a similar function of uniting opposites in *The Tin Drum*—uniting the Apollonian and the Dionysian.[67] However, I argue that in Grass's novel, the Black Cook only embodies Oskar's fears of race and female sexuality. The source of nurturing feelings for Oskar cannot be found in this same black mammy/cook figure but rather in his own grandmother. But what does it mean that Grass has pitted the black mammy against the Kashubian grandmother? Oskar suggests he tries to reconcile the black mammy and his grandmother but is unable to: "And just what, you may ask, is Oskar looking for under his grandmother's skirts? Does he wish to imitate his grandfather Koljaiczek and take liberties with the old woman? Does he seek oblivion, a home, the ultimate Nirvana? Oskar replies: I was looking for Africa under her skirts" (*TD* 113).

In his analysis of Oskar as a protagonist, Peter Michelsen addresses this intersection of blackness, innocence, and Oskar's desire to return to the womb. However, Michelsen does so in a way that supports binary and racist thinking that juxtaposes blackness and whiteness. In accord with my remarks about black music's association with uniting the individual and the collective, Michelsen views Oskar's drum, and arguably jazz, as "a Dionysian instrument . . . a means that triggers intoxicative states, similar to those, which Oskar believes to see in his reading of Rasputin's orgies."[68] Here it is unclear whether Michelsen reads Oskar's drumming as capable of Dionysian orgies because of the scenes described in the Onion Cellar or because of the past German associations between jazz and indecency. Nevertheless, his reading is much more prejudiced toward black culture. Michelsen writes, "Oskar justifies his goal to destroy the world and its forms with his desire to abolish individual-rational consciousness, which he seeks under the skirts of his grandmother: 'Africa is what I was looking for under the skirts' (p. 148)—'Oskar's goal is to return to the umbilical cord; that's the only reason for his efforts . . .' (p. 124)."[69] While I agree that Oskar ultimately desires to flee from the world and return to the safety of the womb, both his flight under his grandmother's skirts and his flight to black culture represent more of a search for innocence and therefore a rejection of the adult world. In Michelsen's view, however, Oskar's goal is not a flight to safety, but the destruction of the world and the "individual-rational consciousness" that Michelsen problematically associates with Africa. The notion that Europe is a space of individuality and rationality and Africa that of the "Dionysian," "intoxication," and in short anticivilization, is a racist stereotype that was propagated throughout the colonial era and in the propaganda films set in Africa made by the Nazis.

While on the one hand Oskar seeks to avoid inheritance and the problems that come along with it, on the other hand he wishes to return to the womb and find safety among his dead relatives. The contrast here is inside versus outside. One (outside/inheritance) is based on the deeds of your forefathers in society, in the outside world. The other (inside/blood) is based on genes. Oskar envisions telling his alleged son Kurt while looking at his grandmother, "Take a look inside, my son. That's where we come from. And if you're very, very good, we may be allowed to return there for a brief hour or so and visit those who await us" (*TD* 330). Oskar later reflects, "According to my theories at the time, it was only inside my grandmother Koljaiczek, or, as I put it in jest, in the grandmotherly butter tub, that true family life was possible" (*TD* 331). If retreating under the skirts and, therefore, symbolically returning to the womb of his grandmother represents safety and warmth—an escape into the familiar—then being turned over to the Black Cook represents being thrust into the outside world, into the unknown, the uncanny, and confronted with the Other face to face, not just through music and mimicry. This association between the Black Cook and the outside world is the only part of Delaney's analysis of this figure with which I would agree.

When the children's rhyme of the Black Cook is mentioned at the very end of the novel, it refers to the point in the game when all of the children except one are on the side of the Black Cook. The sole child remaining is, in this case, Oskar. Now the community points its finger at Oskar. Suspected of murdering a nurse, Oskar flees to Paris (because of travel restrictions during the Cold War, he is unable to flee east to the safety of his grandmother's skirts),[70] presumably to seek refuge under the Eiffel Tower, which he had seen during his stay in Paris with Bebra's troupe and which reminded him of his grandmother's skirts (*TD* 312). He is haunted by the Black Cook from the moment he boards the train. In a Paris Metro station, he takes the escalator to the street, where he intends to get a taxi to the airport. On the escalator ride from the Metro station, Oskar is followed by an old woman who he believes resembles the Black Cook. Like a ladder or a stairwell, the escalator serves as a metaphor for a journey or progression. In Oskar's case, it is the path from childhood to adulthood (from a flight from guilt to acceptance of punishment). Oskar reflects about the experience: "When you're on an escalator, you should really consider everything: Where do you come from? Where are you going? Who are you? What's your name? What do you want?" (*TD* 559). Oskar must decide between youth and maturity, flight and acceptance of punishment. But this is not solely about accepting punishment for the crime of killing a nurse, of which he is not guilty. It is about accepting his legacy, his cultural inheritance. Throughout the entire book, Oskar runs from his legacy, first by doubting his true paternity and then by possibly causing the deaths of both his suspected fathers. Now that he is an adult and feels there is no escape from the Black Cook, he considers accepting responsibility; he describes obligations one would associate with hegemonic German masculinity of the 1950s: "At thirty a man should marry. . . . At thirty a man should start a career. . . . At thirty a man should settle down" (*TD* 560). However, Oskar also entertains the idea of flight to America, where he could establish a new life like his grandfather. Finally, he considers: "I could give in and let them nail me down, go out, simply because I'm thirty and play the Messiah they take me for" (*TD* 560). Surrendering to who he is and where he is from means accepting his cultural legacy. When Oskar equates himself to Jesus, he suggests that, by surrendering, he would be accepting punishment for the collective sins of white Germans.

The Black Cook Oskar sees in the face of the old woman behind him on the escalator is actually an agent of the international police. The world, in the form of the police and the Black Cook, is pointing its collective finger at Oskar, who stands in for the German people. Just as at the end of the circle game, the tables are now turned and Oskar / the white German is ostracized from the larger global community for his implication in fascism. In the Onion Cellar, Oskar's act of appropriating black culture in his drumming changes hegemonic German culture not only by "jazzing up" German nursery rhymes but by making white Germans deal with their past. However, their engagement with the past never directly acknowledges their victims. The Onion Cellar might be a place of collective catharsis, but the mourning that takes place there is done in the privacy of a community of white Germans, and it posits them as victims, mourning over their wartime experience and loss. The fact that the novel ends with Oskar blaming the Black Cook for his bad deeds suggests that Oskar and other white Germans still have not moved past this narrative of victimhood.

None of the versions of the Black Cook nursery rhyme include the infamous words that come toward the very end of the novel: "Du bist schuld . . . und du am allermeisten" (You're to blame . . . and you are most of all) (*TD* 563). In a version of the song from the book *Tiroler Kinderleben in Reim und Spiel*, Grete Horak says that, while the Black Cook points to each girl in the circle, she sings, "Du bist schön und du bist schön und du die aller schönste!" (You are beautiful and you are beautiful and you the most beautiful!).[71] This would go along with traditional fairy tales where the witch seeks to kidnap the most beautiful girl in the village. Grass's use of the phrase "Du bist schuld" (You are guilty) might refer to the fact that the final child remaining typically covered her eyes and cowered before the cook, implying either guilty or fearful emotions. The game actually ends with the final child becoming the Black Cook for the next round. However, in *The Tin Drum*, there is no next round. Oskar is the guilty outsider. His implications in the Nazi regime's crimes do not allow him a second chance.

The protagonist who is the focus of chapter 2, Jochen Rull, is just as eager to escape his cultural legacy as Oskar. However, Rull has a better chance because he belongs to the generation of white Germans who were either too young during the war to feel any guilt or were born after the war. A teenager living in a West German town in 1963, the protagonist of Thomas Valentin's *Die Unberatenen* picks up where Oskar left off—listening to African American jazz, in particular Louis Armstrong.[72]

CHAPTER 2

Waiting for My Band

In this chapter discussion of white German appropriation of black culture begins with Thomas Valentin's novel *Die Unberatenen* (The Unadvised, 1963), which takes place in 1963. The novel is based on Valentin's experiences as a high school teacher in Lippstadt, Westfalen, where he worked from 1947 to 1962.[1] The novel takes place over a short period of time, from March 4 to the 6, and is organized in five chapters, which Daniel Rellstab claims imitate the five acts of a play.[2] Its protagonist, Jochen Rull, is a teenager living in a nondescript West German city.[3] A child of the generation subsequent to Oskar Mazerath's in *The Tin Drum*, Rull picks up where Oskar left off by looking to black popular culture for a means to resist what he perceives as fascist tendencies lurking in the new democracy that is the Federal Republic of Germany. In 1964, Peter Zadek directed a theatrical version of *Die Unberatenen* for the playhouse in Bremen. In 1966, one of the performances in Bremen was recorded for a television broadcast on Nordeutsche Rundfunk, and in 1968, Zadek directed a feature film loosely based on Valentin's novel with a new title, *Ich bin ein Elefant, Madame* (*I'm an Elephant, Madame*).

Die Unberatenen focuses on postwar guilt in the early 1960s, white German fascination with black popular culture, and youth's resistance to hegemonic culture. Zadek's adaptation transports these issues to the counterculture era of the late 1960s. In the movie, Rull becomes representative of the 1968 student movement whose participants, like Oskar, tried to distance themselves from their parents' legacy and culture.[4] However the students' denunciation of their parents' generation, and indictment of the remnants of the country's Nazi past, occurred on a larger and much more public scale than Oskar's individual journey. Zadek's college prep students introduce us to the 1968 German student movement, part of a larger global movement that brought the issues of oppressed people, including African Americans, to the conscience of German youth.[5]

I will not only focus on the link between black culture and rebellious white German masculinity both in Valentin's novel and in Zadek's film, but also question why in both versions, Rull rejects the path in life he is expected to take and tries to avoid inheriting his German legacy. Beginning where I left off in chapter 1, my analysis of *Die Unberatenen* will demonstrate how black popular music in the form of jazz continues to play an important role as a means of resistance for white German youth in the postwar period. In *Ich bin ein Elefant, Madame*, we will see how the birth of rock and roll changes the struggle between advocates of traditional German culture and young rebels who prefer foreign culture.

Hegemonic and Rebellious German Masculinities in the 1950s and 1960s

Before getting into an analysis of *Die Unberatenen* and *Elefant*, it is important to understand the hegemonic and rebellious masculinities present in the 1950s and 1960s as historical context for the conflicts around masculinity taking place in both works. Masculinity in crisis was a major theme of gender dynamics following World War II, and not only in Germany. In the United States, conflicts arose when once-absent husbands who returned home found their wives had grown accustomed to new kinds of freedom. But once the war was over and the men sought to return to their positions both at work and as heads of the household, they found that women were not eager to relinquish their newfound freedom. Just as American pop culture tried to address these shifts in gender dynamics, the same was true for German film and literature. Early postwar texts like Wolfgang Borchert's play *Draussen vor der Tür* (*The Man Outside*, 1946) and one of the first feature films made after the war, Wolfgang Staudte's *Die Mörder sind unter uns* (*Murderers Are among Us*, 1946) feature men who are scarred from the experiences of war, feel they have lost their place in society, and have a hard time relating to civilians, especially women, when they return. Even a more recent heritage film like *The Miracle of Bern* (2003), which attempts to narrate these postwar years for a contemporary audience, focuses on the conflicts between husband and wife and a father and his children. *The Miracle of Bern* addresses an additional element that complicated gender dynamics in the postwar era: the presence of foreign occupying soldiers. While in *The Miracle of Bern* the father only becomes upset because his daughter is dancing with American soldiers, the ultimate transgression at this time was fraternizing with *African American* soldiers.

As one can gage from this brief picture of postwar Germany following the war, the nation lay in rubble, the men were emotionally and physically wounded, and it was common for men to see Germany's loss of the war and its subsequent occupation by foreign forces as a metaphorical rape of the country. This metaphorical rape was, of course, underscored by the estimated half-million rapes in Berlin alone that were committed by Soviet soldiers against German women in the days following Germany's surrender.[6] As Karen Hagemann and Sonja Michel note, "The hardships of postwar fell disproportionately on women, not only because they now outnumbered men in populations decimated by wartime losses, but also because tradition assigned them the role of caring for their families, regardless of the circumstances."[7] In order to rehabilitate German men and German society in turn, West Germany's conservative Christian Democratic government intended to reestablish traditional gender roles, police Germany's youth (including limiting their exposure to American influence), and promote a new "citizen soldier" who was strong, but not overly aggressive like his Nazi predecessor. As Hagemann and Michel explain this period:

> In West Germany, for example, both political leaders and the occupying forces rejected the deeply entrenched marital ideals that were at the core of Germany's hegemonic concept of masculinity of the past. They attempted to recast men as caring husbands and fathers. But to retain the gender (im)balance, they urged women to put their wartime roles behind them as well, to give up any paid work and devote themselves once again to their domestic responsibilities, thereby stabilizing the social order and with it, the gender hierarchy.[8]

In contrast to the "citizen soldier" promoted by the German government, a new breed of rebellious, young, white German men emerged in the 1950s: the so-called *Halbstarken*. The term referred to male rock and roll fans, primarily between age sixteen and twenty-three.[9] *Halbstarke* can be loosely translated as teenager or beatnik, but it literally means "semistrong."[10] The term is used several times in Valentin's novel to refer to the more rebellious students. In the 1950s, the *Halbstarken* were perceived as effeminate because they actively embraced American culture and an African American–influenced dancing style.[11] According to Uta Poiger, *Halbstarken* were strictly opposed to West Germany's rearmament and the new male citizen and soldier. Aside from the conflict that mandatory military service and the disciplined life of a "citizen in uniform" would pose to their leisure time, postwar youth were generally critical of militarism. Texts like Poiger's *Jazz, Rock, Rebels*, Kaspar Maase's *BRAVO Amerika*, and Mark Fenemore's *Sex, Thugs and Rock 'n' Roll* trace the origins of the *Halbstarken* phenomenon and investigate how both West and

East German governments responded to them. According to Poiger, the *Halb-starken* were seen as embodying all that opposed hegemonic German mascu-linity in the Federal Republic of Germany. While the West German government promoted responsibility, a good work ethic, and service to the nation, *Halb-starken* were associated with laziness, consumerism, hypersexuality, and pas-sivism. The fact that the *Halbstarken* willingly embraced American culture was part of why the public demonized them.

Poiger's study of jazz and rock and roll in postwar Germany introduces the category of race, asking how male jazz and rock and roll fans were per-ceived by the wider public through racialized associations with these genres. Poiger demonstrates that, because of white German stereotypes about Ameri-can culture and because of rock and roll's roots in African American music, white male rock fans were viewed as effeminate and white female rock fans as hypersexual. Meanwhile, both groups were transgressing racial and gender boundaries; these were stereotypes that had previously been applied to jazz during the Weimar era. In fact, jazz continued to be popular alongside rock and roll during the 1950s and this was still the case in the early 1960s context of Valentin's novel. Maase claims that a new, postwar nonchalant attitude was widespread among both the working-class *Halbstarken* and the middle-class and upper-class men who preferred jazz.[12] During the late 1950s, films were made in both East and West Germany that addressed the social problems sur-rounding teenage jazz and rock fans. The best-known films from each side are West Germany's *Die Halbstarken* (*Teenage Wolfpack*, 1956) and East Germa-ny's *Berlin, Ecke Schönhauser* (*Berlin Schönhauser Corner*, 1957).

In the late 1960s, new forms of masculinity emerged, as German students in particular became more politicized and interested in antiauthoritarian and liberation struggles taking place around the world. In terms of masculinity, some things carried over from the previous decade. According to Jennifer Clare, the attitude of nonchalance continued: "The 'contemporary fighter' had long hair, loose, formless clothing, and in general had an easygoing posture and flexible movements."[13] And the male 68ers often looked up to the same film and music stars as the *Halbstarken* had, rebellious icons like James Dean and Marlon Brando. Nevertheless, in contrast to the *Halbstarken*'s *Elvis-Tolle* or coif, countercultural men in the 1960s tended to grow their hair long. Fur-thermore, in addition to pop icons, in the late 1960s young men also looked to political figures like Che Guevara as models for revolutionary masculinity. One distinct form of masculinity that emerged during this time is that of the radically chic revolutionary, best embodied by left-wing terrorist Andreas Baader of the Rote Armee Fraktion (Red Army Fraction). This radical wing of the student movement looked toward the American Black Panther Party for both political and stylistic influence. Just as the Black Panthers are remembered for the power embodied in their uniforms with stunning black leather jackets, when Baader is depicted in popular culture, he is often the "cool" terrorist wearing shades and a leather jacket.

While race played a small role in why the *Halbstarken* were demonized, this intensified in the case of the 68ers, whose proximity to racial and ethnic *minorities* made them even more threatening.[14] As Martin Klimke demonstrates, it was from the Black Panthers that the RAF got the notion of conducting urban guerilla warfare. Furthermore, there were figures among the Black Panthers whose notions about gender and sexuality were problematic for a time when women's liberation was on the horizon. Eldridge Cleaver, a Black Panther, was perhaps the most shocking with his suggestions in his famous text *Soul on Ice*, that black men rehabilitate their masculinity by raping white women. And the notion of the rebel who objectifies women is still present in contemporary representations of the RAF, as in the film *The Baader Meinhof Complex* (2008).

Comparing the Two: *Die Unberatenen* and *Elefant*

Several important differences between Valentin's novel and Zadek's film adaptation must be addressed before I can properly analyze each text. First of all, whenever a novel is adapted to a film, stylistic changes must be made. Daniel Rellstab and Hartmut Steinecke describe the novel as realist, because of its attempt to accurately describe the milieu of the high school.[15] While this is true, I consider *Die Unberatenen* a postmodernist text because of Valentin's commitment to multiple viewpoints. The narrative perspective switches between first person and third person and often includes the inner thoughts of both teachers and students. However, we are given no clear indication of whose thoughts are being shared; statements are never preceded by a phrase like "Rull thought." Rather we must determine who is speaking based on the context and content. As Hartmut Steinecke remarks in an epilogue to the novel: "The characters of the novel are primarily characterized by their speech—a large portion of the novel is direct speech, conversations, and discussions."[16] In terms of setting, much of the action is organized according to the school day, as students move from lesson to lesson. And it is never indicated when a lesson ends; the only indication that a new lesson has begun is the perfunctory "Good morning, Mr. ——" that begins each class. These stylistic choices made by Valentin offer a unique look at school life, for one not only gets a sense of the monotony and uninspired school lessons, but also sees how students interact with teachers and with each other. One overhears the most intimate thoughts of the teachers and gets a sense of their disdain for the youth and their job. Zadek's film attempts to convey this aesthetically by, for example, using voice-over to convey inner thoughts and conveying the highly structured school day by using drastic transitional methods between classes, such as a white screen accompanied by loud bell ringing. Nevertheless, Zadek does make stylistic changes that have a significant effect. For example, in the novel no particular perspective is favored, while in the film, Rull's perspective is central. And in the film, we no longer get to see the home life of different students, only Rull's.

Along with these changes, Zadek creates several contextual differences. He moves the story forward several years, to 1967, and sets the action in the city of Bremen, where he worked for years in the theater. He introduces female students to what was in Valentin's novel an all-boys school and he changes the setting from a *Realschule* to a *Gymnasium*.[17] This change in institution has ramifications relating to class and political engagement. The students in Valentin's novel are working class—a detail that the teachers mention when they derogatively refer to the students as *Proleten* (proletarians). As students at a *Realschule*, following graduation they would have had limited options that included an apprenticeship in a trade or at the most working as a civil servant. However, they would not have gone on to attend a university because only graduates from a *Gymnasium* have the necessary qualifications. This has class ramifications because participants in the 1968 student movement were mostly university students and, therefore, came largely from the middle class. Moving the setting from a *Realschule* to a *Gymnasium* allows Zadek to make an easier connection between the narrative and the student movement, which would have been less believable if the characters were working class.

In addition, Zadek makes Rull a much wilder, anarchic, and unpredictable character than the subdued, reflective rebel in the novel. Finally, Valentin's novel ends with a clear resolution; Rull is expelled from school for allegedly drawing a swastika in a bathroom stall, among other offenses, and he moves to Poland. Rull chooses Poland because he feels the country aligns with his political beliefs and because, as a German, he feels a duty to give back to Poland to atone for the crimes of the Nazis. In contrast, Zadek leaves the ending open to interpretation. Rull's fate is to be decided by his peers during a school meeting, a reflection of the political climate of the time. However, during this meeting, Rull derails the interrogations by turning the tables on his fellow students—a scene I will discuss at length in the conclusion of this chapter—and we do not learn whether Rull is formally punished for his transgressions.

Zadek's changes to the novel were likely motivated by a desire to update the story for contemporary times. Though set in 1963, Valentin's novel is largely based on his experiences as a teacher in Lippstadt in the 1950s—a politically conservative time in West Germany. If Zadek had maintained the (sexually) conservative setting of an all-boys school in his theatrical adaptation, the text would have appeared old-fashioned and out of touch for an audience in the 1960s. His choice of Bremen for the new setting clearly suggests that, like Valentin, Zadek draws on his own knowledge of the life in a particular town. Zadek's desire to capture the rebellious energy of the late 1960s would also explain why his interpretation of Rull is much wilder than the portrait in the novel. In Valentin's novel, Rull wishes to become a teacher; a career goal that reflects *some* admiration for his own teachers. This respect for authority figures would seem unfitting in the context of the student movement. Finally, Zadek's open ending can be read as part of the trend in theater and film against resolution and traditional narrative form.

Despite these differences between the novel and Zadek's adaptation, the central premise remains the same. In both texts, Rull rejects the path in life he is expected to take and tries to avoid inheriting his German legacy, in part through his preference in music, particularly black music or music inspired by black popular culture. In the novel, Rull primarily listens to jazz, common for students at the *Realschule* and *Gymnasium* at the time. At the end of the 1950s, jazz and rock and roll were favored among German youth and their affinities for one genre or another were usually determined by class or school. Kaspar Maase asserts:

> The border of collective style ran—coarsely formulated—along the border of the *Realschule*. Many, maybe even most students, who attended the middle and upper institutions liked rock and roll, and individually some sympathized with protest or with the riots of the *Halbstarken*. However, if young people joined group styles (specifically if they could join), then their school milieu was the determining factor.[18]

Thus, in the context of the novel it would make sense that Rull listens to more jazz than rock and roll. Furthermore, as Maase points out, during the 1950s, jazz had become a kind of "collective term," to include anything seen as Western, American, highly sexual, and racially different.[19] In the play, however, Zadek uses both jazz and rock music, reflecting the encroachment of the new genre on youth culture of all classes. But by the time Zadek makes the film *Elefant*, he has erased jazz, and, rather than listening to Louis Armstrong, Rull is often accompanied by the Velvet Underground. While the Velvet Underground consisted of white performers, many of its influences were from jazz, doo-wop groups, and other black predecessors. The band members, who were mainly from suburban neighborhoods in New England, also intentionally moved to neighborhoods in New York City that were heavily populated with African Americans.

In *Die Unberatenen*, blackness functions as a code for not fitting in, and this is articulated in Rull's preference for Louis Armstrong and his inexplicable performance of a black spiritual in one of his classes. In both the book and the play, Rull feels disconnected from his *German* father, and this disconnect is expressed in his preference for foreign music—in particular the music of the black oppressed. In the film, however, this disconnect remains, but the music he gravitates to is emblematic of 1960s counterculture rock music, mainly Velvet Underground's "I'm Waiting for the Man," a track from their 1967 album *The Velvet Underground and Nico*. The song has a number of references to black culture: "Up to Lexington, 125" (Harlem) and "Hey, white boy, what you doin' uptown?" To put it in the film's context, Rull might still identify himself as an Other in the film, but instead of identifying with a black musician, he identifies with white American musicians who themselves get inspiration from "cultural slumming" in black neighborhoods. Indeed, a mystique of black masculinity is still present in the film; it is merely packaged in the form of Norman Mailer's infamous "white Negro"—a figure I will say more about later. Thus by replacing jazz with a white American rock band in the film, Zadek obscures the link between black culture and rebellious white German masculinity.

Rebellion in Valentin's *Die Unberatenen*

Die Unberatenen addresses the generational conflict in West Germany, particularly between former Nazis and collaborators turned civil servants and their teenage students. The sixteen-year-old students try to confront the persisting fascism in West Germany and look for possible alternative father figures who are either foreign or do not believe in the traditional patriarchal society. R. C. Andrews offers a concise summary of the conflict at the center of the story:

> Most of them [the students] are dissatisfied with the education they are receiving, which seems to them to be divorced from all positive values. . . .

Only two or three of the masters seem to have any real interest in their subject and in the boys and to have more than minimal out-of-school contacts with them. A series of interior monologues reveals most of the others to be time-servers dreaming of retirement or ex-Nazis longing to "bring back the birch" and the discipline of the "Arbeitsdienst." Their common terms of abuse are "Jew," "Prole" and "Slav."[20]

The novel's protagonist, Jochen Rull, is expelled from school merely weeks before graduation. His expulsion is decided by the faculty committee after Rull is falsely accused of painting a swastika on the school's urinal; the swastika was actually drawn by an East German agent provocateur. The graffiti was meant to imply that Nazism still lurks in the school in the form of its teachers. Rull is mistaken for committing this offense because the school janitor sees him urinating near the graffiti on the night it was sprayed. The following morning, when the graffiti is found, Rull intends to apologize to the school director for an incident he committed earlier that week: hanging up thought-provoking quotes by well-known German authors throughout the school. But before Rull can say much, the director falsely understands his confession to pertain to the swastika. During his interrogation, Rull maintains his innocence and uses the opportunity to honestly tell his teachers his frustrations about the educational system. Rull is inevitably expelled not because he drew the graffiti, but because the teachers feel his troubling critique of the school and his desire for change pose a threat to the system.

The swastika graffiti is not the only direct reference to the persistence of Germany's Nazi past; the title of the novel itself is a reference to Adolf Hitler. After an argument with his father regarding Rull's communist sympathies and his condemnation of his father's and teachers' Nazi past, Rull reflects in his room: "If he [Hitler] had had another father and just two or three other teachers, maybe our history would have gone differently. Unadvised, poor, wild sow from the Bohemian forest."[21] Rull's comments reflect that he sees Hitler as having once been a misguided youth whose life may have turned out differently if he had had more guidance from adults. Yet the novel is entitled *Die Unberatenen* (plural) not *Der Unberatene* (singular), suggesting Hitler is not the only unadvised one. In fact, when the school's director rants about the many new terms used to refer to Rull's generation, like "teenager" and "beatnik," Rull suggests they be called "Die Unberatenen."[22] By using this title, Valentin suggests that the miseducation or misguidance Hitler received has not changed.

Many of the children coming of age in the postwar era missed their fathers during their formative years, and this emptiness was not necessarily filled when the POWs returned home, for they needed to rebuild the country and provide for their families:[23]

> This absence from home due to work added to the distance created by the time they had spent away from home during early, formative years of their children's upbringing and education, which had left their sons feeling alienated and abandoned. Many boys felt ambivalent about their fathers' return. Years of separation had made them strangers to one another and the father's position as head of household could only be restored by reducing and downgrading the increased freedom and responsibility their sons had enjoyed in their absence.[24]

Furthermore, returning POWs were effeminized in the national discourse. Though they were initially seen as "victims of totalitarianism," it was typical to ascribe to them "the allegedly subhuman features of their former enemies on the Eastern front" and emphasize their lack of sexual desire, which was symptomatic of dystrophy.[25]

While fathers returning from the front could not serve as strong role models, neither could West Germany's leading figures, many of whom were former Nazis. The claim that West Germany's authority figures were incapable of guiding the younger generation because of the crimes of their past would eventually become a major argument of the student protests in the 1960s. Rull's feeling of being unadvised not only suggests that his generation lacks role models, but that those adults who are present are too stuck in their old ways— holding on to belief systems that drove Germany to ruin in the first place. As Heinz Schlüter remarks about the novel, "The times when a teacher knew 'everything' were long gone. After egregious events, many teachers landed on the school bench among the unadvised, between the parents and their sons and daughters."[26] The celebration of POWs as "survivors of totalitarianism" who had endured their desperate circumstances with Christian perseverance, along with the fact that POWs who returned after May 8, 1947, no longer had to undergo the process of denazification, likely contributed to the younger generation's feeling that their parents had not really confronted their fascist past.[27]

Music in Valentin's *Die Unberatenen*

Rull's parents and most teachers at the school view him as a rebel because of his interest in East Germany, his sympathy for communism, and his constant questioning of the status quo. They are also troubled by Rull's taste in music. His teachers accuse him of being a *Halbstarke* because he listens to Louis Armstrong. In the novel, adults' comments about jazz reveal the racism evident in white Germans' early condemnations of the music, discussed in chapter 1. During one lesson, Rull reads a dialogue between a youth and his father, written by another student, which is meant to convey the generational differences in musical taste. In the dialogue, the father remarks, "That jazz! When I was your age, every civilized European would have been ashamed if he had listened to these jungle classics!" (*DU* 177). The description of jazz is clearly a disparaging remark referring to its roots in black culture. The teachers also complain about the youths' new American idols. In Zadek's 1966 theatrical rendition, the teachers criticize an essay by a student entitled "Mein Gott heißt Elvis" ("Elvis Is My God").

In the play, music is used in only three scenes: when Edith Piaf's song "Non, je ne regrette rien" is played in French class, during a scene at a party when students dance erratically to jazz music, and in a café when the Beatles' "You Can't Do That" is played. Rull's interest in Louis Armstrong, a key component in the novel, is completely absent in the play *and* the film. In the novel, besides a preference for Louis Armstrong, Rull's interest in black culture is articulated through a further use of music. During a discussion about Kafka, when one of the more religious students argues that *Der Prozess* (*The Trial*) should be read as a religious tragedy, Rull interrupts the other students by singing the following song in English:

> John Brown's body
> lies a-mouldering
> in the grave
> but his soul
> goes marching on.
> glory, glory, hallelujah
> glory, glory, hallelujah!
> but his soul goes marching on. (*DU* 132)

These lyrics stem from the "John Brown Song," a marching song about the white American abolitionist who led bloody revolts at the Pottawatomie Massacre (1856) and the raid at Harpers Ferry (1859), after which he was hanged.[28] In 1862, the melody was used for the "Battle Hymn of the Republic," and at the turn of the twentieth century for the workers' song "Solidarity Forever."[29] Why does Rull feel the need to perform this song during a discussion of *The Trial*?

Kafka's novel, published in 1925, begins with its protagonist Josef K. being arrested at his residence for reasons unbeknownst to him. Although readers never find out what Josef K. is guilty of, as soon as he is labeled as such, he begins to behave as if he is guilty of something. His initial attempts to find out why he has been arrested lead him down a bureaucratic rabbit hole, and he eventually resigns himself to condemnation and execution.

By performing "John Brown's Song," Rull identifies with the white American abolitionist and therefore expresses his solidarity with oppressed blacks. But by performing the song during a discussion of *The Trial*, Rull seems to suggest that both texts express the same feelings of powerlessness, alienation, and unjust condemnation. The association Rull draws between the two texts exemplifies his desires to think transnationally and consider how the African American experience can help unpack white European issues. Furthermore, considering that many of Kafka's reflections on alienation in his writing related to his status as a Jew in Prague, Rull's performance also sets up a triangulation between Rull the teenage outsider, a Jewish author, and enslaved blacks. This is not the only time Rull seeks a connection to both Jewish and black minorities to articulate his outsider status.

Feeling largely alienated from most authority figures, Rull confides in his history teacher, Herr Groenewold, a German Jew who fled the Nazis, returned to West Germany, but wishes to emigrate to France.[30] The figure of Herr Groenewald is absent from both the play and the film. In the novel, Rull's association with Groenewald, who is an outsider because of his religion and his status as a victim of Nazi violence, makes the student even more of an outsider. Like Rull, Groenewald is critical of the school's teaching philosophy. Groenwald accuses the school of blindly teaching German idealism as if the crimes of the twentieth century had never happened—or as if these crimes had nothing to do with Germany. During a visit to Groenewald's house—an example of the teacher's more open relationship to students—Rull brings a record of Louis Armstrong's "Go Down Moses," which he asks Groenewald to play. Then Rull asks Groenewald to tell him one good thing about West Germany. Later on in the same scene, Rull tries to convince Groenewald that poor countries like Greece or Ireland are better alternatives to West Germany.[31] Rull then asks if he can listen to the record again, and this time, he sings along. Thus, in contrast to his performance of the "John Brown Song," Rull takes the subject position of an African American. After singing, he writes a list of everything that is wrong with West Germany. After Rull leaves Groenewald's house, he heads to the school bathroom whistling "Go Down Moses." And this is where he sees the swastika graffiti. Given how often this song is mentioned it holds considerable significance for Rull.

Rull is preoccupied by questions about his heritage: Whose child am I, and can I choose to be someone else's child? In fact, Rull's French teacher, Herr Violat, suggests that Rull's troubled relationship with his father is the basis of his problems with rebellion. Rull clearly looks to Groenewold, a German Jew, for an alternative father figure. "Go Down Moses" is a Negro spiritual that depicts Moses saving the Jews from Egyptian slavery. In the song, African American slaves identified with the Jews.[32] Linda Williams's discussion of *The Jazz Singer* (1927) is helpful when considering the purpose of "Go Down Moses" in Valentin's novel. In *The Jazz Singer*, Al Jolson, a Jewish American singer and comedian, famously performs the song "My Mammy" in blackface. This performance articulates the protagonist's trials as a Jewish immigrant in America at odds with his parents' generation and their more traditional expectations for their son.[33] By performing in blackface and singing black popular songs, Williams argues, Jolson and other white characters "acquire virtue by musically expressing a suffering that is recognizable as 'black' . . . 'singing black, feeling black' became a testament of white virtue."[34] Similarly, by drawing on diasporic resources like "Go Down Moses" and "John Brown Song," in contrast to his forefathers, Rull acquires virtue as the white German who condemns the Nazi past and seeks redemption by aligning himself with black culture. Through "Go Down Moses," Rull can simultaneously associate with enslaved African Americans, Jews, and his chosen father, Groenewald.

Criticizing national identity through an alignment with victims of racial and imperial violence is a phenomenon that continued on through the student movement of the 1960s when students identified with oppressed victims in the Third World.[35] Rull might attempt to break with his German past through an interest in African American jazz, but his choice of Louis Armstrong still alludes to the German legacy of Weimar counterculture. Although Armstrong was banned from performing in Germany by the Nazi regime, by the 1950s he enjoyed an established popularity in West Germany. In fact, he had five hit songs there between 1956 and 1968.[36] Therefore, in stark contrast to the 1930s, in the 1950s Armstrong could be considered more of a mainstream artist. Thus, what is subversive about Rull's singing "Go Down Moses" is not the musical style but his insistence on speaking from the position of a black man.

Music is also used in the novel during French class when students listen to an Edith Piaf record. In the novel, Valentin does not specify the song, but in the play, Herr Violat announces that the lesson will concern French chansons and puts on a record of Piaf's famous "Non, je ne regrette rien."[37] Valentin's choice of Piaf, and Zadek's choice of this particular song in the play, juxtapose the tastes of the bourgeois teachers with those of the students. When Piaf recorded the song in 1959, she sang it in solidarity with the French Foreign Legion during the Algerian War. Thus, the song's popularity among the teachers stresses their conservative and militant viewpoints. The teachers' inability to sympathize with oppressed minorities is depicted in the novel when they refer to Germany's colonization of Africa as having been superior to that of France. A variety of teachers make statements about German colonialism. In the postmodern style of the novel, these statements are not attributed to any specific character, but rather are meant to provide an image of the kind of national chauvinist and racist attitude that prevails at the school:

> "We Germans are definitely loved in Africa."
> "Because we treated them like human beings!"
> "And not like the French: zappzerapp, so that the Grande Nation could bask on the Riviera and play the strong man in Brussels."[38]

The teachers' insistence that white Germans treated Africans like human beings conveniently ignores white Germans' genocide of the Herero in German Southwest Africa during the Herero Wars from 1904 to 1908.

Rebellion in *Elefant*

Peter Zadek's filmic adaptation maintains the novel's themes of *Vergangenheitsbewältigung* (coming to terms with the past), generational conflict, and identity issues, but these themes are updated to portray the German counterculture of the late 1960s. Besides updating the story, Zadek also makes several plot changes. Valentin's novel features a school that reflects the masculine hegemony of West Germany—all the students and teachers are male except for a female secretary whom everyone has sexual fantasies about and disrespects. In Zadek's film, the school is now integrated, with female students and teachers. Rull is no longer a contemplative young man who tries to provoke a conversation with teachers by posting quotes of Brecht and Nietzsche. Zadek's Rull is a wild, unpredictable character who puts on an array of antics. Most are simply childish, like disrupting his teachers during lessons, wearing a wreath and candles on his head, or climbing into a display case. But two of his antics are clearly motivated by politics: when he wears a Native American headdress at a local protest and when he draws a swastika on a building in the center of town. (While this section will primarily discuss the swastika scene, I also will discuss the performance of Native American identity in the section specifically dedicated to the importance of the Velvet Underground, because their song "The Gift" plays during the protest scene.)

I would like to start by examining the beginning of the film, which showcases one of Rull's rebellious antics. We hear the Velvet Underground's "I'm Waiting for the Man," which will be repeated throughout the film, and we see a close up of a five-story apartment building in Bremen. Of the thirty windows displayed, only one window is lit up, and in an extreme long shot, Rull is framed within it. Even at a distance, one can see a bit of the red that Rull is painting on the walls. In the first full shot of Rull, he stands in the middle of a room that is covered in red blotches, with newspaper covering the floor. Rull is painting his entire room in red, clearly a rebellious act.

By introducing the audience to the film's main character in this manner, Zadek positions him as an unpredictable rebellious force. Like James Dean in his red jacket in *Rebel Without a Cause*, Rull's color of choice signifies defiance. In this opening sequence, Zadek also hints at this young generation's wish to break with the legacy of German culture, while being unable to free itself completely. Although his generation flirts with the idea of choosing new fathers, Rull still seems to hope for some kind of real guidance from his German father. Why else would Rull be waiting for "the man," that is, his father? Toward the end of the sequence we see a close-up of Rull in the foreground, while in the background his father opens the door, sees what Rull is doing, and closes the door again, shutting out both his son and his antics.

The notion that Rull's rebellion is a result of inadequate paternal supervision returns near the end of the film when the teachers discuss whether to expel him, mirroring the scene in the book. The art teacher, looking to the left and right to no avail, says, "The poor boy. By the way, does anyone know his father?" She then pleads to the camera, "Someone should have talked to the boy."[39] These statements acknowledge both the absence of a real father figure and the teachers' refusal to take on this role themselves. In the novel and the play, Herr Violat invokes psychoanalysis, specifically the Oedipus complex, to explain Rull's rebellious behavior. Herr Violat mentions that Rull's father was absent for the first years of his life and did not return from war until the boy was five. Thus, like the *Halbstarken* I discussed earlier, Rull could never really build a relationship with his father. And because it is impossible for Rull to win his father's recognition, Herr Violat believes he rejects anything related to the *Vaterwelt* (world of the father), which includes discipline and order, echoing the claim scholars have made about Oskar in *The Tin Drum*. Here it is worth noting that, in the film, the character of Herr Groenewald is removed completely. Thus, there is no one to offer Rull's character balance or an opportunity to articulate his frustrations.

In a review of *Elefant*, Esther Fischer-Homburger praises the film for its refusal to pick sides in the conflict between students and authoritative figures, as opposed to a similar school drama of the time, Lindsay Anderson's *If* (1969), which directs the audience's sympathy toward the rebellious students and arguably promotes violence.[40] Ironically, writer Peter Hamm came to the opposite conclusion in his assessment of *Elefant*. Hamm felt Zadek portrays both teachers and students as "programmed," and the only individual among them is Rull.[41]

Although she offers some praise, Fischer-Homberger is not entirely happy with the film. She begins her review, "In general one doesn't like to criticize German films . . . Zadek's film is an exception."[42] Fischer-Homberger describes Rull as "a reflector, a young man who doesn't feel right in the institution of school, but refuses to give his discomfort one of the usual names."[43] Instead of a critique of fascism, Fischer-Homburger interprets Rull's swastika graffiti and his other antics as his being interested in "the power and effect of slogans."[44] For Fischer-Homberger, the main point of Valentin's novel—to criticize persisting Nazi tendencies in West Germany—seems to have been lost in *Elefant*. It is possible this point was lost on some viewers because Zadek forgoes much of the dialogue in Valentin's novel, which would have helped articulate this point.

Despite the limited dialogue, Zadek still engages with Germany's fascist past in several sequences of the film, scenes that are not in the novel. During a dinner party with the teachers, the school director confesses a discriminating act he committed toward a Jewish woman during the war. No one responds to his confession. Instead, we see close-ups of the male party guests staring straight at the camera while the women smile awkwardly. The guests continue to chat, and we see the school director in a close-up staring catatonically down at his plate. He is clearly disturbed by his fascist past, but no one else at the dinner table seems fazed by it.

In a later scene, after it is suggested that Rull has painted a swastika on a giant white wall, Zadek cuts to black-and-white grainy tones that suggest documentary style footage to capture real bystanders' reactions. In his autobiography, Zadek claims the scenes were real:

We secretly painted a swastika on the wall of the senate building. We hid cameras all over and waited to see what would happen during the day. As you can see in the film, things got intense right away, because the first person to see the swastika was a visitor from Israel, a young Jew who went into hysterics and screamed, "Six million! Six million! And now this. It's happening again!"[45]

Another reaction included is that of a young woman who is asked for her opinion of the scene. She seems to have no idea what the symbol is or with which party it is associated. In these sequences, Zadek successfully uses the aesthetics offered by film to visualize Valentin's argument that there is a (sub) conscious denial of Nazism among West Germans. Despite the claims in Zadek's autobiography, the film's audience cannot be sure the interviews on the street are not staged. Zadek admits that he included actors in this sequence, so that viewers can never know whether they are watching an authentic or a staged scene.[46] However Zadek's use of grainy film and an unsteady camera suggests that these are authentic reactions, from which one can assume that either white German youth have learned nothing from the country's past or they feel uncomfortable discussing it in public. In both *Die Unberatenen* and *Elefant*, Rull wishes to break with Germany's legacy and construct his own identity out of foreign influences. Rull's desire for different cultural origins and his resulting identity crisis are uniquely conveyed in Zadek's film adaptation, not only in his filmic aesthetics but also through his use of music.

Music in *Elefant*

The most significant musical change Zadek makes to the novel is replacing the jazz with rock.[47] However, music actually plays an even *greater* role in the film, which features numerous songs and artists. First of all, the film's title, *Ich bin ein Elefant, Madame*, refers to a song performed by the Comedian Harmonists, "Ich küsse ihre Hand, Madame" ("I Kiss Your Hand, Madame"). The Comedian Harmonists were a popular all-male vocal group who performed a cappella in Germany in the late 1920s and early 1930s. The group, which consisted of three Jewish and three non-Jewish members, was forced by the Nazis to disband in 1935. The band's founder, Harry Frommerman, was inspired to create his own band after listening to The Revelers, a jazz quintet of white American vocalists with a pianist.[48] The biopic *The Comedian Harmonists* (1997), directed by Joseph Vilsmaier, implies that, by mimicking the Revelers' syncopated jazz style and invoking the same humor, the Comedian Harmonists are able to put a fresh spin on old German songs, jazzing them up. For example, the Revelers' song "When Yuba Plays the Rumba on the Tuba," seems to

be the inspiration for the Comedian Harmonists' "Der Onkel Bumba aus Kalumba tanzt nur Rumba" ("Uncle Bumba from Kalumba Only Dances Rumba)."

Aside from influencing the film's title, "Ich küsse ihre Hand, Madame" is
played in the film when we are first introduced to the school's teachers, suggesting the old-fashioned nature of their musical taste. In another scene, Rull
sings a parody of the song while at the beach. Rull's rendition of the song
contains such illogical lyrics as "Ich bin ein Elefant, Madame" and "Ich habe
keinen Mund, Madame" (I have no mouth, Madame). The music of this same
song is repeated during an unusual animated sequence during which an off-
screen voice tells us about the lives of kiwis. The repetition of the song throughout the film and its ironic use take away from the song's sincerity. By referencing the Comedian Harmonists' jazzed up hit, Zadek invokes the influence of
African American culture on German popular music while also drawing attention to the white German guilt caused by the Nazis' crimes and reaffirming that
music is not immune from politics.[49]

Music has further importance in the film because Zadek updates Valentin's story by replacing Rull's connection to Louis Armstrong with the Velvet
Underground. Using the music of the Velvet Underground, Zadek attempts to
more accurately portray the state of mind shared by white German youth and
other young people around the world growing up in the postwar era. While jazz
was once the preferred music for rebellious youth in the United States and
Europe, by the 1960s, rock and roll had taken its place across the globe. Indeed, Velvet Underground's 1967 debut album, *The Velvet Underground &
Nico* (featuring German singer and collaborator Nico) is considered one of the
prophetic rock albums of the time.[50]

For youth who wished to inherit an alternative to their German legacy,
rock and roll seemed the ultimate choice. Richard Langston argues that, in the
1960s, German students used rock to "deconstruct dominant notions of West
German identity."[51] Rock had an "ability to demarcate the good from the bad,
the genuine from the commercial imitations, and by extension, insiders from
outsiders. . . . Those who made a distinction between 'them' and 'us' according
to musical alliances also delineated the German from the non-German."[52] That
delineation inevitably meant separating German *Schlager* (pop) from foreign
music, most often rock and roll, which, depending on the artist, could be
marked as (African) American or British. When one considers the initial racist
reaction white German critics had to rock and roll, a genre with black pioneers
and black influences on white rock groups,[53] one could argue that white Germans' fascination with rock was a fascination with black popular culture.

As for Zadek's interest in the Velvet Underground, when one considers the band members' biographies, they certainly correspond to the legacy of the "white Negroes" and bohemians decades earlier. Norman Mailer famously addressed this phenomenon in 1957 in *The White Negro: Superficial Reflections on the Hipster*. Mailer attempts not only to describe but to explain the behavior of so-called hipsters: "cool," rebellious white youths who listened to jazz. Mailer stresses the effect that World War II and the Holocaust had on postwar youth. He refers to hip white youth of this generation as "white Negroes" because they take their style from the "Negro," who has always been accustomed to living every day with the threat of death from racial violence: "He kept for his survival the art of the primitive, he lived in the enormous present, he subsisted for his Saturday night kicks, relinquishing the pleasures of the mind for the more obligatory pleasures of the body, and in his music he gave voice to the character and quality of his existence."[54]

The Velvet Underground's members also rejected the "straight world," only this time it was for an urban life of art, drugs, and rock and roll. All four members of the band—John Cale, Lou Reed, Sterling Morrison, and Maureen Anne Tucker—were white and came from comfortable, privileged backgrounds. Reed, Morrison, and Tucker shared a love for black R & B, something Cale—the classically trained musician—would develop while living in New York. The newly formed group was living the bohemian lifestyle in the city, allowing Morrison to proudly claim: "I was hip, not like people living in Freeport, Long Island with their parents."[55] Besides their preference for R & B and their covers of Chuck Berry songs, Tucker also admits trying to express something specifically "African" in her drumming style and even going to Harlem to seek inspiration.[56]

Even the Velvet Underground's formation as a band resonates with the protagonist Rull's disenchantment with authority in the film. Cale, Reed, and Morrison had disappointing experiences with higher education—all three faced punishment for their nonconformity. Their subsequent move to New York City could be read as an attempt to regain a "primal innocence" by going to R & B shows, blues clubs, and black neighborhoods. The song "I'm Waiting for the Man" embodies both this loss of innocence and the equation between black popular culture and freedom, rejecting a traditional bourgeois life and reveling instead in the experience of drug use and venturing to the black part of town, Lexington and 125th in Harlem:

Hey, white boy, what you doin' uptown?
Hey, white boy, you chasin' our women around?
Oh pardon me sir, it's the furthest from my mind

I'm just lookin' for a dear, dear friend of mine
I'm waiting for my man

Whether the lyrics suggest the lyric persona is in Harlem to buy drugs or seeking a homosexual encounter, they *do* reflect something about his difference
from the African Americans around him and his attempts to diffuse the racial
tension by removing the threat of miscegenation. Lou Reed exhibits even more
self-reflexivity about his own whiteness in regard to his desire to appropriate
black popular culture in a later song written during his solo career, "I Wanna
Be Black," from the album *Street Hassle* (1979):

I don't wanna be a fucked up
Middle class college student anymore
I just wanna have a stable of
Foxy little whores
Yeah, yeah, I wanna be black
Oh, oh, I wanna be black
Yeah, yeah, I wanna be black
I wanna be black, wanna be like Martin Luther King
And get myself shot in the spring

This song is an excellent example of how white men engage with or masquerade as the Other, in this case as a black man, in order to explore, reject, or
reconstruct their own identities. Kobena Mercer reads the song as "a parody of
a certain attitude in postwar youth culture in which the cultural signs of blackness—in music, clothes, and idioms of speech—were the mark of 'cool.'"[57]
The last two lines are a blatant critique of this kind of essentialization and
mythologization of black culture without considering the reality of black experience. If being black means one has a greater appeal with women, then it also
means one has to fear racial violence.

The Velvet Underground's Relevance for *Elefant*

If the Velvet Underground is one of many American (and British) rock bands
who idolized black popular music and mimicked black culture, what does Zadek's use of their music say about the film's protagonist, Rull? It is significant
that Zadek would replace Rull's leitmotif of listening to jazz with the Velvet
Underground. There are references to black culture present in "I'm Waiting for

the Man,"[58] but at the same time, by choosing the Velvet Underground, Zadek shows that the Harlem of the 1960s is not the Harlem of the 1930s or 1950s. Instead of Armstrong singing about God, we have Lou Reed singing about drugs, racial tension, and possibly homosexuality.[59]

The Velvet Underground's proximity to Harlem was not a prerequisite for the influence of black culture on their music. Their British contemporaries, for example the Rolling Stones, were also heavily influenced by black musicians.[60] Music critics have suggested that in his on-stage performance—with his hip-swinging and protruding lips—the Rolling Stones' front man Mick Jagger is mimicking the performance style of Tina Turner. Jagger and the Rolling Stones even traveled to Chicago early in their career in order to record at the legendary Chess Records so that they could imitate the sound of their blues idols.[61]

As a contemporary rock group, the Velvet Underground also reflects the student movement's desire to use rock to break away from German history, for it is a genre that did not exist prior to the end of World War II. But considering the rebellious nature and black cultural influence of their British contemporaries, Zadek could have easily used another Anglo-American rock group to serve the same purpose. When the film was made, the Velvet Underground. unlike the Rolling Stones, was not even very popular in America's mainstream music industry.[62] Contrasting the musical relevance of the Velvet Underground with their popularity, Joe Harvard states:

> Any survey that concerns itself with rock *as it is now played* tends to place them in the top two or three. *Spin* magazine's April 2003 list of the "'Fifteen Most Influential Albums of all Time (. . . not recorded by the Beatles, Bob Dylan, Elvis or the Rolling Stones)" is typical in placing *The Velvet Underground and Nico* first. Yet on the Top 100 Album countdowns that Classic Hits radio stations frequently conduct, the Velvet Underground are usually conspicuous by their absence or low position. A reflection of the almost total radio (and press) blackout the group faced for most of its life, the mainstream airwaves today remain nearly Velvet-free.[63]

It is unclear whether the Velvet Underground ever toured Germany in the 1960s. Yet one significant difference between the Velvet Underground and their contemporaries was their German connection through singer Nico, born Christa Päffgen in 1938 in Cologne. Nico left Germany at age sixteen to work as a model and actress in Paris, and she left for America to further pursue her acting career in 1959.[64] After being introduced to Andy Warhol in 1965, Nico was invited to sing with the Velvet Underground, the house band for Warhol's

Exploding Plastic Inevitable show. Nico was well known for lying about her past. She seemed desperate to create an identity for herself. "She lied so often about almost everything to do with her identity that she managed through it to turn herself into a mythic being."[65]

Part of Nico's invented history seemed geared toward fashioning herself as a victim rather than the heir of a Nazi perpetrator; her father served and was killed in the war: "Nico told many stories about her father, reflecting her own conflicts. She told her son that her grandfather was a Turk who died in Belsen for helping Jews. . . . This is an embellishment of her most usual story which was simply that her father had died in Belsen. He didn't. Wilhelm Päffgen was killed in action in 1942."[66] Nico's desire to fabricate a foreign past for herself recalls Erik Erikson's theory, developed in the 1950s, of identity diffusion and negative identity. For his study, Erikson interviewed a girl of Middle Eastern descent who, after making friends with Scottish immigrants, had invented a fictional Scottish past for herself and affected a Scottish brogue. When asked what motivated her, she responded, "I needed a past."[67] Nico needed a past that would position her as a victim rather than a persecutor. For example, she also claimed to have been raped by a black GI during the postwar years, for which no corroborating evidence has been found. It's certainly possible that young white Germans struggling with their own identity saw themselves reflected in Nico's troubled relationship to her past.

The film's credits attribute all of the music in the film to the Velvet Underground—a claim that is actually false. Aside from "Waiting for the Man," one further Velvet Underground song is featured in the film: "The Gift" plays during the student protest. During the protest, Rull shows up dressed like a Native American: topless, wearing a feather headdress, holding a spear, and with a painted face and a necklace of teeth. Rull speaks to his fellow students in a pseudo-pidgin form of German. Off-screen, the Velvet Underground's "The Gift" plays as nondiegetic accompaniment. The song consists of a rock instrumental behind a short story written by Lou Reed and narrated by John Cale.[68] The story is about a young man named Waldo who misses his girlfriend Marsha, a student at a college in another state. Lacking money for travel, Waldo hides in a package and mails himself to his girlfriend. While opening the package, Marsha and her roommate accidentally decapitate Waldo with a sheet metal cutter. When playing off-screen during Rull's Native American performance, the absurd lyrics of the song, as well as the deadpan delivery by John Cale, intensify the juvenile nature of Rull's behavior.

Despite the prominent use of the Velvet Underground, other songs in the film from three British artists go unacknowledged: Donovan, the Rolling Stones, and the Nice. Perhaps Zadek intentionally misled his audience or did not consider these songs as important. Or maybe Zadek could not afford the rights to excerpts from more famous musicians. It is also possible that Zadek wanted to justify German counterculture by specifically drawing a link to American counterculture—considered the more authentic source as the birthplace of rock and roll. I believe Zadek's preference for the American Velvet Underground mirrors the underlying questions of *Die Unberatenen*: Whose culture must/can we inherit? Can we choose our own legacy? Whose children are we?

These questions of legacy and inheritance are actually present in the Weimar-era film *Ich küsse Ihre Hand, Madame* (1928), which Zadek's title also references. Thus, although Zadek uses the Velvet Underground as a medium for discussion about counterculture, race, and identity, he does not do away with the Weimar references tied to jazz in the novel. In his autobiography, Zadek denies the significance of the song "Ich küsse Ihre Hand, Madame" and of a parody of the song in the film's title. He claims to have listened to Weimar jazz at the time of filming and found the title humorous.[69] And in the novel, Rull is referred to as the "Elefant im Porzellanladen" (elephant in the china shop).[70] Nevertheless, I believe one can make a legitimate connection to the themes of the Weimar-era film, which features Marlene Dietrich. The main character, Count Lerski, is an exiled Russian aristocrat working as a waiter in Paris. He finds love with Dietrich's character, Laurence, despite her misunderstandings about his true identity that make her suspicious of him. The film inevitably reinscribes conventional understandings about class for Laurence realizes how much she loves Lerski only after his wealthy past is revealed. But the title song is also instrumental in their reunification, for it provokes Laurence's sentimental reactions to Lerski. Apparently the film was created for the sole purpose of promoting the song—Lerski lip-synchs to a recording by the original artist.[71]

When Rull sings a parody of the Weimar hit on the beach, by changing the lyrics he is able to criticize the previous generation, turning its cultural possessions into something incoherent and absurd. At the same time, the song serves as evidence of the continuation of pre-1945 sentiments. Furthermore, despite its reinscription of traditional class boundaries, the Weimar film still deals with questions of identity: Who are you really? Does identity depend on where you come from? Or what you currently are? Can you create a history for yourself?

Conclusion

In a 1970 article entitled "Reflections on the Dissent of Contemporary Youth," Erikson claimed the large-scale destruction at the end of World War II meant that young people were destined to challenge their fathers and had to find a new way to do so that was not simply borrowed from the modernist revolutionary forms that had failed.

> The large scale utopias which were to initiate a new kind of history in the post-world war period . . . have all been followed by holocausts as coldly planned as were the gas chambers and Hiroshima. . . . Thus also ended the unquestioned superiority of the fathers, whether they had obeyed and died, or survived and thrived. If then, as it always must, rebellious youth borrows roles from past revolutions it must now avoid the temptation to settle for any previous consolidations.[72]

In the same essay, Erikson describes young people as aligning themselves with other oppressed and repressed peoples forming a collective "Revolt of the Dependent." Erikson claims the "Revolt of the Dependent" directly challenges "all those existing institutions which monopolize the admissions procedures to the main body of society. . . . All this, too, dissenting youth now seeks to provide for itself in newly improvised and ritualized self-graduations, from musical happenings to communal experiment and to political revolt."[73] But the students in Valentin's novel have not yet reached this radical stage. By 1968, students' musical and political interests would coalesce to create *counterpublics* where young people formed communities they intended to operate outside of society. But while the student movement of the late 1960s included agitation, public demonstrations, and eventually the terrorist violence of the RAF, the most trouble the *Halbstarken* were known for was rioting in movie theaters and breaking chairs. And as I suggested earlier, based on their interest in jazz and their enrollment in a *Realschule* rather than a *Gymnasium*, the students in Valentin's novel would likely not even be involved in these types of activities.

In this section, I would like to discuss the conclusion of each text and consider how their different endings contribute to differing arguments that are tied to historical context. In the novel, one of the reasons teachers offer for expelling Rull is his proximity to "primitive," "non-Western" culture, which poses a threat to the other students. Interestingly, Rull's attraction to Otherness is raised only after Herr Violat offers his psychoanalytical explanation for Rull's rebellion. To recap the discussion I briefly addressed earlier in this chapter, Herr Violat claims that, because Rull did not see his father for the first five years of his life—his father was in a Soviet POW camp—Rull never got to establish a stable attachment to his father: "What the boy is missing, like so many today . . . is recognition of a father figure. To put it simply: he loves his mother and hates his father. Not really his own, biological father, but the world of the father, the world of authority, order and legitimacy" (*DU* 271).

It is the German teacher, Dr. Nemitz, who draws the link between Rull's "father issues," his attraction to Otherness, and the danger he poses for the other students. Dr. Nemitz states Rull fights "against everything that is considered of value in the school, and in every school of the Western world. . . . Gentleman, we are close to falling victim to one of the most affecting defects of civilized man: his predilection for the primitive!" (*DU* 273). Dr. Nemitz goes on to say that if they keep Rull in the school, they are welcoming a Trojan horse in their midst.

However, besides the way Rull is Othered, most important is that Rull is not really expelled because the director actually believes he drew the swastika graffiti. And he is not expelled because he hung up a few thought-provoking quotes around the school. While the swastika graffiti is a potential embarrassment for the school, ultimately the director and teachers argue for Rull's expulsion because he openly critiqued the teachers' lesson plans and commitment. As one teacher rhetorically asks, "Where would we be, if every student had an opinion about our teaching—and actually wanted to express it? That is the dark side of democracy, men, and not the only one" (*DU* 269).

This leads me to the final significant diversion between the novel and the film. Germany's Nazi past and its continuing racism are ongoing themes throughout the novel. And this is reconfirmed at the conclusion of the teachers' meeting about Rull. When the teachers argue that expelling Rull would be a defense of decency, Groenewold challenges their assumption that decency is always a positive thing. Without prior warning, he plays a recording of a Heinrich Himmler speech, during which Himmler defends the "final solution" with the following words, "To have persevered—except for a few exceptions of human weaknesses—to have remained decent, that is what made us hard! This is a glorious chapter in our history that hasn't been written and will never be written" (*DU* 280). By playing this speech, Groenewold suggests that allegedly universal values like "decency" can be redefined so that they justify all kinds of actions. This move also allows Groenewold to make a connection between the Nazi period and the present day, in a way that both highlights his status as victim and outsider and ascribes victim status to Rull as well, aligning him with German Jews.

Despite this final act of protest on Groenewold's part, by ending with Rull's dismissal by the teachers, *Die Unberatenen* appears to be most of all a critique of the teachers, whether in regard to their Nazi past or their fear over the changes on the horizon of this new West German democracy. The students' behavior is depicted as a reaction to the lack of guidance and the hypocrisy of their teachers. Valentin is in no way critical about the students' interest in and appropriation of foreign culture; he does not problematize their proximity to Otherness. Throughout the novel, students might maintain racist ideas about blacks while appropriating black culture, but this problematic is never addressed. Rather, Valentin's novel seems to accurately reflect a cultural landscape of postwar Germany, where much like white Americans and Brits, white Germans see nothing wrong with consuming black culture and using derogatory terms like *Neger* in everyday interactions. Part of the reason for this might be that these young white Germans never actually come into contact with black people, a problematic that I will explore in the next three chapters.

In contrast to the novel, the film's ending is more reflective of the politics of cultural appropriation. Zadek provides a critique of both German authority figures *and* the students who hope to flee their historical legacy by identifying with foreigners. The film concludes with a section titled *Reifeprüfung*—a reference to the traditional, state-authorized school exams. The fact that, even after all of their subversive antics throughout the film, the students ultimately submit themselves to be judged in a state exam that will allow them to find their way in society, suggests some kind of failure to break with the past. This seems to be the underlying argument in one of the last scenes of the film. Rull is at a school assembly where his fellow students are to decide whether he should be expelled. One of the main student agitators, Klaus Rohwedder, wishes to give Rull a chance to explain why he chose to draw a swastika. Rull curiously turns the tables, taking on the role of interviewer himself and begins asking Rohwedder whether he played soccer for a team in Eimsbütteler. When Rohwedder denies this, Rull asks whether it was his father. At first, these questions seem completely out of context and an indication of yet another of Rull's antics. Finally, Rull says, "If I think about it more precisely, it must have been your grandfather. Was he also named Rohwedder?" Until now, this questioning has been filmed in the form of shot / reverse shot between Rull and Rohwedder. Yet this final question is followed by a shot of Rohwedder's room, covered in political posters, which is accompanied by off-screen booing and hooting. Through his seemingly meaningless questioning, Rull is actually reinstating a German legacy Rohwedder had attempted to escape. Otto Rohwedder (1909–1969) was a soccer player for the Nazis' national team. It is unclear whether the Rohwedder in the film is Otto's grandson. But Rull's suggestion thereof brings back the point that, despite Rohwedder's self-fashioning as the perfect revolutionary, he cannot deny his paternal legacy.

Zadek's critique of the good versus bad / us versus them mentality demonstrated by the students is also visible in the protest scene discussed earlier where Zadek takes aim at the students' performance of rebellion. During this scene, the audience gets a bird's eye view of students confronting policemen as if in a playful cat-and-mouse game. Rull's Native American costume suggests the silliness of the spectacle that is put on by policemen and students. The reason for their protest seems both unclear and arbitrary. The policemen lock arms, and from an aerial camera angle, we see a group of three students who continuously charge the police, only to be thrown back as if they were playing the game Red Rover. Rull's Native American costume might also be a reference to the genre of the western, critiquing the tendency of both sides to view the conflict in a binary of good versus bad. This reference to westerns resurfaces when Rohwedder's presence on screen is accompanied by a western musical theme.

I believe it is Zadek's critique of students' binary thinking that leads him to end the film with, of all things, a counterrevolutionary *Schlager* song, Freddy Quinn's "Wir," which was recorded in 1966. Even at the time, the song was known as reactionary response to the student movement. In his lyrics, Quinn criticizes students for their reckless behavior and pointless desire for destruction of German traditions and values. Quinn constructs a binary of "us" versus "them." And ironically, despite these critiques, in the end, Quinn attempts to highlight some similarities between himself and the rebellious students, insisting that he is not merely an old-fashioned square. Although the song attempts to draw a line between "us" and "them," Zadek once again intentionally blurs this line as well as that between "good" and "bad." During the entire film, the juxtaposing song sequences have suggested that students seek comfort in rock music, the music of the foreigners who are good, and they wish to escape German *Schlager*, which is bad. Yet, in Zadek's final montage, the foreigners are not always the "good" guys; we might see images of the rebellious Beat poet Allen Ginsberg, but we also see footage of the Ku Klux Klan. It is also unclear who "us" and "them" refers to in this music video. Does it refer to Quinn's lyrics concerning the obedient versus the rebellious, old versus the young, or the Germans versus the Americans? By blurring these boundaries, Zadek seems to suggest that students' denial of or resistance to their German legacy is too black and white. The references to Weimar throughout the film also suggest that Germans can look outside national boundaries for role models, but they still have to deal with the legacy of their parents because it is an imminent part of them. Zadek confirms this by ending the film with the titles "Wir," then "Made in Germany." This German identity might not be an easy one to carry, but "to merely exercise the father signifie[s] denying his internalization and thus the continuation of his reign."[74]

The next chapter takes us into the 1970s with Ulrich Plenzdorf's *Die neuen leiden des jungen W.* (1972). While the first two chapters have concentrated on the appropriation of black popular culture in West Germany, chapter 3 examines two texts set in East Germany, one written prior to, and the other following, reunification. I will consider similarities and differences between how West Germans and East Germans appropriated black popular culture to reject the traditions of their forefathers. Not just a means to rebel against tradition, black culture remedies feelings of confinement in the East, as we will see, and counters feelings of emasculation.

CHAPTER 3

Of Blues and Blue Jeans: American Dreams
in the East

In this chapter, I turn my attention to how black popular culture can function as a counterexample to hegemonic *East* German masculinity in Ulrich Plenz- dorf's novel *Die neuen Leiden des jungen W.* (*The New Sufferings of Young W*, 1972) and Michael Schorr's film *Schultze Gets the Blues* (2003). Although Plenzdorf's novel was written while the German Democratic Republic (GDR) was still in existence and Schorr's film is set in a postunification East German village, both texts share an emphasis on the important role black popular cul- ture plays for white characters with limited opportunities for rebellion within their highly structured and monitored communities. While white West Ger- mans' alternately fond and fearful memories of African Americans often re- sulted from direct contact with black GIs following World War II, East Ger- mans were relatively isolated by their government from contact with Americans and their ostensibly capitalist and imperialist culture. Nevertheless, exceptions were made for U.S. minority groups, like Native Americans and African Amer- icans, who were treated as potential allies in the fight against American impe- rialism. One can imagine that the official East German injunction to despise white, but not minority, Americans was not always easy to abide by, especially given the endurance of prewar prejudices about race.

One of the best examples of East Germans' ambivalent relationship to- ward African Americans is from Reiner Kunze's *Die Wunderbaren Jahren* (*The Lovely Years*, 1978), a collection of sketches describing the contradictions of life in the GDR. The following excerpt is from "Nine-Year-Olds":

PASTOR: So let's say, a man comes from America . . .
FIRST PUPIL: That can't be. He would be shot by tanks immediately. (Gestures using a machine gun) Bang—bang—bang—bang! (The other pupils laugh.)

PASTOR: But why?
FIRST PUPIL: Because Americans are enemies.
PASTOR: And Angela Davis? Didn't you make a poster for Angela Davis?
FIRST PUPIL: She's not American. She's a Communist.
SECOND PUPIL: Nope, she's a Negro.[1]

In the pupils' worldview, the East and socialism are good; the West and capitalism are bad. However, the existence of American Communists and the fact that not all Americans had the same power within American hegemony complicated this simple binary, since the East German state did its best to advocate for the culture of such "good" Americans by such acts as promoting abolitionist literature from the nineteenth century, promoting African American theater, and even producing their own socialist westerns.[2]

Considering the GDR's investment in stressing the failures of American democracy, it is not surprising that African American activists, particularly those with ties to the communist movement, were also promoted in East Germany as allies.[3] What Kunze's sketch also illustrates is a racist manner of thinking, which had been widespread in Nazi Germany and during the Wilhelmine era, that held blacks as a separate and unequal race. Finally, this excerpt shows that, despite the national rhetoric of socialist solidarity in East Germany, racism did exist. As historian Quinn Slobodian states, "On the one hand East German authorities officially denounced 'race thinking.' On the other hand, they continued to rely on stereotypes of phenotypical and folkloric difference to illustrate themes of internationalist solidarity."[4] In theory, East German scholars "followed the UNESCO statement [from 1950] in discarding racial hierarchy while preserving the kernel of hereditary racial difference," but by maintaining the existence of *some* racial difference, they allowed for old prejudices and fears to still be maintained.[5] Regarding antiblack racism in the GDR, there are many accounts of African students, workers, and orphans, who might have been invited to the GDR to study and work but were nevertheless segregated from the East German population.[6] The assumption prevailed that Africans in the GDR were there only for a short time and were tolerated under the assumption they would eventually take their skills back to their respective countries to further the socialist cause.[7]

African Americans in the GDR tended to be present as public figures either visiting or seeking refuge from racism in the West. On several occasions, large crowds of East Germans turned up to see Angela Davis, Martin Luther King Jr., and Paul Robeson. A handful of black GIs serving in West Germany even fled to the GDR after deserting the U.S. Army. In the East they were given political and vocational training and were championed as proof of socialist countries' superior treatment of minorities.[8] However, even these prominent African Americans were able to pick up on the discrepancy between East Germany's official stance on race and the opinions of average white citizens. For example, African American singer Aubrey Pankey addressed the "pseudosympathetic voices for negroes, behind which in reality racist attitudes [were] concealed."[9]

Despite the GDR's official efforts at erasing racism and discrimination from public view—in 1950 GDR leader Wilhelm Pieck officially declared there was no more racism in the country—the everyday reality was quite different.[10] Peggy Piesche coins the term "socialism of difference" to refer to the disjuncture between the GDR's official welcoming policy toward foreign blacks and the reality of how these workers and students were really treated.[11] Regardless of the government's claims that racism was only a symptom of capitalist oppression and therefore could not exist in their socialist state, even the African Americans who praised the GDR reported incidents of racism. Oliver Harrington, who lived in the GDR from 1961 until 1991 translating American classics for the Aufbau publishing house, claimed that "living in East Germany, he was 'insulted on the streets on an average of about 5 times a day.'"[12] Even the director of the Cultural Commission of the Politburo,[13] Alfred Kurella, claimed that white East Germans had "'pseudosympathies' with blacks." In a letter to his colleague Albert Norden, Kurella went even further, alleging that "behind the very loudly proclaimed propaganda for the 'poor Negro' and his 'culture' that certain people propagated, there actually lay a 'racial hatred with inverse indicators.'"[14]

Plenzdorf's *The New Sufferings of Young W* and Schorr's *Schultze Gets the Blues*, separated as they are by thirty years, allow us to examine more closely the ways in which black popular culture, or more specifically black music and black masculinity, were received in the GDR and how these attitudes changed or persisted after reunification. Both texts are concerned with white male protagonists who have grown up in and were socialized in the GDR, yet feel estranged from their communities. Both Edgar (the protagonist of Plenzdorf's novel) and Schultze are faced with a crisis of masculinity that is linked to their conflicts with modernity. They find solace in listening to black popular music. And finally, the blues—a genre that has a long and significant history in East Germany's countercultural scene—is an important motif in both texts. In this chapter, I will provide a detailed discussion of these texts' historical and cultural contexts, unpack them individually, and then consider them in relation to each other.

Cold War Masculinity: Military Service, Work, and Family

In many ways, the masculinity promoted in East Germany is similar to that promoted in West Germany. As I stated in chapter 2, during West Germany's rearmament in the 1950s, the need arose for a "citizen soldier" who could be present at home but was prepared to defend his country against communism if necessary. The GDR promoted a similar "citizen soldier," but the indoctrination of this role began much earlier. Several institutions existed that were meant to teach children socialist values and the necessity of armed resistance. From the Ernst Thälmann Jungpioniere (Ernst Thälmann Young Pioneers) to the Freie Deutsche Jugend (Free German Youth, FDJ), the state made it clear to East German youth that their workers' paradise was under constant threat from the West and it was their responsibility to protect the state.

Based on the *Wandervogel*—a "back to nature" youth movement created in the late nineteenth century—the FDJ's traditions were not very appealing to young people, who increasingly preferred "street culture" to hiking and "dropping out" to group activities. According to historian Mark Fenemore, by 1969, "As many as 85 per cent [of youth] said that they found spontaneous, informal groups a more fulfilling source of leisure than the FDJ."[15] Furthermore, Fenemore claims, "The increasing accessibility of consumer items like transistor radios, TVs, bicycles, and mopeds made the nature opportunities provided by the FDJ appear unnecessary and redundant."[16] Indeed, technology is key for Schultze's and Edgar's involvement with alternative culture: Edgar uses a tape recorder to record his messages and songs for the outside world, and Schultze's radio draws him into broadcasts of zydeco and Cajun cooking shows.

A year after the Berlin Wall was built in 1961, conscription was implemented in East Germany and "all eighteen-year-old males had to submit to military training and discipline."[17] The Volksarmee (People's Army) was run in the strict Prussian military tradition with regimented routines and no privacy or freedom.[18] This perpetuation of German military tradition reflected East Germany's failure to deal with the legacy of Nazism as thoroughly as West Germany had.[19] In fact, Fenemore discovered many continuities in the construction of masculinity from the Nazis to the GDR. This was not only a result of East Germany's denial of any culpability for Nazism but also a consequence of the country's rhetoric of victimization and the importance it placed on violence. Fenemore states,

> Communist attempts to foster support and willingness to defend the GDR
> led them to foster the same masculine ideals and values as those cherished

by previous German regimes, not least the Nazis. They sought to use masculinity to generate hegemony. Boys continued to learn that "traits such as strength, competitiveness, inexpressiveness and aggressiveness" were expected of them as males. Literature and propaganda portrayed images of an idealized masculinity based on strength, courage and willingness to defend socialism.[20]

While this was the ideology supported by the state, Holger Brandes stresses that because of the "low acceptance of its own army and its military service . . . the military ideal of masculinity was only very 'conditionally hegemonic.'"[21]

Just as in West Germany, when it came to rebellious masculinities in East Germany the problems began with the father. As discussed in chapter 2, both West and East Germans believed that the separation of sons from their fathers (especially those fathers killed in action or interned as POWs) made young men rebellious. Boys allegedly had more freedom living under the rule of their mothers, and they did not want to relinquish this freedom when their fathers returned. Both protagonists in the texts lack fatherly guidance. Plenzdorf's Edgar, whose parents divorced early on, has not seen his father since age five. Schultze's father is dead, and the film suggests that the only tie that he has to his father is his accordion playing.

Although gender equality was an important part of the socialist program, in reality many of the inequalities that existed in the West were also present in the East. As Brandes points out, "The highest executive committees of the GDR were almost exclusively composed of men."[22] East German girls did participate in youth organizations, but when it came to military service, the most common scenario was that young men went to the military, and the women remained at home awaiting their return. In Plenzdorf's novel, Edgar's love interest, Charlie, awaits her fiancé, Dieter, who is serving in the military. Gender participation was more equal in the workplace, with studies showing that a higher percentage of East German women worked than West German women.[23] However, despite the state-run *Kinderkrippen* (nurseries), the responsibility of childcare and other domestic duties still weighed on the shoulders of women.

A final key to understanding masculinity in East Germany was that, as Fenemore states, "the workplace and not the family was to be the key site for reconfiguring citizenship" and manual labor was respected more than intellectual and artistic careers, which were valorized only to the extent they were seen as in service to the workers.[24] Artists' task was to present workers with a utopian image of their lives and of the state in the style of socialist realism:

In the GDR, a male habitude dominated, with clichés of the working-class hero, which originally was anchored in classic industrial work and its quality characteristic of bodily engagement, discipline and endurance. . . . In [R. W.] Connell's sense, one can perhaps speak most appropriately in relation to this of a proletarian-petty bourgeois shaping of hegemonic masculinity in the GDR. At its core, the point was that the GDR not only unofficially defined itself as a *Arbeiter- und Bauernstaat* ("Worker and Peasant State") but was also shaped up to the most banal forms of daily life by a corresponding habituality. . . .[25]

Because of Edgar's rejection of the workplace and Schultze's forced retirement, both are displaced from the most valued social roles. Furthermore, the fact that Edgar and Schultze are drawn to the arts makes them stand out even more as the opposite of the East German male ideal.

"Race Music," Style, and Masculinity

In the GDR, Western/American culture was deemed "nonculture" that could only criminalize youth. These views were not only part of anticapitalist propaganda, but were also based on the kinds of American culture that found its way into the East. Mark Fenemore notes, "From comic book characters like Tarzan and Superman to the inarticulate cowboys of Westerns and suave spies like James Bond, the West bombarded East German youth with its own visions of heroism."[26] None of these models were considered acceptable in the workers' state.

A further source for East Germans' critique of rock and roll culture was its roots in black popular music. In *Sex, Thugs and Rock 'n' Roll*, Fenemore reprints a police poster with portraits and profiles of *Halbstarken* to demonstrate how subcultural groups "were made to function as racialised others."[27] The manner in which the photos are presented with explanations of their hairstyles is reminiscent of Nazi-era eugenicist descriptions of non-Aryans. One can also see the racialized discourse surrounding the *Halbstarken* in the manner in which authorities described their clothing. Like racial minorities in American cities during World War II who embraced the zoot suit craze, white East German men wishing to rebel against stiff military styles donned flashy clothing. The racialized terms used to describe this clothing were *Affenpalmen*, literally "ape palm trees," referring to a pattern printed on shirts and *Niggihemden*, likely slang for "Negerhemden" (Negro shirts) and possibly the origin of the East German slang term for T-shirt, "Nicki." Rock and roll was also called

Affenmusik (ape music). Furthermore, since rockers were more concerned about personal style and fashion than was normally expected of males, their behavior was perceived as emasculated and homosexual.[28]

While some youth tried to defend their preference for rock and roll as an expression of their solidarity with oppressed African Americans, the state's position was that it had no problem with "authentic" black popular music, which rock and roll was not. Negro spirituals were officially endorsed as an authentic cultural form, especially since they were promoted by leftist hero Paul Robeson. Heavily influenced by Robeson's own opinions about jazz, East German music critics believed that while Negro spirituals were a reflection of authentic black culture, popular genres like jazz and rock and roll were the result of black musicians' exploitation by music executives.[29]

Aside from rock and roll and spirituals, another genre of black popular music that was very popular in the GDR was the blues, a genre of particular importance in this chapter because both Plenzdorf's novel and Schorr's film pick up on the motif of the blues. In postwar Germany, the blues was alternately received as the source of jazz or a mere side note to jazz.[30] Blues enthusiasts, in the West and East alike, tended to mythologize it as an authentic music of proletarian blacks. The corresponding argument that the blues had been ruined once it reached Broadway, where it was altered to cater to a white bourgeois market, served the GDR's socialist ideology well.[31] However, this view of the blues essentializes it, disregarding the European influence in early African American music and the fact that not only white Americans but some middle-class black Americans also were offended by the music's subject matter and dark tone.

Just as rock and roll fans practiced *Halbstarken* culture, blues fans developed their own scene as well. In West Germany, what connected young people with the blues scene was a critical opinion of German society, feeling like an outsider and the desire to explore alternative lifestyles and occasionally experiment with drugs. According to historian Detlef Siegfried, the West German blues scene "culminated around 1970, as a widely ramified 'counterculture' that emerged out of the nonconformist subcultures of the sixties—beatniks, provos, communes, drug scenes—and the student movement that saw itself as a counterforce to the traditional majority."[32] The blues-rock scene in East Germany was of equal importance. Michael Rauhut describes it as

> not only the most vital and enduring youth scene in the country, but also an explicitly Eastern phenomenon. It was born out of the reverberation of Woodstock and only lost its relevance during the 1980s under the com-

petitive pressure of punk, heavy metal, and other attractive alternatives with which youth could identify. The model that the generations of "Bluesers" who came after one another followed remained the ideals of the hippie era. Freedom, authenticity, and nonconformity were the primary values that were reflected in behavior, artistic preferences, and outfits.[33]

By the end of the 1980s, there were over fifty clubs in the GDR promoting blues. Although the state might have promoted blues music, the style of blues-rock fans was often as provocative as the *Halbstarken*. Since the Bluesers evolved from the hippie movement and the folk rock revival of the 1960s, their scene developed later than the *Halbstarken*. Nevertheless, Bluesers' long hair, jeans, and parkas were just as much a thorn in the government's side. From his self-description, Edgar of Plenzdorf's novel likely associated with this youth culture. In the novel, his clothes consist of "his burlap jacket that he'd sewn together himself, with copper wire, and his old jeans."[34] Neither the *Halbstarke* nor the Bluesers corresponded with the state's idea of model socialist masculinity.

Child of Mittenberg

For its time,[35] Ulrich Plenzdorf's novel was a controversial and stylistically innovative work that narrowly evaded censorship, having benefited from a change in East German politics that occurred shortly before it was published. In December 1971, the leadership in the GDR changed hands from Walther Ulbricht to Erich Honecker, who announced a new phase in East German arts that allowed for more stylistic freedom, as long as the subject matter remained socialist.[36] Plenzdorf's novel was published a year later in the literary journal *Sinn und Form*.[37] By 1973, in light of such nontraditional works as Plenzdorf's, Honecker regretted opening the floodgates and retracted his earlier promise.[38] Plenzdorf's text was controversial not only because of its stylistic experimentation, which eschewed socialist realism, but also for its subject matter, which Peter Hutchinson described as the "failures and limitations of GDR society: especially the denial of individuality, aversion to alternative lifestyles, stress on the work ethic, the pressures to conform, the failure to cultivate critical thinking, [and] the endorsement of socialist realism as the only acceptable form of writing."[39]

The text references parts of Goethe's *Die Leiden des jungen Werthers* (*The Sufferings of Young Werther*, 1774) in order to make larger arguments about East German society and East German literary history. Goethe's *Werther* was a prime example of *Empfindsamkeit* (emotionalism), an eighteenth-century artistic movement that complemented Enlightenment thinking by promoting feeling instead of pure reason. Like Oskar, Goethe's Werther rejects the professional path his father lays out for him. Instead of returning to the city to pursue a career, Werther remains in the countryside to pursue a young woman named Charlotte (Lotte) with whom he falls in love though she is engaged to a man named Albert. Werther eventually shoots himself because he cannot bear the pain of living without Lotte and being forced into a conventional life. *Werther* was Goethe's most popular text, inspiring a frenzy of young people who sympathized with the protagonist's emotions and even mimicked his dress.

Plenzdorf's decision to use *Werther* as an intertext was no doubt an attempt to mock the GDR's valorization of eighteenth-century literary style. The GDR's promotion of eighteenth-century styles was part of an effort to establish links with older German culture and demonstrate that the GDR was not a successor to the Third Reich.[40] By critically engaging with a canonical text from this period, Plenzdorf could conform to the regime's desires while simultaneously ridiculing the state by drawing a comparison between eighteenth-century bourgeois society (based on the one period text that East Germans did not want their children reading) and East Germany's "worker's paradise." Plenzdorf claims that "Werther was never on the lesson plan."[41] According to Ute Brandes and Ann Clark Fehn, East Germans favored Georg Lukács's reading of *Werther*. Lukács claimed *Werther* revealed the contradictions between "narrow bourgeois institutions, as epitomized by the marriage of Lotte and Albert, with the bourgeois ideal of self-realization."[42] Brandes and Fehn add that "much of the controversy of the Plenzdorf text for GDR readers lies in the very suggestion that sufferings comparable to those of the idealistic, alienated Lukács-Werther are possible in the socialist state."[43] Ultimately, the subject matter of Goethe's text helped Plenzdorf argue for individualism and nonconformity and aided him in legitimizing the feelings of East German youth because Plenzdorf put Edgar's feelings about society on par with Werther's sufferings.[44]

In Goethe's *Werther*, readers learn about Werther's plight from letters he writes to a friend, which are preceded and followed by an explanation from this friend after Werther's suicide. Plenzdorf's text opens with obituaries about Edgar, followed by Edgar speaking from the grave, but we do not yet learn how he died. Throughout the course of the novel we learn about Edgar from tapes he recorded and sent to his friend Willi, passages of Goethe's novel that he quotes, interviews his father conducts with friends and relatives after Edgar's death, and from Edgar's thoughts from the grave, which offer a wiser perspective on his earlier behavior. Although Edgar makes several critical remarks about the GDR, both before and after his death, the lack of an authoritative narrative voice makes it difficult to pin down whether Plenzdorf is defending or challenging socialist structures.[45]

Just as in *The Tin Drum* and *Die Unberatenen*, black popular culture is more an accent than a central theme in Plenzdorf's novel. Nevertheless, to the very extent they appear incidental, Edgar's references to black popular culture establish, for the text, a naturalized link between rebellious white East German youth and black popular culture. As in Oskar's and Rull's cases, it is instructive to examine Edgar's notions of black popular culture more deeply. Edgar Wibeau's outsider status in East Germany is already apparent from his last name, which he discusses at length at the beginning of the text. This name is a point of dispute and frustration at the workplace, since the name Wibeau is of French origin, stemming from the Huguenots who settled in Berlin in the seventeenth century. Edgar is a metalworker's apprentice, and his instructor at the factory, Flemming, insists on calling him *Wiebau*. This provokes Edgar to drop a metal foundation plate on Flemming's toe and flee his hometown for fear of the repercussions. From the grave, Edgar reflects on his actions:

> I mean, after all, every person has the right to be correctly called by his correct name. If you don't attach any great importance to it—that's your business. . . . What's the matter with the name "Wibeau"? If it'd been "Hitler" maybe, or "Himmler!" That would've been truly decent. But "Wibeau"? "Wibeau" is an old Huguenot name. So? (*NS* 6)

Edgar insists that Wibeau cannot be as offensive a name as Hitler or Himmler. At the same time, however, he suggests his coworkers might have preferred those "truly decent" names because they would have been more German and easier to pronounce. This accusation is even more scandalous in East Germany, since the official rhetoric claimed there were no Nazis, and that the state had been built by antifascists directly descendant from the democratic Weimar Republic, thus free of the guilt of the Third Reich.

Although Edgar's running away is preceded by his dropping a metal plate on his instructor's toe, until this act, Edgar had actually been a model student. It is not his behavior, but his beliefs that pose a danger to the system. On the morning of his rebellious act, Edgar's peers attempt to pass off machine-filed foundation plates as their own. As usual, Edgar does not participate in these antics. Nevertheless, he defends his peers' actions by challenging the factory's educational methods. When Flemming suspects the plates are from the filing machine located in a neighboring plant, Edgar responds, "OK, let's assume there is a machine there. Can be. You have to ask yourself, why do we have to file down those foundation plates then? And that in our third year" (*NS* 5). Flemming defends his teaching methods with the argument that only when the boys can file a watch out of a piece of iron by hand will they have surpassed the stage of apprentice. Rather than merely questioning the best way of becoming a watchmaker, Edgar challenges his entire apprenticeship, noting, "But we didn't really want to become watchmakers" (*NS* 5). Edgar suggests that none of the boys really want to do this job and might have other aspirations frustrated by a state that left its citizens little leeway regarding occupations.

His instructor, Flemming, is representative of the regime's stubborn dogmatism, which Edgar describes as "[an] attitude out of the Middle Ages: the era of handmade articles" (*NS* 5), an irony considering the regime's support of socialist industrialization. Additionally, the East German school system, as Edgar describes it, seems to favor memorization over critical thinking, making him a star pupil given his talent for memorization. But rather than being proud of this skill, Edgar would prefer to be a free thinker. He refers to his penchant for memorization as "a real pain. . . . It had its advantages of course, in school for example. I mean every teacher is satisfied when he hears a passage from a book he knows. I couldn't blame them. They don't need to check if it's all right, like they do with their own words. And they were all satisfied" (*NS* 30). His teachers' preference for memorization over critical thinking is representative of the state's resistance to experimentation and new ideas, a struggle at the center of the novel.

Rebellion, Youth, and Nature

In his efforts to rebel against the status quo, Edgar applies binary thinking to every aspect of his life, and he is constantly seeking to present himself in a manner that is farthest away from the East German ideal. Similar to the *Halbstarken* and blues fans who were an eyesore for the East German regime, Edgar's rebellious character is externalized in his wardrobe. For Edgar, jeans are the most important symbol of youth. He believes real jeans wearers are young and slim and have a carefree state of mind that one loses as one ages: "People shouldn't be allowed to get older than seventeen—or eighteen. After that they get a job or go to college or join the army and then there's no reasoning with them anymore" (*NS* 14). To be an adult and wear jeans is an oxymoron, just like "card-carrying Communists [who] beat their wives" (*NS* 14), a statement that reveals some of the contradictions that might have existed in the GDR.

In his work life, Edgar prefers being an artist to working in construction, because art is not determined by preconceptions and cannot be judged scientifically: "A pair of pliers is good if it grips. But a picture or something like that? Nobody really knows whether it's good or not" (*NS* 24). His desire to escape preconceptions leads him to idolize childhood, which he associates with innocence. For Edgar, childhood is an undetermined, pure state, in which an individual has not yet been corrupted by society. That is why above all, Edgar values artwork done by children "Children can really bore you but they can paint so it'll just knock you over. If I wanted to look at pictures I'd rather go to a kindergarten than a stupid old museum" (*NS* 27).

When Edgar runs away from his small town of Mittenberg, he goes to East Berlin, where he takes refuge in an abandoned garden house belonging to the family of his friend Willi. Edgar fancies himself an artist and initially spends his time making abstract art. In the outhouse of the garden colony where the house is located, Edgar finds a copy of Goethe's *Werther*. Ironically, because he uses the book's title page as toilet paper, he never discovers what he has been reading. According to Susan E. Hunnicutt, "By having Edgar strip the book of cover, title page and afterword, Plenzdorf was stripping it of all previous associations and interpretations, in particular of the Lukacsian interpretation. . . . Plenzdorf essentially allowed Edgar to read Goethe without interference from State sanctioned interpretations."[46] Although Edgar is at first put off by Goethe's "impossible style," he is drawn to the text and feels his thoughts are reflected in it. In Berlin, Edgar meets a young woman whom he calls Charlie (a reference to Werther's love, Charlotte). When Charlie confronts Edgar with his claim to be an artist, he rebukes her with a quote from *Werther*: "Uniformity marks the human race. Most of them spend the greater part of their time in working for a living, and the scanty freedom that is left to them burdens them so that they seek every means of getting rid of it" (*NS* 30). Edgar uses yet another passage from *Werther* to counter Dieter, Charlie's fiancé, who suggests he must learn the rules of drawing before he can be an artist. Edgar suggests instead that rules might make someone accepted by society, but they also destroy everything natural:

> One can say much in favor of rules, about the same thing as can be said in favor of civil society. A person who trains himself by the rules will never produce anything absurd or bad . . . can never become an intolerable neighbor . . . on the other hand any "rule," say what you like, will destroy the true feeling for nature and the true expression of her! (*NS* 41–42)

By quoting Werther's critiques of society in several conversations with others, Edgar is able to secretly criticize the GDR and plant subversive ideas in the minds of his interlocutors, who are busy trying to decipher Werther's archaic language. It is understandable that Edgar, a frustrated teen in the GDR of the 1970s, would be drawn to *Empfindsamkeit*. For those East German youths who wished to "drop out" of society and seek an escape from the regimented daily life in the GDR, *Empfindamkeit*'s "turn inward" and retreat into nature would be appealing.[47] In fact, Edgar's opinions about freedom and nature and his fascination and elevation of black culture over hegemonic German culture, both of which I discuss later, resonate with *Empfindsamkeit*. In Karl von Eckartshausen's short story from this literary period "Isogin und Celia, eine Geschichte von einem unsrer schwarzen Brüder aus Afrika, von einem Mohren" ("Isogin and Celia, a Story about One of Our Black Brothers from Africa, about a Moor," 1787), Eckartshausen addresses the alleged differences between European and African culture in order to express similar opinions to that found in *Werther*. Not only does Eckartshausen criticize the rules of German society, but he seems to hold Africans in higher regard than Europeans because Africans supposedly follow the rules of nature as opposed to man-made rules:

> I do not know whether it is really true that Europeans are the more civilized peoples: I doubt this more and more each day. The name *barbarian*, with which we so like to label other peoples, sounds strange to me. I think we've fooled ourselves, that we may be mistaken. Could it be that we actually have earned the name *barbarian* more than some native, who at least, even if he does not have other laws, stays true to the laws of nature?

Here the white European's tragic alienation from nature is contrasted to the "noble savage's" harmony with it. Eckartshausen also shares Edgar's opinion about education:

> When I think back to what the state and what education have made out of me, I often find an odd thing: a creature who was alienated from nature starting in his youth through thousands of endeavors, whom people filled with knowledge that was of little use to him and made him familiar with a system that does not exist in nature and that forces some opinions onto people that under great scrutiny are revealed as lies.[48]

Despite his essentialist view of Africans, it is still remarkable for the eighteenth century that Eckartshausen sees Africans as "brothers" rather than a separate race.

The sensibility movement, in stark contrast to East Germany's emphasis on collectivity, encouraged self-reflection, perhaps even self-absorption. Along with de-emphasizing the individual, the affective character of bureaucratic East Germany was decidedly cold and rational. For example, the obituary published about Edgar in the local newspaper callously condemns his alternative lifestyle and ascribes his accidental death to his "careless tinkering with electric current" (NS 1). His mother describes the messages he recorded and sent home as "strange messages. So affected" (NS 3). In them the only comfort she can find is their indication of his ability to work: "No matter, at least they [the tapes] told us one thing. That Edgar was well. That he was even working, and not wasting his time" (NS 3). The state's turn from feeling and nature to reason and efficiency is most dramatically externalized in the fact that the garden colony where Edgar hides out is scheduled to be demolished to make room for new high-rise apartment complexes. Ironically, such garden colonies are remnants from the Weimar Republic and were conceived as creating green spaces in the city where the working-class could find rest, fresh air, and exercise—an attempt to reconcile the modern subject with nature.

Romantic Notions of Black Popular Culture

Throughout the novel, Edgar tries to portray himself as a rebel, only to admit that he has consistently given in to authority figures like his mother, who was against his artistic ambitions and wanted him to learn a "decent job." His mother's dedication to normalcy—fueled by the stigma of her divorce—even led her to try to train the left-handed Edgar to write with his right hand, which ultimately failed. He reflects, "I was just sick of running around as living proof that you can raise a child very well without a father" (NS 11). Having been a very obedient son, an artistic lifestyle and blues music represented a way to break out of his normal routine. The reason he gives for his rebellion makes him seem like one of Norman Mailer's "white Negroes" who decides "to accept the terms of death, to live death as immediate danger, to divorce oneself from society, to exist without roots."[49] Before running away, Edgar suddenly realizes that if he were to die, "If [he'd] suddenly croaked, smallpox or something . . . what would [he] have gotten out of life" (NS 11). Like the "white Negro," Edgar equates danger with experiencing life, with really living.[50] It might seem contradictory that a fictional character in an East German text would share the same valorizing notions of blackness and desire for a life of danger as a famous, white, American author like Mailer. My comparison between Edgar's and Mailer's views reveals that Plenzdorf's text interrogates assumptions about East German culture in a way that disturbs the status quo. If Edgar were a truly socialist realist character, he would be content with his job, not feel stifled by the security offered by the state. By fashioning Edgar in this way, Plenzdorf suggests that the tenets of socialism—employment, security, and equality—are not enough to make people content with their lives. Furthermore, the similarities between Mailer's idolization of black culture and the way black culture is valorized in Plenzdorf's novel also suggests that the presence of a socialist political system does not automatically eradicate racism. Plenzdorf might posit black culture as more exciting than hegemonic German culture, but in order to do so black culture must be characterized as something primitive and inherently separate.

The topic of security brings me back to a comparison between Edgar and Werther. While Werther's suffering was caused by his alienation from society, Edgar actually suffers from too much attention. As Hutchinson states, "Werther was a misfit and very much alone in his society; despite his anti-social behavior, Edgar does not lack support."[51] In fact, it is the overwhelming support, guidance, and smothering nature of the state and society that drive Edgar to rebel. Hutchison comments that East Germans "are helpless victims of a state which overcontrols them and persuades them they are better off as they are—protected and secure. Yet the desire to break free from such 'protection' is clearly at the heart of Edgar's problem."[52] East German society's paternal nature is highlighted, for example, when Edgar is short on money in Berlin and easily finds a job at a construction site where the workers take him under their wing despite his lack of talent for the work.

In his short life, Edgar constructs himself as the underappreciated artistic genius. When he brings his portfolio to an art school in Berlin to apply for a spot, the professor suggests he become a draftsman, but Edgar wants to be a "real" artist, not a part of the GDR's system.[53] Part of Edgar's fantasy is the belief that his father is an avant-garde painter, when in fact his father is just a movie extra.[54] Edgar's resentment toward his mother stems, in part, from her determination to limit his contact with his father, whom he calls "der schwarze Mann von Mittenberg." Literally this would be translated as "the black man from Mittenberg," but in German slang it really means, "the bad man." In Edgar's imagination, his father led the kind of artist's life for which Edgar strives. He describes his father as "the slob who drank and chased women. The bad man from Mittenberg. Him with his paintings that nobody could understand" (*NS* 10). W. Barner notes that Edgar initially sees his father as "a role model . . . an artist with whom he can orient himself. But this proves to be an illusion. The son has to find his own path."[55] And since his father is not a suitable model for rebellion, Edgar turns to black popular culture instead.

Not incidentally, Edgar's fantastical description of his father sounds a lot like the mythical blues musician—reckless, decadent, and dangerous—so admired by white fans and by Edgar, who shows particular respect for blues and jazz musicians.[56] Edgar claims his favorite artist is Louis Armstrong, whom he familiarly refers to as Satchmo. Even in his musical preferences Edgar resists the regime, since East German musicologists dismissed Armstrong's music as fodder for the culture industry. Edgar writes a "Blue Jeans Song" that he sings in the style of Armstrong. He asks that readers imagine "all of that [the lyrics of the song] in this very rich sound, in *his* style. Some people think *he's* dead. That's bullshit. Satchmo can't be killed, because Jazz can't be killed" (*NS* 15). In the film, this comparison is articulated with Edgar ending a performance of his "Blue Jeans Song" with a Louis Armstrong impersonation.

In Plenzdorf's text, Edgar also describes himself as a cross between Robinson Crusoe and Louis Armstrong (*NS* 15). This combination might seem odd, but at closer look, both characters embody a somewhat tame version of rebellion. Crusoe represents a romantic ideal of white European masculinity that is in danger of succumbing to weakness at the dawn of the modern era. Stranded on a desert island, Crusoe is forced to reestablish a connection to nature for survival, but he still maintains his distinctly European intelligence, which is contrasted to the "primitivism" of his black servant, Friday. Thus, like Tarzan, Crusoe is appealing to young white boys because he is a very masculine character, but he is saved from abject difference thanks to his whiteness. Armstrong also embodies this contradiction of difference and familiarity. On the one hand, his difference is anchored in his status as African American jazz musician. On the other hand, as one of the more popular musicians of his time who appealed to white audiences, Armstrong was also considered servile to many of his African American contemporaries. Thus, like Crusoe, Armstrong is different, but his difference has been made safe, in Armstrong's case by his commercial appeal. Two further heroes of Edgar's—Sidney Poitier and Charlie Chaplin—also embody this ironic combination of "safe difference" or "safe rebellion." For Edgar, the roles these actors play position them as "advocates for justice for the small and the humiliated."[57] But one could also argue that Edgar's desire for a difference that is not too unfamiliar is an indication that he is not as willing to leave the familiarity and comfort of East German culture as he suggests.

Edgar does not only listen to music by American artists. When he is not recording messages for his friend Willi, Edgar listens to the band MS-Septett. Frank Schäfer claims that "MS-Septett refers to MSB—the Modern Soul Band, founded in 1968. . . . MSB were the 'Blood, Sweat and Tears' of East Germany."[58] Edgar's love of soul is reflected in his description of himself as "Edgar Wibeau, the great rhythmist, equally great in Beat and Soul" (*NS* 32). In Berlin, he frequents music clubs, and besides the MS-Septett, he enjoys hearing East German jazz and soul songstress Uschi Brüning, whom he describes as not "any worse than Ella Fitzgerald" (*NS* 33).

Edgar also expresses an admiration for blacks and black culture when he laments his failed dancing abilities. He claims he cannot dance in public because the music is always interrupted by breaks, and in order to really get into a groove, two bands would have to play interchangeably, "Otherwise no one can get into proper form. The Negroes know that. I mean the blacks. You should say blacks" (*NS* 32). In the German text, Edgar's self-corrects himself by switching from "Neger" (Negroes) to "Afrikaner" (Africans); while in the translation Kenneth Wilcox uses the term "blacks." The switch in the original German text reveals a self-consciousness about racial terms that expresses Edgar's desire to side with and show respect for the oppressed, a sentiment he shares not only with white East German youth, but with many young leftists in West Germany as well.

Wilcox, translator of the English text, renders, as we've seen, "Afrikaner" (African) as "black," which significantly alters the meaning. Like Oskar, Edgar attributes a feel for rhythm to blacks generally, but to Africans in particular. By changing "Afrikaner" to "blacks" Wilcox ignores the fact that Edgar is not in that instance talking about blacks as a nondescript racial group, which could include, for example, African Americans or black Brits. It is possible Edgar refers to Africans because, considering the African orphans, students, and workers present in the GDR, he was more likely to encounter Africans than African Americans. Therefore, although black popular culture in his imaginary is very much influenced by African American culture, his actual contact with black individuals might be limited to Africans.

Edgar Sings the Blues

Plenzdorf's text is called *The New Sufferings of Young W[ibeau]*, and the blues seem an appropriate trope for Edgar because of his numerous sorrows. Edgar's "blues" are, however, quite insignificant. Barbara Currie does not consider Edgar a tragic character; rather, she argues that he merely flirts with the idea of being an outsider.[59] The insignificant nature of Edgar's troubles might be a result of his young age. Furthermore, despite his nonconformity, as a white, heterosexual German male in the GDR, his displacement from the hegemonic majority is purely voluntary. Despite his odd behavior, his colleagues at his new job on the construction site in Berlin seem eager to integrate him.

Aside from the burden of his robotic memory, Edgar also claims to suffer from not being able to wear long hair:

> As a genuine model student in Mittenberg I naturally wasn't even allowed to have a shag, much less *long* hair. I don't know if you can imagine what a pain that was . . . having long hair was a nonstop hassle. Just the way people looked at it. I don't know if you know what I mean, people. That face that they make when they tell you that you can't have long hair in the shop or someplace else, for safety reasons. Or else head protection, hairnets, like the women, so you look branded, like you're being punished. (*NS* 33–34)

Edgar's lament recalls the comparison white West German students made between being discriminated against because of one's long hair and being black in the United States.[60] Such a comparison seems audacious, which begs one to ask whether Edgar's attachment to blues is as superficial as his sufferings.

Another of Edgar's sufferings is avoidable—the cough he develops from not heating the garden house in the winter. Edgar does not have to remain in the house. He could return to his mother, who pleads with him to come home and, as a compromise, suggests that Edgar find work in a different factory. But Edgar likes the idea of being a sickly struggling artist:

> Not that I was sick or anything, at least not really. I did have a cough. Probably I'd gotten it rummaging around in the old subdivision. Maybe I should've started heating the place. But I could've stopped coughing if I'd wanted to. Only that I'd sort of gotten used to it. It had such a splendid effect. Edgar Wibeau, the unrecognized genius, selflessly works on his newest invention, his lung half eaten away, and he doesn't give up. (*NS* 62)

Edgar's acknowledgment that his suffering was avoidable draws yet another comparison to the "white Negroes" who fetishized black popular culture without recognizing the tangible bodily pains blacks faced in reality.

The final symptom, from which Edgar suffers, is his unrequited love for Charlie. Throughout their friendship, Edgar perceives hints of mutual affection from Charlie, but he can never be entirely sure how she feels. And for Charlie to break off her engagement to a veteran and college student in order to begin a relationship with a *Gammler* (bum) like Edgar would be social suicide. Nevertheless, shortly before Edgar's fatal accident, he shares an intimate moment with her when the two go off for a motorboat trip in a rain storm, leaving her recently returned fiancé, Dieter, at home to work on a homework assignment. Edgar and Charlie stop at a small island so that she can relieve herself. Afterward, sitting next to each other, completely soaked, Charlie asks Edgar if he would like a kiss.[61] Edgar accepts her offer and the experience leads him to draw the following comparison: "In some book I once read how this Negro, I mean this black, comes to Europe and gets his first white woman. He started singing, some song from his homeland. . . . With Charlie I really could've started singing. I don't know if you know what I mean, people. There was no saving me" (*NS* 76).

Once again, the translator replaces "African" with "black" for reasons unknown.[62] For Edgar, the permission to kiss Charlie is the most significant form of recognition he can imagine. Frantz Fanon describes the significance of the white woman for black men in *Black Skin, White Masks*. Speaking from the perspective of the black man who desires white women, he says:

> I wish to be acknowledged not as *black* but as *white*.
> Now—and this is a form of recognition that Hegel had not envisaged—
> who but a white woman can do this for me? By loving me she proves
> that I am worthy of white love. I am loved like a white man.
> I am a white man.
> Her love takes me onto the noble road that leads to total realization.[63]

Even though Edgar analogizes himself to an African, it is hardly an act of meaningful solidarity. Edgar feels like an African only in the sense that his lowly status as a *Gammler* makes him feel inferior to Charlie, the ideal and noble beauty. This attempted identification with black men reinforces the notion that they are inferior to white women. This scene ends in disaster, for Charlie abandons Edgar shortly thereafter, never to speak to him again. Eventually, Edgar realizes he has misread her signals and that she had only been using him to upset Dieter.[64] Heartbroken, Edgar returns to his garden house, where he makes a final attempt to repair an automatic paint sprayer, which he wants to show off at the construction site. But the sprayer explodes, killing Edgar instantly, with the narrative leaving it unclear whether it was an accident or suicide.

In a broader sense, Edgar dies because he cannot meaningfully be integrated into the socialist ideal. Edgar's confrontation with modernity is a losing battle. He is unhappy with the prospect of being yet another worker on an assembly line—another cog in the wheel—preferring to withdraw into nature and into himself. At the end, one could argue that, by resolving to fix his foreman's failed invention—an automatic paint sprayer— Edgar gives in to modernity by seeking to create a device that makes work easier. On the other hand, if the sprayer had worked properly, Edgar would no longer have had to earn his living painting rooms. The time he could have saved painting at construction sites could have been devoted to his art. But when the machine explodes, it kills him and any hope of reconciling his frustrations with GDR life.

Susan Hunnicutt questions readings that interpret Edgar's death as an accident. She points to Willi's statement that Edgar was successful at inventing things, arguing that Edgar chose to let the machine explode to make his death look like an accident. In a state where the official statistics on suicide were kept secret, if Edgar's death were clearly a suicide, then his life and death would have been silenced.[65] I do not disagree with Hunnicutt's argument, but I believe Edgar also lets the machine take his life to make a point about the cold-hearted rationalism of the state. Edgar may have actually developed a talent for working with machinery, but that is not the path he *chose*. Therefore, he allows a machine, a representative of modernization and industry, to take his life as an act of protest. Edgar's death seems a testament to the GDR's failure to allow its citizens sufficient freedom. At the end of the novel, his foreman gives the following explanation to Edgar's father for his death: "According to what the doctors said, it was something electrical" (*NS* 83). This statement recalls the ending of Georg Kaiser's expressionist play *Vom morgen bis mitternachts* (*From Morning to Midnight*, 1912). In Kaiser's play, the protagonist is simply named Kassierer (cashier) after his profession. Faced with the troubles of modern society, the cashier concludes that money is the root of all evil and succeeds at breaking out of the orbit of money and bourgeois culture altogether. Yet, shortly thereafter he dies. Before his death, he makes the following observation about his mechanical life: "From morning to midnight I chase round in a frenzied circle—his beckoning finger shows the way out—where to?"[66] Because the cashier no longer values society's rules, he is able to liberate himself; however, as a result, he is disconnected from everyone else and therefore dies. The only explanation the policeman can offer is, "There must have been a short circuit."[67] This short circuit suggests that the cashier might have rebelled, but inevitably his protest against society and his death will not disrupt the greater system; the order remains. The same is true for Edgar: In the authoritarian society of East Germany, exercising his independence can only lead to his death.

When one considers that Edgar is literally killed by a machine, a final comparison emerges between him and the black people he so idolizes. Black culture has often been conceived of as preindustrial and related to the premodern world. And later on in this chapter, I further discuss how African American men's association with preindustrial economies made their transition from slavery to employment even more difficult. Thus, if Edgar's death is supposed to indicate his association with the preindustrial and premodern, further underscoring his association with black culture in a rather problematic way, then Plenzdorf may also be arguing that despite their vastly different political systems, both the United States and the GDR are highly industrialized nations that leave no place for outsiders, whether they are Othered by their race or by their beliefs, as in Edgar's case.

"You're Never Too Old for a Revolution"

Plenzdorf wrote *The New Sufferings of Young W* in the 1970s,[68] a time when East Germany was economically stable.[69] In contrast, Michael Schorr's film is set during a time of economic depression in the East. Following reunification, after East Germans overwhelmingly voted in favor of joining the Federal Republic of Germany in 1990, nearly the entire East German system was dismantled by West Germany. This restructuring meant that many East German businesses were bought by their West German competitors and then shut down. East Germany suffered an intense rise in unemployment, from which it still has not recovered. Thus, while Edgar suffers under the East German philosophy of a *Recht auf Arbeit* (right to employment), after reunification many East Germans lost this right.

Furthermore, animosity between East and West Germans that for years had been fed by Cold War rhetoric did not end with the GDR. In the early days of reunification, the press depicted East Germans as naive newcomers to capitalism who had quickly traded in their bankrupt state for a few hundred German marks as *Begrüßungsgeld* (welcome money) for shopping. Once the euphoria of change subsided, many East Germans felt duped and even today feel disappointed by and highly distrustful of democracy. Twenty-seven years after reunification, East and West Germans still sense an enduring separation between them, whether in the differences in pay scale and unemployment rates or persisting animosities and prejudices on both sides. After four decades of isolation, East Germans soon learned that reunification not only brought welcomed change and opportunity but problems as well. The immobility they had experienced in East Germany, such as the inability to travel to Western countries, may have been done away with, but for many of those who remained in the East, it was replaced by a different kind of upward *immobility* linked to a lack of opportunity.

Set in postunification Germany, *Schultze Gets the Blues* tells the story of a middle-aged miner who lives in the small East German town of Teutschenthal in Saxony-Anhalt. Saxony-Anhalt is the location of the Harzgebirge (Harz mountains), an area of small villages that were previously dependent on mining. According to Annette Erler, "Today, because of the limited industry, the region's economy is mainly supported by tourism."[70] Compared to Edgar, Schultze's life seems to have followed a more traditional path. He is well integrated in the community, having worked as a miner and been a member of his local music club. In contrast to Edgar, at first, Schultze does not appear dissatisfied with the provincial lifestyle. The film opens with an establishing shot of the countryside; the mise-en-scène is empty aside from a lone windmill to the left of the frame, and a distant mountain and a few telephone poles in the background. The patient turning of the windmill and the lack of action conveys the slow-paced life of the village. The camera remains still as Schultze enters the frame from the left and exits on a bicycle. In the next shot, we see Schultze and his coworkers Manfred and Jürgen waiting at a railroad crossing on their bicycles. Their immobility and conflict with modern technology is emphasized not only by their bicycles, but also by their inability to move after a train has passed because they must wait for the rail operator to manually raise the bar. While Schultze is one of the group in this shot, the camera's prior focus on his solitary movement relays his potential for mobility and change.

After the credits role to the upbeat sound of a zydeco tune sung in French Creole, the next shot is of Schultze riding a mining elevator to the surface. The film begins on the day that Schultze, Jürgen, and Manfred have been made redundant. If the three men began their careers, like Edgar, in their teens, one suspects they have been working in the mine for well over forty years. After devoting most of their life to their work, they are forced to retire and sent packing, accompanied by their colleagues' singing of the traditional *Bergmannslied* (miners' song) "Glück auf, Glück auf! der Steiger kommt" (Good luck, good luck! The foreman's coming) and with gifts of lamps made out of salt rock. Schultze and his friends clearly are not satisfied with these events. Their retirement ceremony scene is shot from outside the room where the festivity takes place. From the standpoint of a voyeur, while Schultze and the other miners are limited to their own perspective, the audience can see the bigger picture. Schultze, Manfred, and Jürgen sit around a small table with their heads bowed down;

the salt rock lamps sit in the middle of the table. The other miners stand around the table as they sing. The scene resembles a religious ceremony with Schultze and his friends in prayer, and the choir of miners accompanying them. Schultze and Jürgen wipe away tears as if their careers were being laid to rest. This scene conveys the men's frustration with their early retirement and the important status mining has held in their lives.

They are likely forced into retirement because the region's industry is suffering. Not only does Jürgen say the firm "took the piss out of them" and they were "thrown out,"[71] but several scenes suggest that they did not voluntarily retire. First, Manfred's wife is shown looking for a new job for him in the newspaper shortly afterward, and the jobs that she tries to convince him to take are low-paying and rather unattractive, like construction, truck driving, and working in a sausage factory. Second, Schultze complains about getting a raw deal from his employer. When they leave the mine on their last day, rather than follow the three men, the camera focuses in on the silence and the objects left behind: a table and chairs, a kettle and pot of sausages, a coat rack with a single coat—all testaments to the simplicity of their daily lives. The emphasis is placed on the disassembly of the industry—as the young people move away and the older residents die, all that remains is silence and abandoned objects.

Without work, their core bonding activity and the most important communal activity in the former GDR, their daily routines seem to become meaningless. Jürgen and Manfred find distraction at home with their loved ones—Jürgen has a wife, and Manfred has a wife and a son whose motocross career he encourages. Schultze, however, has neither a wife nor children. He is shown, instead, lovingly caring for his garden gnomes. From the silent scenes of Schultze in his small garden house, it slowly becomes apparent that Schultze is not the model East German citizen one might have suspected. Aside from being a good worker, another important component of postwar masculinity in East and West Germany, was marrying, having children, and caring for a family—essentially becoming a producer-provider-protector. In Robert Pirro's analysis of the film, "For Schultze, the end of mining work does not disrupt his life of routine: solitary meals, meeting his pals, Jürgen and Manfred, over beers at the local pub or fishing with them from a bridge, and playing accordion (as his father had before him) for the town band."[72] However, the silence of these sequences shows how empty and meaningless Schultze's participation in these rituals has become. By losing his job, he has lost what was traditionally his key function in East German society and that which defined his manhood.

Not only does Schultze not have a wife and children, but his own family is anything but idyllic. His mother lives in a nursing home. He may visit her regularly, but she is in a catatonic state and seems incapable of conversing with him. His father has passed away and all that remains is a portrait of him with an accordion. The accordion symbolizes the pressure of the past. It is, in Emily Hauze's words, "a paternal tradition. The image of his father, of whom he feels pressured to be an exact duplicate, looms, with phallically extended accordion in hand."[73] Thus, playing the accordion is the only connection left between Schultze and his father and perhaps the only area in which Schultze, the eternal bachelor, has not disappointed him. Schultze tries to escape his father's view and judgment by turning his picture to face the wall, but the frame falls down, revealing his father's picture and reasserting his presence.

Interestingly, Schultze spends a lot of time in a garden house that resembles where Edgar lived after running away. Unlike his friend Jürgen, who is forced to interact with a rude neighbor next door, Schultze likes to be on the outskirts of town, isolated from everyone else and surrounded by his garden gnomes. Therefore, despite Schultze's participation in collective activities, he appears to be somewhat of an outsider. Perhaps Schultze is the man Edgar would have become had he tried to make a compromise with his mother and take on some other kind of work in his hometown.

Mobility versus Immobility

There are several reasons why Schultze seems an unlikely rebel: he is old, retired, and a quiet man who never argues or raises his voice. In terms of style, his plain appearance—bald head, glasses, worn-out jeans, plaid shirt and hat— gives him the look of a farmer who would hardly turn any heads in his village. Although his retirement theoretically ushers in the opportunity for change in Schultze's life, he seems like an improbable candidate for change. He is a man of routines and traditional conventions. He spends his days engaging in the same activities he did while he was working: going to the local pub, fishing, working in his garden, visiting his mother, and playing the accordion in the local music club, Harmonie. His life is so regulated that even his fellow members at the music club poke fun at his stagnancy, although they themselves are also conservative. They could never imagine Schultze playing something other than his traditional polka, which one man suggests should be renamed the "Schultzepolka." During the planning for the music fest to commemorate the music club's fiftieth anniversary, when Schultze suggests he play something besides his polka, one of the club members provokes Schultze, asking him what on earth he would play as an alternative, "techno or something?" This provocation points out the apparent absurdity of someone as old as Schultze becoming interested in such a new musical genre, which is usually only associated with younger people.

In contrast, there are several other individuals who seem more likely candidates for rebellion. For example, there is Frau Laurent, his mother's roommate at the nursing home. Frau Laurent does not equate herself with the other nursing home residents, to whom she refers as "alte Leute" (old people). Frau Laurent's cosmopolitan nature is embodied by her taste for Irish whiskey and her French name, which the nursing home workers have difficulty pronouncing, just like Wibeau. Frau Laurent behaves much more candidly than the other nursing home residents. She wears revealing dresses, flirts with Schultze, and enjoys sneaking off to the casino. Her fire for life makes her sudden death all the more unfathomable for Schultze.

Another person who seems discontent with the confines of the village is Manfred. Manfred has dreams of his son going to America and competing in motocross. He believes that America is where there is opportunity and fortune. He says about his son, "He should have it better than me, when he's over there riding motocross."[74] Manfred's obsession with America is expressed in the American flags decorating his home and the high-tech American products he buys.

Finally, there is the mysterious new waitress at their local pub named Lisa. She arrives in town in order to work at the music festival. Much like Frau Laurent, Lisa has an open and outspoken nature, and she enjoys flirting with Schultze. Upon their first meeting, she boldly jumps onto one of the barroom tables and does a flamenco dance, shocking and intriguing Schultze and his friends at the same time. When Schultze admits that he likes the Spanish music playing in the background, she responds, "I'm going there." Thus she is yet another cosmopolitan trapped in the constraining boundaries of the town. Characters like Frau Laurent, Lisa, and Manfred seem to represent those people who treat cultural contact as an escape. Frau Laurent and Lisa want to escape their boredom, while Manfred wants to escape the lack of economic opportunity.

In contrast to Frau Laurent, Manfred and Lisa, Schultze seems quite content with his life in the village. His static lifestyle is best conveyed in a scene that juxtaposes the mobile with the immobile and the modern with the traditional. In this scene, Schultze is on his way to the grocery store on a bicycle with a small wooden cart attached. Schultze does not seem to own a motor vehicle, and it is unclear whether most residents in his town do, since most of them are shown riding bicycles. In this scene, everything that is associated with Schultze is archaic and unprogressive. He is an old man on an old bicycle, careening down a grass-covered path. Suddenly, a youth enters the frame, parallel to Schultze. In contrast to Schultze, the youth is on a motorbike going much faster. The youth is even positioned higher than Schultze on the screen as if to stress his superiority compared to Schultze. The two figures meet at the same position in the frame for just a brief moment before the youth passes Schultze up as anticipated.

Both Schultze and the youth on the motorbike continue moving forward in the same direction but at different speeds and at different heights, forming a parallel. Thus, instead of representing contrasting images, Schultze and the boy could possibly be mirror images of each other. Based on Schultze's age, appearance, and behavior, one would expect him to remain stuck in tradition. Nevertheless, Schultze is approaching something new and exciting in his life, perhaps even faster than his younger equivalent. In this scene, he is actually on the way to the grocery store to buy ingredients for jambalaya. While the town's youth might dream of going to America to compete in motocross and earn money, Schultze reaches America before them. In the end, it is actually the youth of the town who are stuck, which is represented by Manfred's son, who is left behind with a motorbike that does not start during one of the competitions. The agent that helps Schultze step beyond his traditional boundaries and gain more mobility is zydeco.

Increased Mobility through Music

Schultze's first encounter with zydeco immediately changes his life and propels him beyond his usual boundaries. One evening, Schultze, who appears to be having trouble sleeping, enters the kitchen in his pajamas to get a late-night snack. He turns on the radio, and upon hearing a news report about miners suffering from lung cancer, he changes the dial with a disturbed look on his face.[75] Schultze continues changing the dial past a classical music station and yet another news station reporting about an event that happened in 1936, until he happens upon the song "Zydeco 1988" by the band Zydeco Force. Music scholar Martin Stokes has explored how radio has been implemented by states to help construct a national identity; a method that he claims is "seldom foolproof."[76] The fact that Schultze does not stop at the classical music station or the history station symbolizes his emerging lack of interest in the German past and German national identity. He is literally searching for something new, and by chance he discovers zydeco on German radio.

Zydeco may in fact be an old musical genre within the context of American history, but since it is not German and Schultze has never heard it before, it represents something brand new. Once Schultze hears the zydeco, we get a close-up of his face as he pauses several times with a contemplative expression. It seems as if he is trying to listen more closely in order to discover the music. He most likely recognizes the use of his own instrument, the accordion, but cannot quite identify the musical style. Schultze's curiosity is, however, still shrouded in an air of suspicion. He turns off the radio and gets as far as the kitchen door. Yet the music haunts him to such a degree that he returns to the radio to turn it back on.

Each time Schultze turns on the radio, a light simultaneously goes on in the room. The light is perhaps a metaphor for Schultze's own enlightenment, indicating that his encounter with zydeco will bring a bit more light or knowledge into his life. Once again, we see Schultze contemplating the music, even stepping back from the radio, as if this music could pose a threat to him. After he turns off the radio a second time, he then enters his living room, picks up his accordion, and attempts to play the song he just heard. He starts off slowly, trying to imitate the melody, creating a Germanized polka version of the song. Nonetheless, he gradually becomes more confident in his playing and starts playing faster and faster. As Schultze begins to nod his head and close his eyes, one sees that he is clearly enjoying the music, even if there is still a bit of distrust with it. Afterward, he sighs while looking down at his accordion, as if he knows that his new interest will soon make waves in his small community.

Racism, Tradition, and Resistance to Zydeco

Directly after he hears zydeco for the first time, the next scene shows Schultze at his doctor's office with his accordion. Apparently, Schultze's interest in zydeco has made him concerned about his health. His doctor tries to reassure him:

> My dear Schultze, a changing taste in music isn't an illness. I mean, I'm not a psychologist, but it's not life threatening to not play polka for once, more the other way around. But let's be serious; be happy that for once something happens in your life. You truly now have all the time in the world. Think of it more like a gift.

The doctor then admits that he had actually wanted to become an opera singer before opting to become a doctor. This suggests that, while most people in the town have chosen a decent job, perhaps everyone has a secret inkling in them to do something different, be someone or somewhere else. Local confines seem to trump transnational/transcultural ambition. Schultze's doctor praises him for having the courage, at his age, to do something different. Schultze's short response, "If you think so, Doctor," shows that he is clearly still reluctant to pursue this newfound interest. This is, however, only the beginning of Schultze's battle with himself and the rest of the town concerning zydeco. Despite Schultze's hesitancy in engaging with zydeco, he decides to play some of what he learned for a small audience at his mother's nursing home, including his own mother. In conclusion of his performance, members of the audience merely stare blankly at him and then each other. Frau Laurent is the only person there who encourages Schultze to continue to play zydeco: "Don't look like that Schultze. Don't let them get you down. They don't have any idea, they're old people," Frau Laurent says, as she leans toward Schultze so that his mother cannot hear.

For the most part, Schultze keeps his transformation to himself, revealing hints of his new interest to his friends here and there. It is not surprising that Schultze is reluctant to be more vocal about the changes in his life. His town's conservatism is perhaps best represented by the music club. Music clubs play a very important role in small towns in the region where Schultze lives. Participating in the music club is a way of solidifying one's part in the community. The music club is a symbol of his village and its traditions. Even his village's partner city in America, New Braunfels, Texas, is an indication of Teutschenthal's lack of desire to explore something new. New Braunfels is a town anchored in German heritage and home of a yearly German music fest modeled after the Munich Oktoberfest. Thus, even when Schultze's music club demonstrates a willingness to engage with America, their engagement is with a town that emulates German culture. Even though they have contacts in America, the music club has never really left its traditional boundaries. Therefore, when Schultze suggests he play "was Amerikanisches" (something American) at the upcoming festival, it is immediately met with displeasure. The music director is already upset that Schultze wants to play something other than his "Schultze-epolka." The fact that it is American is even worse: "Das auch noch?" (That, too?), the director responds. The director then poses the question, what would Schultze's deceased father think if Schultze were to abandon the polka? The music director's response stresses how much the town refuses to let go of the past, preferring to face the dead rather than the future.

Schultze's performance at the music festival is preceded by a choir, which performs a very traditional *Volkslied* (German folk song), "Kein schöner Land" ("No Country More Beautiful"), written in the nineteenth century. According to Philip V. Bohlman, German folk songs have long been important for creating a German national identity:

> Imagined during the late eighteenth-century *Aufklärung*, the German Enlightenment, and invented during the romanticism of the early nineteenth century, German folk song became a visible player in the struggle to construct German nationalism. . . . By coining the term *Volkslied*, or folk song, in the 1770s, Johann Gottfried Herder consciously engaged in an act of naming a previously unnamed quality of Germanness. From its Enlightenment beginnings, folk songs served to connect language to place.[77]

"Kein schöner Land" is a particular favorite among folk song enthusiasts, and it was part of the repertoire of the Spielschar Ekkehard; a group of young singers led by antirepublican conservative, Gerhard Roßbach, during the Weimar Republic.[78] The group's performances of folk songs, mystery plays, and classical music were meant to promote the kind of German identity Roßbach endorsed—an identity that was characteristically non-Jewish and antimodern.

In the film, the music festival is actually the second time a song from the nineteenth century is performed by the town's inhabitants. As I mentioned earlier, during his modest retirement ceremony at the beginning of the film, Schultze's colleagues sing "Glück auf, Glück auf! der Steiger kommt," a traditional miner's song also written in the nineteenth century. Opening the film with a *Bergmannslied*, a subcategory of folk song that specifically speaks to the region's mining tradition, establishes the setting of the film and the importance of tradition for its characters. As the choir at the music fest attests their country's beauty and God's grace, "Kein schöner Land" evokes pastoral and idyllic images typical of the *Heimatfilme* (homeland films) of postwar West Germany. Pirro claims *Schultze Gets the Blues* invokes *Heimatfilm* because it places regional dialects, rural life, and local traditions on display. However, he qualifies this comparison: "Unlike those [*Heimat*] films, *Schultze*'s embrace of homespun values is multicultural, not provincial, extending to a foreign place and people."[79] And it is Schultze's engagement with zydeco that provides this multicultural perspective.

Bohlman suggests that "German folk songs did not simply represent German national identity, they were agents participating in its formation and implementation."[80] When the music club and choir perform these traditional songs, they are doing just that—forming and articulating a particular kind of white German national identity, which Schultze inevitably contrasts with his performance of a foreign music, zydeco. Campbell remarks that present-day fans of *Volkslieder* praise the music's ability to uphold a hegemonic German identity "that has endured unsuccessful democracy, economic chaos, fascism, war, and now successful democracy."[81] Schultze's fellow villagers would likely add unification, unemployment, emigration, and foreign influence to that list of ailments.

One of the Harz region's dearest tourist attractions is its *Volksmusik*. In fact, instrumental music clubs had been an important part of communities in East Germany. According to Annette Erler, "The solidarity of the choir community is prized as being more important than choir practice."[82] After reunification, the clubs were needed not only to bring the community together, but also to offer everything from "leisure to distraction from unemployment and lack of prospects."[83] During the days of the GDR, music clubs in the Harz region were dependent upon their *Landwirtschaftliche Produktionsgenossenschaften* (LPGs; agricultural production cooperatives).[84] After reunification, however, the LPGs were dismantled and music clubs found themselves with a lack of funding and a lack of gigs, resulting in the disbandment of many. Members of East German music clubs in the region blamed reunification for the deterioration of their clubs, claiming that members must now work more and had little time for music. Supposedly, members also preferred going window-shopping in the West instead of band practice. The deterioration of East German music clubs through the influence of the West is also evident in the fact that more and more of the remaining music clubs no longer play the traditional workers songs, but rather their routines have been increasingly influenced by American music. Placing Schultze's story in the context of the real tension between music clubs in East German mining towns postunification and Western or foreign influence makes Schultze's story seem all the more relevant.

When Schultze plays zydeco at the village fest, although his small group of friends enthusiastically clap for him, the other villagers are so shocked by his performance that, when he is finished, the once cheerful crowd falls totally silent. One villager angrily refers to Schultze's playing as "Scheißnegermusik" (shitty Negro music). This outburst invokes past perceptions of black popular music when white Germans often referred to jazz as "Negermusik" in the 1930s and 1940s.[85] The choice of such a derogatory word to describe zydeco gives us a hint at one of the reasons why the villagers are so opposed to it.

As shown in the previous chapters, racist responses to black popular music have a long tradition in German encounters with American culture. In the film, the waitress Lisa defiantly counters this outburst, raising her glass with the toast "auf die Negermusik" (to Negro music). The word *Neger* stems from the end of the seventeenth century, when the new flow of Africans coming from the West Coast of Africa via the transatlantic slave route initiated a shift in European sensibility toward blacks, who were no longer associated with the exotic "Moor."[86] For Germans, while Moors were seen as possibly more culti-vated than Europeans, thanks to their impressive Islamic culture, *Neger* were seen as primitive and in need of colonization. As Peter Martin claims, Euro-pean engagement with the West Coast of Africa was so different than previous contact with Africans because, while the Moors had sought to conquer Europe, in this case Europeans felt superior and that they had the right to invade black societies.[87] Thus, describing zydeco as "Negermusik" almost suggests a case of reverse colonization. Instead of Germans bringing culture to Africa, now African Americans were bringing culture to East Germany by way of Schultze. Lisa's toast to the "Negermusik" might support Schultze, but it still explicitly marks zydeco as Other, black and therefore non-German.

Why Zydeco?

The townspeople's labeling of zydeco as "Negermusik" actually conceals the fact that zydeco, like many musical genres from the United States, is a product of contact between African Americans and Europeans. There are several rea-sons why Schorr may have decided to use zydeco music in this film instead of another (African) American genre. First of all, zydeco—which combines Afri-can, Caribbean, European, and American influences—is both threatening and innocuous simultaneously. It poses a threat to the locals, not only because it is new and foreign, but because it is American. The fear of zydeco's intrusion into Schultze's town may symbolize the fear of the Americanization of Germany. For the town residents, this music is both that of the "oppressor," the Ameri-cans, and that of the "oppressed," African Americans, giving them even more reason to reject it.

On the other hand, one could see zydeco as less threatening because, al-though it is American music, it is marginal American music. In his article "Dis-juncture and Difference in the Global Cultural Economy," anthropologist Ar-jun Appadurai suggests that a community is more afraid of being dominated by its neighbor's culture than a culture that is farther away. Although zydeco's "invasion" of Schultze's life and his village can be read as Americanization, it is a different kind of Americanization than the current popularity of hip-hop. Zydeco is the local music of a marginal Creole and Cajun southern commu-nity; thus it would most likely be categorized as "world music" rather than more popular genres of American music. By listening to zydeco, Schultze can engage in a music style that does not follow the familiar formula of other popular American genres, which makes it seem less American.

Furthermore, zydeco implements the accordion, providing Schultze with enough of an aspect of familiarity to make him interested. Emily Hauze recognizes the accordion in both *Schultze* and Werner Herzog's earlier film *Stroszek* (1976) as a "metaphor for dreams that might be realized in America and for the mobility required to realize them."[88] And zydeco is rural music that is very much tied to farm life.[89] Therefore, as someone living in a rural setting, Schultze could perhaps better identify with it. Pirro explains:

> Musically, Zydeco was formed when Creole music from south-central and southwest Louisiana was crossed with rhythm and blues in the years after World War II. . . . In his [Schorr's] commentary on the film made available on the DVD release, he explained his need for an American music "basically connected to the kind of polka accordion music Schultze plays" and his discovery that Zydeco, like polka, has "the accordion as the lead instrument."[90]

In addition to Schorr's explanation, one must also consider that zydeco was actually already quite popular among *West* Germans in the 1960s. Thus, Schultze's interest in zydeco can be read as an anachronistic case of the mass consumption of zydeco in West Germany. The fact that it took nearly four decades for zydeco to reach Schultze's town points out just how isolated it had been. Additionally, the song Schultze listens to, "Zydeco 1988" by Zydeco Force, does not have much text, and therefore, his lack of English skills does not pose a barrier to enjoying the song.

Finally, considering the long history of blues in the GDR, one could even say Schultze's engagement with zydeco, a form of blues, is a means of reclaiming an earlier dissident East German culture. In this way, Schultze reinstates a history of rebellion that is often overlooked when remembering the GDR. Furthermore Schultze's actions pose the question of whether listening to blues in a postunification East German village is *not German* or whether the genre of the blues has been a part of East German culture for so long that it is no longer a foreign entity. One significance of Schultze listening to contemporary zydeco is that he does not fall prey to the tendency among white blues fans of respecting only the roots of a genre. By listening to a more contemporary form of zydeco, Schultze is not the white expert of black popular music who does not allow the music to change.

Same Game, Different Field

Once he has heard it, Schultze's urge to play zydeco becomes so great that, even when he tries to play his traditional polka, hints of zydeco seep into his performance. The broadening of Schultze's musical taste is soon followed by an attempt to cook jambalaya. These are all changes in Schultze's character that would have been unthinkable prior to his encounter with zydeco. Performing zydeco and eating jambalaya are Schultze's attempts to participate in a community that exists beyond his immediate boundaries. But these activities are not enough to satisfy him. Soon he is doing odd jobs for additional money and going to a travel agency to inquire about flights to Louisiana. He finally decides he would like to travel to the United States. Previously, Schultze even resisted the idea of a visit to the United States as the music club's representative, a trip Manfred would love to make. This provokes Jürgen to ironically comment, "One can go and doesn't want to. The other wants to go and can't."

Despite the feelings of suspicion, confusion, and even disgust brought on by Schultze's performing zydeco, his music club still decides to send him as its representative to its partner city, New Braunfels, Texas, in honor of his birthday. There are many possible reasons behind this generous act. Perhaps the members know Schultze did not have the money for a trip to the United States and wanted to do something nice for him. It is possible they wished to excise Schultze's foreign influences from the community in order to restore the harmony promoted by the club. Regardless of the reason, the gesture shows some willingness to understand Schultze's interest and support him despite other members' personal beliefs.

Schultze, like many *young* Germans, leaves Saxony in search of more experiences. By the time Schultze travels to New Braunfels, he has already established his own fantasies of what the southern United States is like. He has been listening to and playing zydeco, cooking jambalaya, and reading his book about the South, *Kings of Swamp Music*, that Lisa gave to him. What Schultze encounters at the Wurstfest, however, is a music festival that seems like a parody of hegemonic German culture. He finds no trace of zydeco, jambalaya, or even many African Americans. What he encounters are white Americans, most likely of German descent, who are wearing Texan attire—cowboy hats and boots—but dancing to polka performed by a Lederhosen-clad white American accordion player. Schultze, however, is in search of an "authentic" experience with southern American culture. But being at the Wurstfest makes him feel as if he had never left his town. Upon hearing a rendition of the German national anthem, Schultze leaves the fest for good.

Before traveling to the United States, Schultze did not realize that despite its location, New Braunfels is probably the best cultural equivalent to his hometown one could find in America. New Braunfels was founded in the late nineteenth century by German immigrants who were not afraid to settle in the notoriously dangerous area. It is also the site of the first statewide *Saengerfest* (singer fest), held in the 1850s. At the time, *Saengerfests* provided German immigrants of central Texas with a social context to come together. However, they soon roused suspicion and opposition by the surrounding white Americans after a *Saengerbund* in San Antonio criticized the institution of slavery because it was contradictory to democracy. Afterward, tensions ensued between the English-speaking and German-speaking Texans, the latter of which withdrew into their own community. Although this tension persisted through the Civil War and both world wars and many music clubs became obsolete, some music clubs, as well as the New Braunfels Wurstfest, still exist. According to Chester Rosson, "These events can be seen as efforts by the german [*sic*] community to reach out to the larger American community and involve it in the European cultural tradition."[91] This offers yet another example of music functioning as a tool of social integration. Although the musicians of these Texan-German music clubs may have added a few new instruments like the accordion, they are still rather conservative in their musical preferences, "choosing tried and true nineteenth-century pieces, mostly by secondary composers over any newer material."[92]

Emily Hauze believes that Schultze "is content to find glimmers of himself, and of his European heritage, reflected in a country that, ultimately, is not 'really he,' but welcoming to him."[93] However, I would argue that Schultze anticipated "authentic" southern culture and is disappointed to find an American version of the music fests he knew from Germany. Disillusioned, Schultze sets out in search of "real" southern culture, only to discover that there is no such thing. Rather than a monoculture, Schultze encounters various hybrid cultures like the Bobby Jones Czech Band, a Texan band that plays Czech polkas and waltzes, country music, and Cajun music.

On his quest to find zydeco, Schultze acquires a motorboat and travels along the Gulf Coast until he reaches Louisiana. It becomes more evident how much Schultze has changed since the beginning of the film. He acquires a motorized vehicle and tries his best to communicate with the people he encounters, despite his poor English skills. He is also not too shy to interact with women. As Robert Pirro points out, Schultze's very first interaction with an American is with an African American woman with whom he shares a hot tub at his motel, the Edelweiss Inn, which is decorated in German *Fachwerk* architectural style. Schultze's initial reluctance to get into the hot tub seems less a fear of difference than about exposing his whiteness. He enters the frame wearing a bathrobe. After the woman in the hot tub, Josephine, encourages him to get in, from behind we see Schultze disrobe and then turn to face the camera, exposing his protruding beer belly. Richard Dyer remarks that part of the power of whiteness is its ambiguity. One can never define what whiteness *is*, only what it is *not*. Because of its ambiguity, the marking quality of whiteness is hardly ever noticed. Exposing himself to this black woman perhaps helps Schultze recognize his own whiteness. As Hauze notes, his bathing in the hot tub resembles a kind of rebirth. When he emerges and later goes to the German American festival, he cannot bear to take part in this performance of a traditional German identity.

Conclusion: The Blues, Modernity, and Masculinity in Crisis

Michael Rauhut and Peter Wicke, prominent German musicologists who have written extensively on the reception of black popular music in Germany, suggest German fans' search for an "authentic" blues relates to a desire to hold onto something old when faced with a changing society.[94] The blues represents a form that African American music took during Reconstruction (after slavery was abolished by the Thirteenth Amendment in 1865) when newly freed slaves were faced with all kinds of new challenges. Richard Middleton describes blues as "corresponding to culture shock: mobility, uprooting, alienation and freedom,"[95] therefore making it the perfect soundtrack for the "losers of modernization, black and white alike."[96]

Keeping the origin of the music in mind, Wicke points out that the popularization of blues and the notion of "authentic" blues have a lot to do with the myths spread by white ethnomusicologists, such as John and Alan Lomax, who recorded black blues singers in southern prisons between 1933 and 1939.[97] What attracted the Lomaxes to incarcerated musicians was the desire to find music performed by blacks who were cut off from society and whose music supposedly had little or no European influence. Therefore, the music labeled "authentic" blues did not necessarily reflect the nuances or variety of the genre; rather early blues history was written by whites who believed in a narrow notion of blues in the vein of Herdian *Volksmusik*. This blues myth was later revived in the 1960s by white folk music enthusiasts and record collectors and quickly found its way to Germany. For example, in 1962, the American Folk Blues Festival (AFBF) was started by the West German concert agency,

Lippmann and Rau. At the time, African Americans criticized the AFBF for solidifying blues and only including older blues musicians instead of incorporating its many contemporary forms. Charles Keil called the festival a "third rate minstrel show" because of its stereotypical portrayal of African American musicians.[98] Jimi Hendrix expressed similar concern for white fans' essentialization of black popular music:

> You know the trip: after a few years they [the record executives] drop you like a hot potato. Then you're lying in the street. If you're lucky, some whiteys will get turned on to the stuff you used to do years ago. Then the fat manager pigs will get you from the docks, where you've had to work, give you a new set of teeth and a guitar and earn money off of you like crazy—just like they're doing now with the old blues singers.[99]

In Plenzdorf's novel and Schorr's film, the myth of the blues is utilized as a means of dealing with modern changes and the characters' resulting masculinity crisis. Despite the thirty-year difference between these texts, both protagonists find themselves at odds with their community and unable to fulfill East Germany's masculine ideal. Edgar prefers to be an artist and not the manual laborer his country demands. He does not win the girl; he loses her to Dieter, the less intelligent army veteran. Schultze is emasculated when he loses his job, and he has neither wife nor children to rehabilitate his masculinity. For both men, the blues becomes an important leitmotif. Yet the connection made between these men and blues music does not rest on lamentation about their problems. In order to further investigate the significance of blues for these protagonists, we must turn briefly to the music's origins.

In his seminal work on black popular music in America *Blues People*, Amiri Baraka locates the birth of blues in the era of U.S. Reconstruction. There are several significant differences between the earlier slave songs (ballits and field hollers) and "primitive" or country blues. Slaves songs were collectively sung, dealt with the problems of the social group, and often focused on the afterlife—achieving redemption for one's suffering in heaven—and the prospect of returning to Africa. Blues songs, however, were much more individual.[100] During Reconstruction, those freed slaves "lucky" enough to work a plot of land typically worked alone. Therefore, the lament each man sang was about his unique situation.[101] I consciously refer to men singing country blues in the fields because most country blues singers were men, as opposed to classical blues singers like Ma Rainey and Bettie Smith.

This gender imbalance has to do with the difficulties black men in particular faced during Reconstruction. During slavery, it was not uncommon for slaves to be taught a trade because white men did not worry about competition with blacks on the job market. Once slavery was abolished, however, black men had difficulty finding any work and when they did, it was agricultural labor.[102] Black women, on the other hand, typically had little trouble finding domestic work.[103] Under the paternal institution of slavery:

> The black man in America performed an integral function in the mainstream of white American society. One that was easy to ascertain, and almost as easy to provide for. . . . With the old paternalistic society of the South went the simple role of the Negro in the Western world. Now the Negro was asked to throw himself into what was certainly still an alien environment and to deal with that environment in the same manner as his newly found white "brother" had been doing for centuries.[104]

Black men's failure to provide for their women is a common theme in blues songs. Faced with high unemployment and migration to find agricultural work, black men in particular had become "isolated from the mainstream of American society."[105] Thus, country blues tends to thematize this alienation from American society and the desire to find recognition.[106] Baraka's history of the blues does not contradict Wicke's claims. Rather, while the primitive blues of Reconstruction likely developed according to Baraka's history, blues as an independent genre was not recorded until 1902–1903, and by then it had made its way to white audiences. Therefore, the blues that was promoted as "authentically" non-European in the 1930s was more likely the result of musical exchanges between the black and white communities of musicians and fans.

It's not that Edgar and Schultze's outsider status is equivalent to the precarious position of the black man during Reconstruction. For freed slaves, aside from poverty, unemployment, and lack of education, discrimination and racial violence were everyday realities. In contrast, Edgar and Schultze have relatively comfortable lives and have, Schultze more successfully than Edgar, found ways to become recognized members of their societies. Nevertheless, Edgar and Schultze also suffer from a feeling of alienation that has to do with their failure to fulfill masculine expectations. For both Edgar and Schultze, their primary failure as East German men—their lack of meaningful work—has been caused by modern changes. However, they have opposing relationships to the modernization of their environments. Edgar is a creative young man who wishes to technically revolutionize how East Germans work. When he fails at his ambitions to be an artist—a profession that would grant him little recognition in the worker's state—he turns his aspirations to building a machine that can paint a room by itself. But his efforts are not taken seriously, for by the 1970s, the GDR's established political leaders were slow to promote technological innovation. While Edgar becomes an agent of modernity, attempting to make the GDR more technically modern, the recently unemployed Schultze is more of a victim who is weathering the changes of reunification and globalization. Despite these characters' opposing relationships to modernity, their age difference, and differing historical contexts, each develops an affinity for black popular culture to cope with his struggles. The blues, or more specifically, the "myth" of the blues, becomes an outlet for them to express their outsider status, and its exotic nature fulfills their longing for freedom.

In postwall eastern Germany, increasingly influenced by global capital, older trades that depend on manual labor are becoming less prominent as the service industry grows in importance. At first, Schultze's confrontation with modernity also appears to be a losing battle; for at the very start of the film, he loses his job and appears to be a stagnant and lonely individual. Just like Edgar's blues music, zydeco helps Schultze cope with the impending modernism and globalization. Through zydeco, Schultze is able to engage with American culture in a form that is less threatening. Furthermore, in contrast to Edgar, Schultze does not romanticize or exoticize black popular culture, and his engagement with zydeco does not remain a form of escapism, like Edgar's dancing to blues by himself. Schultze actually seeks out a community of zydeco enthusiasts in the United States.

After stealing the boat, he happens upon an African American woman and her young daughter living on a houseboat. Initially, he only asks the woman for a glass of water, but she invites him in for dinner. After dinner, the woman offers Schultze a glass of whiskey, which alludes to his earlier relationship with Frau Laurent that was cut short by her untimely death. When he accepts the whiskey, an awkward Schultze blushes after the woman sends her daughter away, telling Schultze the two adults will take the liquor upstairs. Her request to "go upstairs" is clearly read as sexual innuendo by the blushing Schultze. However, the director then cuts to Schultze and the woman sitting and innocently chatting upstairs, which turns out to be the boat's upper deck instead of a bedroom, and the sexual tension is instantly relieved. Schultze stays with the family for several days and sends pictures of himself on the boat to Manfred and Jürgen. Toward the end of the film, Schultze finally gets to experience a live performance of zydeco when the family takes him dancing. Schultze is seen dancing vigorously with another African American woman, until he nearly collapses because he is unable to breathe. Robert Pirro observes, "After the visit to the dance club and while Schultze sleeps on the houseboat deck, she [the African American female friend] tucks a blanket around him. These arguably maternal gestures on the part of African-American women characters raise the possibility of notions of the nurturing and caregiving 'mammy.'. . .[107]

Although he dies in his sleep atop the houseboat, in contrast to Edgar, Schultze accomplishes something that is confirmed when the African American family attends his funeral in Germany. For Schultze, zydeco was a way of getting outside his bubble. Pirro reads Schultze's engagement with zydeco as leading to the integration of outsiders into his Saxon community. Additionally, his death also marks a transition to the villagers' acceptance of modernization. During the funeral service, Manfred's cell phone rings, and he jokingly pretends that Schultze is calling him. This interference by technology lightens the mood of the more serious and traditional service, and, as Pirro argues, "To the extent that the cell phone has become one of the icons of globalization, Schultze's 'call' evokes his community's newfound capacity to manage the intrusive presence of global technologies and even integrate them into local practices."[108]

At the end of the film, Schultze's funeral procession leads the way from the cemetery as the local music club plays a German polka rendition of "Zydeco 1988." As was typical of nineteenth-century jazz funerals in Louisiana, the band plays a slower, more somber song on the way to the funeral and a lighter, upbeat song leaving the cemetery. Schultze's village has adopted zydeco and made it their own, and one gets the feeling the people have become more open and more capable of bracing the changes globalization will bring. The East German community appropriates this black performance to articulate its mourning over Schultze. Finally, Schultze's trip to Louisiana helped him regain his masculinity. The African American mother and her daughter stand in for the spouse and child he lacked in Germany. Their presence at his funeral is a testament to their having become his family. Schultze's is a story of rebellion *and* alternative social integration. Edgar, however, does not get the girl or the family, and his marginality ends with his death.

CHAPTER 4

Two Black Boys Look at the White Boy

In this chapter, I turn my attention to two African American authors who have dealt with postwar German fascination with blackness. Instead of white German protagonists, their work centers around African American protagonists in Germany. These texts are Paul Beatty's novel *Slumberland* (2008) and Mark Stewart's Broadway musical, based on his Tony Award–winning script, *Passing Strange* (2009). Paul Beatty was born in Los Angeles and received an MFA in creative writing from Brooklyn College. Beatty first garnered attention for his poetry when he regularly performed at the Nuyorican Poets Café in New York, where he became the Grand Slam Poetry Champion in 1990. *Slumberland* is based on his experience living in Berlin for a year and a half during the 1990s while on a fellowship.[1] Mark Stewart is a singer-songwriter who was also born in Los Angeles and goes by the name Stew. In the 1990s, he formed the band The Negro Problem, which released five albums between 1997 and 2012. *Passing Strange* was his first rock musical and is semiautobiographical. It debuted at the Berkeley Repertory Theater in 2006 and opened on Broadway at the Belasco Theater in 2008. In 2008, the musical was nominated for seven Tony Awards and won the award for Best Book. And in 2009 a DVD of the musical was released, based on a performance filmed by Spike Lee.

The protagonists in *Slumberland* and *Passing Strange* are Ferguson and Youth, respectively, two African American men from Los Angeles who feel constricted by their middle-class upbringing and go to Germany to rebel through music. Ferguson is a DJ who goes to Berlin to find a long-lost African American jazz musician for whom he can play his perfect beat. Youth goes to Berlin because he is an aspiring musician who considers Europe the epicenter of counterculture and hopes to reinvent himself there. By sending these black men to Germany to rebel, Beatty and Stewart invoke the long history of African Americans seeking freedom in Europe, in particular the freedom from institutional racism in the United States. From W. E. B. DuBois, who studied at the University of Berlin (now Humboldt University) from 1892 to 1894, to innovative director Melvin van Peebles, who moved to France in the 1960s to get his first break as a filmmaker, there are many African American men who recognized that racial bias in the United States would hinder them from pursuing their goals. Maria Höhn and Martin Klimke's aptly named book, *A Breath of Freedom*, gets to the heart at why Germany in particular has symbolized liberation for African American men. Höhn and Klimke quote Colin Powell, who served as a lieutenant in Germany from 1958 to 1959. Powell says that being stationed in Germany at that time, compared to the racist treatment he felt back in the United States, felt like a breath of freedom.[2] And this is exactly what Ferguson and Youth seek. A large part of this history is the freedom to date white women, an action that, during the Jim Crow era, was deadly in many parts of the United States. But the kind of freedom I am highlighting here is the chance to reinvent oneself, which is what these protagonists hope to find in Berlin—far from home, cut off from friends and relatives, and detached, they hope, from expectations of how African American men are supposed to behave. However, as soon as they reach Berlin, they realize that white Germans also have specific notions about African Americans, and these stereotypes are perhaps just as confining as the rules left behind in America.

In the first three chapters I demonstrated that white German characters' appropriation of blackness as a means of rebelling against hegemonic German culture is problematic because of the binary it establishes between black and German that forecloses the possibility of being both black *and* German. In the chapters 4 and 5, by examining texts by African American and black German artists, I *reverse the gaze* and examine an African diasporic perspective on this phenomenon. There are not many fictional texts by black authors that address the experience of African Americans in postwar Germany. The most famous is perhaps William Gardner Smith's *Last of the Conquerors* (1948), based on his experience serving in the U.S. Army in Berlin as a clerk-typist and as head of the motor pool from 1946 to 1947.[3] A more recent novel is *Halfblood Blues* (2011), written by Ghanian-Canadian author Esi Edugyan, which jumps between Nazi-era Berlin and postwall Berlin to narrate the story of a black German jazz musician. And most recently, Darryl Pinckney published *Black Deutschland* (2016), a novel about a gay African American man who shuttles between his hometown of Chicago and Berlin and struggles to deal with family conflicts and substance abuse.

In this chapter I examine Beatty's and Stewart's work in particular because of their historical setting in Berlin in the late 1980s. Pop music undergoes an important shift during the 1980s. While pop music in the previous decades was heavily influenced by African diasporic music genres—the blues, R

& B, and soul—the rising popularity of electronic music in the 1980s ushers in the first genre of music in decades that is not necessarily tied to black culture, a point that I will elaborate on later in the chapter. The other reason I chose these texts is the central role music plays in each text. *Slumberland*'s protagonist is an exceptional DJ who goes to Berlin to seek out a missing African American jazz artist and in the meantime works as a self-proclaimed "jukebox sommelier" at the Slumberland bar. In *Passing Strange*, the protagonist, Youth, is an aspiring musician who quits his punk band in Los Angeles to seek freedom and adventure in Berlin. Both the protagonists of *Slumberland* and *Passing Strange* are African American artists from Los Angeles who have come of age in "postsoul" black America.[4] Their versatile identities and experiences are an example of the diversity possible, but often denied, within the African American community. Quintessential "soul babies," these young men feel unfulfilled by LA's false happiness, and they travel to Germany to escape the narrow confines of middle-class (black) American culture. By traveling abroad to Germany, they "reterritorialize" the white man's space, but also participate in a transnational exchange between Germany and black America that has been going on for centuries.

The final reason I chose to put these texts into dialogue is because Beatty's and Stewart's texts challenge both German and American essentialist notions of blackness. The German texts in the last three chapters depict blacks as an anonymous oppressed mass and associate black culture with rebellion. But Beatty and Stewart introduce complexity to the African American experience. Their characters are middle-class, educated black men from suburban communities. These characters rebel by going to Europe and they give us insight into how African Americans felt or feel about the impact German notions of blackness have for black men, in particular those with mobility and agency that are rare in fictional texts. A further purpose of including perspectives of black artists is to counter cultural appropriation with cultural autonomy; to find out how African Americans and black Germans define themselves in a German context and see where these competing representations come into conflict.

Finally, Beatty's and Stewart's texts acknowledge not only diversity within the African American community but also the complexities of German identities. Ferguson and Youth are just as guilty of stereotyping Germans as Germans are of stereotyping them. And Beatty and Stewart craft narratives that demonstrate awareness that their black protagonists are anything but perfect. Beatty and Stewart are very reflective and very critical about identity politics, regardless of whether black or white characters are concerned.

In the next three sections I will address *Slumberland* first, in particular why Ferguson is so concerned with making blackness passé, why his experiences in Germany present a challenge to this goal, and how reunification makes German racism even more apparent to him. Then I will introduce *Passing Strange*'s coming-of-age story. Like Ferguson, Youth is also aware that blackness does not always signify coolness; however, Youth believes he can find a more authentic self in Europe. I explore what in Youth's middle-class, suburban lifestyle he finds so uncool and constricting and why he believes Europe will grant him a freedom that is impossible in the United States. Ironically, when Youth reaches Germany, instead of embracing a more authentic self, he absorbs German stereotypes about blackness in order to appear cooler. Thus Youth readily adopts the very stereotypes Ferguson attempts to debunk. Here I must clarify that while I can distinguish between white and black Germans in *Slumberland*, in *Passing Strange* all of the German characters are played by black actors, so I can only refer to them as "Germans"; which conveys a great deal about Stewart's intervention into discussions of race in Europe. I conclude this chapter by arguing that while both texts add an important perspective to how black culture is perceived in Germany, ultimately, *Passing Strange*'s exploration of constructed versus "real" identities does a better job of exploding categories and breaking with essentialist expectations for both men and women. In contrast, because Ferguson's goal to become unmarked is made possible by his male and class privilege, *Slumberland* liberates its protagonist while keeping black women imprisoned in stereotypical roles.

DJ Darky Lays Blackness to Rest

Throughout his work, Paul Beatty has shown a concern with challenging essentialism, and much of Beatty's criticism of essentialism and multicultural politics is echoed in the thoughts of *Slumberland*'s protagonist, Ferguson. Ferguson came of age in the 1970s and 1980s, a time when African American protest culture was heavily commodified thanks, in part, to laws like the Civil Rights Act of 1965, which began to dismantle the discrimination that had made it difficult for African Americans to escape poverty and move up to the middle class. African Americans enjoyed increasing geographic and economic mobility. Mark Anthony Neal describes this period as a second migration.[5] Unlike the Great Migration of African Americans from rural southern towns to urban northern cities, now the black middle class was leaving urban areas for the suburbs.

Ferguson, a DJ who goes by the name DJ Darky, has been working on what he describes as the perfect beat. But rather than selling it to one of the mediocre hip-hop artists he knows in LA, he would like to use this crowning achievement as an opportunity to collaborate with the great Charles Stone. Stone is an avant-garde jazz musician, known as the Schwa, who went missing in the 1960s. Ferguson's idea comes about one night while he is playing a newly crafted beat for his group of music connoisseur friends, the Beard Scratchers. His friends are so impressed, they suggest Ferguson find Charles Stone to have it "ratified" as the perfect beat. What points Ferguson to Berlin is a mysterious pornographic film he receives in the mail that is set to Stone's unmistakable music. The return address for the film is

> "Schallplattenunterhalter Dunkelmann" at the Slumberland Bar at Win-terfeld Square in West Berlin. Assuming that "Schallplattenunterhalter Dunkelmann" is the name of the person who sent the film, Ferguson calls the Slumberland asking to speak with this mysterious person. A female bartender responds: "There are many *dunkel* [dark] men here."[6]

In fact, the Slumberland is a bar favored by dark men of all kinds, including GIs, ex-pats, and African immigrants who mingle there with their white girl-friends. Ferguson heads to Germany to track down Charles Stone. In order to get a work visa, Ferguson proposes he work as a "jukebox sommelier" at the Slumberland. The bar accepts his proposition, and he takes his record collec-tion to the walled-in city.

The novel actually begins at least a decade after Ferguson first arrived in Berlin. Reflecting on his experiences in Germany, Ferguson addresses white Germans' preconceived notions of black popular culture. However, he does not speak to them directly; rather he talks *about* them, presumably to a black audi-ence. The first line of the novel reads, "You would think they'd be used to me by now. I mean, don't they know that after fourteen hundred years the charade of blackness is over?" (*SL* 3). Ferguson's tone places him in a higher position of authority than his white German subjects. *He* and his audience are in on the charade, and he is surprised that white Germans have yet to catch up. Most likely, this "charade of blackness" is the many stereotypes I have discussed throughout this book: black popular culture is primitive, naive, childlike, free, innocent, in close proximity to nature, authentic, wild, and—the description that is most false, according to Ferguson—"cool." Throughout the novel, Fer-guson's main project is to declare blackness passé, which has to do with his belief that coolness is not solely an attribute of black popular culture. Follow-ing Gilroy's lead in *The Black Atlantic*, Ferguson tries to reinstate the influence of European culture present in black culture. He stresses that the evolution of "cool" includes many cultures, and he recognizes the constellations connecting past and present vanguard movements.

While black popular culture might have been considered "cool" among white German rock fans in the 1950s and among leftists during the 1960s and 1970s, Ferguson believes that, by the 1980s, black popular culture has lost its outsider appeal. Ferguson's opinion possibly is informed by the shifts that had occurred in black popular music and African American communities since the civil rights movement. In the 1970s, the burgeoning black middle-class urgently sought corresponding representations of themselves in the media, and they were especially attracted to a more commercial and polished brand of soul music with crossover appeal.[7] As historian Alice Echols explains, "Having gained a foothold in a more integrated America, bourgeois blacks struggled to live as though they were colorless. Consuming crossover became part of the great beige way."[8] A part of this crossover craze was the commodification of black popular culture in the form of afros, dashikis, and other marketable symbols of African American culture. For critics, these shifts reflected a watering down of "black, urban-based working class" culture.[9] However, Echols defends this transformation. In her opinion, middle-class African Americans wished to embrace integration and the new economic mobility it brought instead of being frozen in whites' glorification of mythological black hardship.

Ferguson insists now that black popular culture has been depoliticized and African Americans feel free to try on different identities, "The Negro is now officially human" (*SL* 3). He does not lament the demise of black coolness. On the contrary, for him, if blacks are perceived of "as mediocre and mundane as the rest of the species" (*SL* 3), it would be a testament to a new stage of equality. Rather than being essentialized for the stereotyped traits, Ferguson believes, if black popular culture is passé, blackness will no longer be perceived as tied to some inherent identity; rather, it can be as fluid and shifting as white identity. This new freedom is eventually represented in Ferguson's collaboration with Charles Stone at the end of the novel. When he and Stone perform what he calls the "Berlin Wall of sound," Ferguson proudly proclaims that, because their collaborative beat is of "indeterminate blackness" and "*out* of character," blacks will no longer be judged by the color of their skin (*SL* 16), and finally the ghosts of Josephine Baker, Langston Hughes, and the Black Panthers—all black icons who were infamous in European society—can rest in peace. Ferguson appears to embody what, in 1989, Trey Ellis defined as the "new black aesthetic" (NBA). Ellis describes members of this new aesthetic as "cultural mulattoes":

Just as a genetic mulatto is a black person of mixed parents who can often get along fine with his white grandparents, a cultural mulatto, educated by a multi-racial mix of cultures, can also navigate easily in the white world. And it is by and large this rapidly growing group of cultural mulattoes that fuels the NBA. We no longer need to deny or suppress any part of our complicated and sometimes contradictory cultural baggage to please either white people or black.[10]

Now that blackness is passé, one of Ferguson's newfound freedoms is trips to a tanning salon. These sessions are a means not only of coping with the gray Berlin winter, but of invoking his right to be a blank slate. In his opinion, his naturally dark complexion does not undermine his actions. By tanning, he joins the ranks of whites that, for decades, enjoyed the freedom of being unmarked and for whom tanning signified privilege. Like the postmodern man masquerading in women's oppression, whites who tan can momentarily experience being "black," but inevitably return to their unmarked state. Ferguson thus stakes his claim to being unmarked.[11] The fact that the experience reminds him of his mother suggests he equates the tanning bed with the womb: "The ultraviolet radiation substitute[es] for [his] overprotective mother piling blanket after blanket on her baby boy. The warmth from the lamps becomes indistinguishable from that of [his] mother's dry, calloused hands" (*SL* 7). If his tanning symbolizes a return to the womb, perhaps Ferguson hopes to emerge reborn as an unmarked man. However, his identity is entwined with how others see him, and, regardless of his self-perception, white Germans' projections keep him in chains.

Trapped in the Black Box: White German Perceptions of Blackness in *Slumberland*

When Ferguson arrives in Berlin he feels "as happy as a runaway slave" (*SL* 51), like many African Americans who have found a certain kind of freedom in Europe. Yet despite black GIs' claims that postwar Germany was a racial utopia compared to the United States, Ferguson is not delusional about the extent of white Germans' hospitality; as he remarks, "Everyone was so nice—to a point" (*SL* 51). He understands that, as an African *American*, he is received with a certain degree of friendliness as long as he is believed to be staying in Germany for a short while—long enough for them to "pick [his] brain about jazz and American racism" (*SL* 51), but not long enough to take root.

This feeling of freedom soon subsides; however, as Ferguson grows increasingly aware of the burden of black popular culture he must carry in Germany. White Germans' objectification of him makes him feel akin to a group of emperor penguins on display at the Berlin zoo. He praises the animals for "rebelling in penguin defiance in the face of the curious stares and the stereotyped expectations of the outside world" (*SL* 56). His equivalence between himself and the penguins at the zoo recalls the *Völkerschauen* (literally "people shows" or human zoos) that Carl Hagenbeck organized in the nineteenth century, when he put indigenous peoples, including Africans, on display in German zoos. Ferguson later applies this metaphor to an African American security guard he meets at the *Amerikahaus*.

The *Amerikahaus* was introduced to German cities in 1946 by the U.S. Information Service. It was instrumental in making Germans familiar with the kinds of American culture that the USIS deemed representative of America's colorful democracy.[12] It is not coincidental that a black man has been chosen as a gatekeeper in the novel. He stands inside a "glass-enclosed vestibule" that Ferguson describes as a cage. Ferguson does not view the long history of cultural exchange between African Americans and Germans from a solely positive perspective. He muses, "The tall African-American watchman belonged to the long legacy of freak show blackness, including the Venus Hottentot" (*SL* 57). This nameless black guard, who is armed only with a badge that says "Security," conforms to stereotypes of the childlike black who is not trusted with serious jobs and therefore not with a weapon. Ferguson riffs on these stereotypes of the happy-go-lucky black man by saying of the guard that he "disarmed intruders with his smile" (*SL* 57).

Like the men Ferguson encounters in the Slumberland bar, the security guard seems to be a remnant of a bygone era—black GIs who chose to remain in Germany long after World War II. This might explain the bar's name. With its red lighting, bamboo blinds, banana trees, reggae, and sand-strewn floors, the Slumberland is described as a hyperreal location that simultaneously signifies both every white German's fantasy of an exotic getaway and nowhere at all. The men who frequent the Slumberland, although Germany *and* America have changed significantly since the 1950s, are still convinced that "Germany is the black man's heaven" (*SL* 58). As an outsider coming into this "racial utopia" with the post-civil rights mindset of the new black aesthetic, Ferguson remains skeptical. The security guard, on the other hand, suggests that in exchange for the freedom to date white women, black men in Germany must give in to their essentialization and objectification. "You have to let them love you," he advises Ferguson (*SL* 58).

One of the first assumptions Ferguson encounters is that black popular culture is free and innovative—as if it was more of a bricolage than other postmodern, pop-cultural phenomena. One white German man tells him, "You know, jazz improvisation comes from the slaves having to improvise in order to survive" (*SL* 52). Ferguson counters this naive romanticization of black popular culture by reinvoking the physicality of the black experience. His counterargument demystifies black popular culture, stripping it of the white German's attractive notions: "Making a holiday meal from pig innards isn't improvisation; it's common sense to throw whatever's left into the fucking pot" (*SL* 52). While "improvisation" comes from a place of luxury, like Dada poet Richard Huelsenbeck's "African" drumming at the Cabaret Voltaire in the 1910s, survival tactics are what men resort to in the face of oppression. Slaves did not drum purely as a means of artistic expression but as a necessary means of communication.

It is in the area of music, however, where Ferguson is most confronted with essentialist notions about blacks. He is a DJ and "jukebox sommelier," and white Germans' ideas about black popular culture are tied to music. After reunification, during his first gig in East Berlin he is surprised to see his DJing event labeled as "BLACK MUSIC!" (*SL* 122).[13] As Ferguson sets up his equipment, "It dawned on [him] that [he] and not [his] music was the entertainment, the atmosphere" (*SL* 122). When he realizes that the crowd wants to watch him "perform" black popular culture, Ferguson spins a mixture of "unsung American and German funkateers: Shuggie Otis, Chocolate Milk, Xhol, Manfred Krug, and Veronika Fischer" (*SL* 122). By playing white jazz vocalist Manfred Krug and *Schlager* star Veronika Fischer under the label of "black music," Ferguson questions the felicity of such labels. Is "black music" music by black artists? Music originating in the African diaspora? Or somber music? In chapter 3, we saw that labeling zydeco "Negermusik" obfuscates its European influences, and this is the case for most musical genres labeled "black music" in contemporary Germany.

Wir sind ein (weißes) Volk

As an African American familiar with the race and class conflicts in the United States,[14] Ferguson offers a unique, outsider perspective on discrimination in postunification Germany. Ferguson's encounter with reunification happens by chance one day while he is searching for Charles Stone. When he stops to watch Berliners dismantle the wall, a middle-aged East German runs up to him, hugs him, and shouts, "'Ich bin frei!' *I am free!* Then, cribbing from Kennedy's famous speech, he whispered in [Ferguson's] ear, 'Ich bin ein Negro. Ich bin frei jetzt' (I'm a Negro. Now I'm free)" (*SL* 118). This encounter reminds Ferguson of something his "father would say whenever he'd come across a hard-luck colored person in a witness box, cardboard box, or coffin box before his time. He'd say, 'Lincoln freed the slaves like Henry Ford freed the horses'" (*SL* 118). This equivalence relates to my closing argument in the last chapter about the difficult circumstance of freed slaves. Ferguson's father suggests that both slaves and horses lost their purpose for the system. Once horses were no longer the primary means of transportation, they became good only for sport. And when a horse is worn out on the racetrack, its fate is to be slaughtered and repurposed, either as food or glue. Emancipation freed the slaves from forced labor, but those who did not become sharecroppers (enslaved by debt) had grave difficulty finding work. And in time, sports would become one of the few venues where black men were assigned worth.

Ferguson draws an equivalence between freed slaves and East Germans. After reunification,

> Germany changed. After the wall fell it reminded [him] of the Reconstruction period of American history, complete with scalawags, carpetbaggers, lynch mobs, and the woefully lynched. The country had every manifestation of the post-1865 Union save Negro senators and decent peanut butter. Turn on the television and there'd be minstrel shows— tuxedoed *Schauspieler* in blackface acting out *Showboat* and literally whistling Dixie. . . . There were East Germans passing for West Germans.[15] (*SL* 134)

Ferguson echoes my argument in the last chapter, equating East Germans with freed slaves because, with reunification, East Germans were also thrust into modernity (in the stage of late capitalism) and expected to compete with West German "brothers" who had been at the game much longer.

George Blaustein suggests that Beatty's choice of Berlin for the setting of his novel is a metaphysical move. Blaustein reads *Slumberland* as Beatty's answer to Kenneth Warren's question, "What is African American literature?" Warren believes African American literature was dialectically dependent on the Jim Crow era and, therefore, ceased to be after Jim Crow was abolished. According to Blaustein, Beatty "uproot[s] the African American drama from its national bearings and graft[s] it, however awkwardly, onto divided and reunited Germany," and this revives African American literature because it "allows for surprising displacements and projections of familiar American historical narratives."[16] Similarly, Elisa Schweinfurth believes *Slumberland*'s "comparison of post-Wall Germany to the post–Civil War United States suggests that the German setting is not only used to address the problematic relations between East and West Germans but also to approach racial tensions between black and white people in the United States through displacement."[17]

While I agree with Blaustein's and Schweinfurth's argument that *Slumberland* allows its readers to grapple with African American issues in an alienating setting, it is limiting to think of the novel as merely displacing American issues to Germany or comparing the conflict between East and West Germans with the racial conflict between black and white Americans. Instead, I would like to highlight the value in considering how the discussion of reunification in *Slumberland* allows for West Germans, East Germans, and African Americans to "touch tales."[18] The collisions between their experiences in the novel enable a critical reflection on not only white West German embodiment of black popular culture but also the tenuous solidarity movement of white East Germans with African Americans' fight for civil rights.

As I mentioned in the last chapter, prominent African Americans who viewed their fight for civil rights within the larger international solidarity movement were celebrated in the GDR even though antiblack racism was still present there. It is, therefore, not surprising that despite the similarities Ferguson recognizes between the East German and the African American experience, reunification brings a rise of overt nationalism and racism with it. As an African American, Ferguson experiences reunification much as black Germans do. Many Germans of color claimed that reunification revived German nationalism—the "we" in the common phrase "Wir sind ein Volk" did not include immigrants or dark-skinned Germans.[19] As black German poet and activist May Ayim stated, after reunification,

> Concepts such as homeland, people, and fatherland were suddenly—again—on many tongues. Words came back into official circulation that had not been used without hesitation in either German state since the Holocaust. . . . In the first days after November 9, 1989, I noticed that there were hardly any immigrants and black Germans visible in the city landscape. . . . Our participation at the party was not requested. . . . I found the "receptiveness" and "hospitality" toward white GDR citizens duplicitous considering the constant warnings to our so-called foreign fellow citizens that the "boat is full."[20]

Reflecting on the troubling nationalism that he notices in his German lover Doris's speech, Ferguson's feelings reflect Ayim's:

The way she [Doris] bandied about *Jews* made [Ferguson] miss the Wall. Before reunification no one called [him] *Neger* to [his] face or said *Jew* as a pejorative. . . . Needless to say, the black expat population longed for the Wall's return. . . . Reunification and the rise of neo-Nazi activity had given the West German asshole the freedom to show his true colors. (*SL* 138–39)

This observation sheds light on Charles Stone's protest against the wall's dismantling. Stone, whom Ferguson finally encounters as he is collecting stones in order to rebuild the wall, wears a placard proclaiming, "How can we read the writing on the wall, if there is no wall" (*SL* 140). L. H. Stallings views Stone's effort as a desire to hide truth and resist change.[21] I argue, however, that Stone is attempting to fissure the German unity that has led to a solidity within and rejection of Others without.

Arguably, it was the wall's dismantling that revealed the true colors of both Germanies. After it was built in 1961, West Germany had even more reason to invite guest workers from abroad. They were needed to counter the labor shortage that resulted from the lack of migrants from the East. Meanwhile, the Socialist East also had guest workers, but because East Germany saw itself as free of racism and exploitation, these workers were referred to as "Socialist friends." The East even argued that the problem of neo-Nazi violence, which existed in both Germanies, was a Western import. With reunification came new financial burdens and intensified fears that there would not be enough resources available for Germans *and* foreigners, including "foreign-looking" citizens. The writing on the wall revealed Germany to be an imagined community that did not consider people of color a part of the fold. Before I can conclude with an overall interpretation of the novel and the theme of essentializing blackness, I turn to *Passing Strange* and bring the musical into conversation with Beatty's novel.

Punk and Circumstance

Similar to *Slumberland*, Mark Stewart's musical *Passing Strange* also confronts Germans' stereotypes about black popular culture.[22] However, while Beatty dramatizes the conflict around national identity between white Germans and black Germans, *Passing Strange* outright rejects a German identity dependent on whiteness given that all of the characters are played by black actors. Presenting an all-black Europe also challenges the reader's notions of a stable identity because the same actors who play black Los Angelenos at the start of the musical become Dutch in Amsterdam and German in Berlin.

The (in)stability of race and identity is a theme that *Passing Strange* has in common with *Slumberland*. The protagonist of *Passing Strange* is simply referred to as "Youth." Since it is a semiautobiographical piece, the name suggests that this is the younger self of the narrator, who is played by the musical's creator, Mark Stewart.[23] The generic name "Youth" could also be a reference to the common practice of using such general names for characters in Weimar-era expressionist and later in the situationist street theater of the late 1950s and early 1960s. The name makes the protagonist a universal figure with whom many can identify. After all, Youth's progression from adolescent rebellion against his background to acceptance and love for his family is a common journey across many cultures.

Although *Passing Strange* begins several years earlier than *Slumberland*, in the late 1970s, there are several similarities between Youth and Ferguson. Youth is also an African American male raised in a middle-class family with a love of music, and he, too, has grown dissatisfied with LA's eternal sunshine and feigned happiness. Youth describes himself as coming from "a big two-story, black middle-class dream [with] . . . manicured lawns, [and] some saving bonds,"[24] a stark contrast to the poverty-stricken images of African Americans that circulated in Germany in the 1960s and 1970s. Youth's conflict with his mother arises because he does not want to follow the straight-and-narrow path laid out for him. While he wants to play music and travel the world, his mother would be happiest if he would go to church regularly and marry the upstanding Edwina. A carbon copy of his mother, Edwina portrays their future life together as living in "a sprawling two-story house fulla African sculptures from tribes we know nothing about, kente cloth couch covers, and Malcolm X commemorative plates lining the walls of our airy, peach-colored breakfast nook!!!" (*PS* 19). While these objects are supposed to ground Edwina's middle-class dream in black popular culture, they are still dehistoricized, decontextualized, and stripped of any political meaning connecting them to African American history.

Youth's mother is most representative of the strict African American tradition, and it is through her that Stewart plays with familiar stereotypes of black popular culture. At the beginning of the musical, the character "Mother" is introduced to the audience speaking black vernacular in a southern accent: "Lawd ham mercy, child, look at cho head! Look jus' like a feathuh bed! Now let go dat pillow! Leave dat dangerous dream be. Jump outta dat bed 'n come a churchin' with me!" (*PS* 2). In Brechtian fashion, the narrator interrupts this performance to point out the Mother's artifice: "She drops the Negro dialect and speaks in her natural voice" (*PS* 2). According to Brandon Woolf, this scene demonstrates *Passing Strange*'s response to the limits of African American theater and the narrow notions of black popular culture in general: "*Passing Strange* is Stew's refusal. It is his refusal to accept the traditions of (black) musical theatre, the strictures of racial authenticity, and any neat and tidy process of identity formation."[25] Thus, from the beginning, *Passing Strange* introduces the possibility of different black identities that not only exist in the black community simultaneously, but can be performed, referred back to, and undermined by individuals.

Youth feels his middle-class suburban surroundings have grown so comfortable as to be uncomfortable, to the point of becoming "chains." Instead of being himself, he claims he is forced to dress "phony" and go to church because that is the convention—even if the churchgoers are unhappy. Youth's experiences reflect Mark Anthony Neal's description of the conservative nature of postsoul black America. "Efforts to create the most 'positive' historical read of the black experience and its various icons have often denied a full exploration of the humanity of black folks."[26] When Youth's offbeat choir instructor, Mr. Franklin (who is coded as gay by his performance), discusses his own struggle with black conformity, it ignites a spark of rebellion in Youth.[27] Mr. Franklin describes them both as "just two brothers . . . (Thinks for a sec or two) passing. (This epiphany hits him hard . . . Mr. Franklin is perhaps growing a bit angry now) Like your high yellow grandma back in the day, only we're passing for black folks. Good, lawn trimmin', tax payin', morally upstanding, narrow-minded Christian black folk!" (*PS* 25). As the son of the pastor, Mr. Franklin's dreams of exploring Europe have been suspended by his dependence on his father, who is also his employer. He reflects: "You could say he's [the pastor's] paying me to . . . not be myself" (*PS* 24). But Mr. Franklin would not call himself a slave. "Because . . . slaves . . . ha ha ha . . . SLAVES! Yes, that's it!! Slaves got options! Options, ya dig? I'm talking escape . . . revolt . . . death. (*Pause*) Options. (*Pause*) But cowards ain't got shit. Cowards only have . . . consequences" (*PS* 24).

Unlike the slave willing to risk death for freedom, in his own comfortable black middle-class life in LA, Mr. Franklin is not willing to risk failure and alienation to follow his dreams. To survive, he and Youth pass for the dominant notion of what it means to be black, middle-class males in 1970s America. But Youth soon grows tired of passing, and he quits the choir to express himself in

punk, which to him is more "real" than Mr. Franklin's "spicing up the spirituals" (PS 29).[28] Speaking on behalf of his band, the Scaryotypes, Youth tells Mr.
Franklin: "The double life shit's not working for us anymore . . . we're gonna
live . . . the way you . . . just talk" (PS 29). After an acid trip with his two bandmates, Sherry and Terry, Youth concludes they must go to Europe to be really
free. "If we're gonna deal with the real, we gotta tour Europe. America can't
handle freaky Negroes" (PS 31). Yet Sherry and Terry are too afraid to leave the
confines of their neighborhood, so Youth makes the journey on his own.

Along the Yellow Brick Road: Youth's Fantasies of Europe

Youth's first stop in Europe is in Amsterdam, which in the musical is introduced
by bright, colorful lights and a happy, upbeat song. In one of the city's quintessential coffee shops, he encounters Europeans' stereotypes about blacks for the
first time. When he declares that he is a musician, Christophe and Joop ask him,
"Do you play jazz?" "Do you play duh blues?" (PS 44). Youth's biting response
is, "Do you live in a fucking windmill? Do you wear clog shoes?" (PS 44). He
may take offense at their assumptions about his music, but he, too, is not free of
essentialist thinking. Youth believes that Europe represents "real" culture and
accepts the old stereotypes differentiating between high (European) and low
(American) culture. For him, America is new, artificial, and kitschy.

In Amsterdam, Youth meets Marianna and is immediately taken into her
"family" of artists and outsiders. At first, he revels in how friendly and trustful
the citizens of Amsterdam are compared to people in LA. Youth soaks this up.
His uninhibited sexual encounters help him learn to accept his body and (he
thinks) himself. Nevertheless, Amsterdam soon becomes as comfortable as
LA. Youth yearns to move on because he believes the "Real" cannot be found
in paradise since paradise, whether in LA or Amsterdam, makes people com-
placent, and instead of *really* living, one just goes through the motions. Truth-
fully, in Amsterdam, Youth's songs are much more cliché and sentimental than
his punk lyrics were in LA. He believes true songwriting comes only from pain
and that he cannot write songs when he is comfortable. Only in Berlin will he
learn that the clichés plaguing his song writing have little to do with where he
is and more to do with the influence of both the formulaic pop songs he once
viewed as rebellious and his avoidance of feeling real emotions.

Berlin at the time was still a hot spot of conflict where the superpowers of
the Cold War faced off. The narrator's description of Berlin as "a black hole
with taxis" (PS 57) conveys the effect of political conflict on the divided city's

atmosphere. Located in East Germany and surrounded by a wall, the city was physically cut off from the West; however, its political and cultural ties to the Western world, and its appeal for American and British artists and tourists, made it a bastion of capitalism in the East. Appropriately, Youth's first encounter in Germany is with a border guard at Checkpoint Charlie:

> BORDER GUARD: Ausweiss!!!
> YOUTH: Huh?
> BORDER GUARD: Identity! Your identity!!!
> YOUTH: My identity?
> BORDER GUARD: Pass! (Youth *attempts to pass him.* Border guard *grabs him, really pissed.*)
> YOUTH: I don't understand—
> BORDER GUARD: Your PASS-PORT! (*PS* 57–58)

Youth's confusion in this scene is partly based on cultural misunderstandings. The border guard's poor English leads him to translate *Ausweis* (identification card) as "identity." As Brandon Woolf points out, beyond a misunderstanding attributed to poor translation,

> Youth's seemingly innocent moment of confusion at Checkpoint Charlie is indicative of the more complex relation between national and racial identity for which *Passing Strange* is arguing. In the most literal sense, "identity" is strictly associated with Youth's national affiliation: he is an American with an American passport, and he must claim this identity to pass through the border. Youth's identity is also his pass(age) itself, formed in and through his movement from one place to another.[29]

A further source of linguistic confusion is the border guard's demand for a "Pass," which is German for "passport." Youth mistakes it as the imperative "Pass!" for his allowance to pass into Berlin. This reference to passing, however, has to do not only with physical movement, but also with performance. Woolf continues:

> In a third sense, Youth's identity is his "pass," his ability to masquerade as something other than what the picture on his passport says he is: African American. Youth's confusion—his "I don't understand"—implies that no one notion of identity is sufficient here and that the moniker "African American" is too reductive, too stagnant.[30]

Ironically, although Youth's journey at the beginning of the musical begins with his resistance against a stagnant (black) identity, he falls prey to this very practice. For it is in Berlin that he passes as a poverty-stricken ghetto youth in order to find acceptance.

Youth arrives in Berlin on May Day, which since the 1980s has seen battles between protesters and police on the city's streets, specifically in the district of Kreuzberg. It is during one of these riots that Youth meets the Nowhaus Collective. The Nowhaus consists of Hugo, a music critic and part-time bartender; Sudabey, a director of pornographic films; Mr. Venus, a cabaret artist; and Desi, the founder of the collective, with whom Youth falls in love. The collective's name is a play on Bauhaus, the Weimar-era leftist architectural collective founded by Walter Gropius. While the Bauhaus designers intended to combine art and technology in products for a mass market to "alleviate environmental deprivation and improve living and working conditions for the urban masses,"[31] the Nowhaus's stance *against* mass culture is indicative of a shift from modernism to postmodernism and from a belief in ideology to Mr. Venus's conclusion, "What's inside is just a lie. There's only surface" (*PS* 62).

Mr. Venus's assertion recalls arguments made by philosopher Jean Baudrillard in *Simulations*, originally published in 1983. According to Baudrillard, simulation "is the generation by models of a real without origin or reality: a hyperreal."[32] He uses the analogy of feigning an illness to elaborate the difference between dissimulation and simulation:

> To dissimulate is to feign not to have what one has. To simulate is to feign to have what one hasn't. . . . "Someone who feigns an illness can simply go to bed and make believe he is ill. Some[one] who simulates an illness produces in himself some of the symptoms." [Émile Littré, *Dictionnaire de la langue française*] Thus, feigning or dissimulating leaves the reality principle intact: the difference is always clear, it is only masked; whereas simulation threatens the difference between "true" and "false," between "real" and "imaginary."[33]

Thus, if the characters of *Passing Strange* simulate an essential black identity, black vernacular is one "symptom" of black popular culture. By speaking this vernacular and then switching into her "real voice" at the start of the musical, the Mother demonstrates how black popular culture can be simulated.

Following Baudrillard's notion of simulation, one could argue that there have been so many images of blacks produced and circulated for centuries—images that continue to be recycled and quoted today—that it is no longer clear what is real. Today's images of black popular culture have become so detached from any reality that they are hyperreal. While a modernist might have argued that past images—like whites in blackface, *Uncle Tom's Cabin*, and Hagenbeck's *Völkerschauen* (human zoos)—distorted the real black experience, today one would reject any notion of authentic black culture. Baudrillard's description of reality TV sheds some light on this issue. Speaking of a reality TV show where a family was filmed in their home, Baudrillard repeats the producer's claim, "'They live[d] as if we weren't there.'"[34] Baudrillard points out the impossibility of this statement. Of course, the family was always aware of the cameras, and their behavior naturally changed due to the presence of an audience. The pleasure the audience gets from watching such television is "a thrill of vertiginous and phony exactitude. . . . Here the real can be seen to have never existed."[35]

The same could be said about Hagenbeck's *Völkerschauen* or Josephine Baker's performances. The behavior of the Africans, African Americans, and black Germans in these "shows" was always mediated by the presence of an audience, like the photo on the cover of Tobias Nagl's book, *Die unheimliche Maschine*, which depicts an African "astonished" by a camera. As Nagl points out, what is obviously present but not openly referred to is the fact that the African, and the camera he is looking at, are subjects of yet another camera. Thus, rather than an "authentic" encounter between "primitive" man and technology, as the caption of the photo claims, this is an African man posing with a camera for a picture.[36] However, rather than thinking of this as a performance, the Weimar audience viewing this photo likely thought of itself as invisible—not an audience at all. For the white viewer is an objective bystander merely looking in on the "natural" behavior of blacks, but what they're really observing is mimicry with no origin. And when the sophisticated Josephine Baker wore a banana skirt on stage during her European performances, the joke was really on the audience. Baker's audience expected to see a black woman in "authentic" garb, but Baker's skirt is a prop in her performance of primitivism.

The Sound of Rebellion: Electronic Music and the Disavowal of Authenticity

At first, the Nowhaus's ideas about culture and society come as a shock to Youth. The narrator astutely points out the conflict between Berlin's postmodern cynicism and Youth's naïveté:

NARRATOR: Now, say you sounded like this:

YOUTH: Don't try to hide . . . [This lyric is accompanied by slow, romantic music. Youth's singing, his drawing out the vowels, is clichéd.] The truth is inside . . .

NARRATOR: And then you heard this . . .

MR. VENUS: WHAT'S INSIDE IS JUST A LIE!!! [This is set to hard rock industrial music.]

NARRATOR: It would have to make some kind of impression on you, wouldn't it? (*PS* 63)

In the musical, when Youth subsequently claims that "the Real that [he's] been searching for . . . is in the beauty of these burning streets [of Berlin]" (*PS* 65), his cry for revolution is accompanied by romantic piano music, and he quickly falls back into his old singing style. Youth has traveled to Berlin to find "the Real," only to be told that there is no real. During the song "Surface," the Narrator and Mr. Venus turn Youth's world upside down by revealing his intimate lyrics to be a mere product of the culture industry:

NARRATOR: . . . according to the Nowhaus manifesto and I quote: ". . . what we mistakenly call *our* thoughts, *our* feelings and *our* dreams, have actually been put there by a system, therefore . . ."

MR. VENUS: What's inside is just a lie . . .

NARRATOR: Our minds have been invaded, conquered and occupied. Hence:

MR. VENUS: What's inside is just a lie.

NARRATOR: And like a catchy refrain that gets trapped in your head . . .

MR. VENUS: What's inside is just a lie. . . .

NARRATOR: And so the only way to become your true self . . .

MR. VENUS: What's inside?

YOUTH: I'm starting to feel real . . .

NARRATOR: You gotta create your true self.

MR. VENUS: What's inside?

YOUTH: I'm starting to feel real. (*PS* 63–64)

Youth soon finds himself swept up by the Nowhaus's postmodern cynicism, and before he knows it, their politics begin to influence his own music, exemplified by his performance art piece set to electronic music instead of the earlier sentimental piano playing. It is no coincidence that Mark Stewart links Berlin to Youth's rejection of authenticity and his departure from pop lyrics.

While genres like soul, blues, and R & B might have still appealed to the white leftists and Afro-Americanophiles of the '68 movement, by the early 1970s, white German musicians began experimenting with the notion of embracing their cultural heritage and singing in German. What also differentiated these musicians from the folk and rock acts of the 1960s was their turn *away* from black popular music. Electronic musicians "no longer invoked exclusively blues and rock and roll, rather . . . [they were] influenced by German masters of electronic music like Karlheinz Stockhausen and Oskar Sala."[37]

Besides electronic music, other burgeoning genres of popular music in West Germany were punk, which had made its way from Great Britain around 1977, German new wave (NDW, a more experimental and less aggressive version of punk that grew out of the art scene), and hip-hop, which had been brought over by black GIs. This is the musical landscape of West Germany onto which Ferguson and Youth set foot. And like the African American DJs who were inspired by Kraftwerk's electronic sound, Ferguson and Youth are most interested in learning what German music, including the industrial, minimalist sound similar to that of band Einstürtzende Neubauten, has to offer them.

The German postwar music scenes that I have discussed thus far—jazz, rock and roll, blues, and zydeco—all have strong ties to African American (rhythm &) blues. Although Germany's first electronic musicians may have been reacting against much *earlier* musical traditions (romanticism), their attempts to distance themselves from Nazism via electronic music resulted in a simultaneous break from postwar genres heavily influenced by black popular culture. If the West has historically thought of black culture as more "primitive" and "authentic," then the postmodern rejection of authenticity could have led musicians away from black musical influence. Reacting against the Anglophilia and political sensibilities of the student movement, white NDW musicians felt comfortable discarding Anglophone pop aesthetics, which coincidentally were strongly influenced by black culture.[38] Perhaps this new trend enabled musicians, both white *and* black, to experiment more with music, art, and identity, giving them the courage to break away from notions of authenticity. Thus, musicians who previously were influenced by R & B, such as Iggy Pop, Lou Reed, and David Bowie, ultimately traveled to Berlin to strip away their notions of authenticity and recreate themselves.

Likewise, both Ferguson and Youth believe Berlin can emancipate them from a static, essential notion of black popular culture. Considering that both *Passing Strange* and *Slumberland* are set in the late 1970s and 1980s, the musical genre one would expect to be most prominent in each narrative is hip-hop, which emerged precisely during this period. But neither text makes hip-hop a central theme. Rather than the soundtrack to the African American experience of the post-disco era that hip-hop has come to represent, in *Slumberland,* hip-hop becomes one of *many* musical options in Ferguson's repertoire.[39] And in *Passing Strange*, hip-hop is not mentioned at all. Instead of something mandatory, hip-hop becomes just another option to listen to.

Passing (as from the) Ghetto

Despite his budding relationship with Nowhaus founder Desi, Youth is told that he can only remain in the collective if he can contribute to their goal of creating *"an anti-bourgeois living community / That stands in opposition to capitalist society"* (*PS* 65). Even after his philosophical discussions with the collective have opened up his mind, it takes time before this has an audible effect on Youth's music. Mr. Venus addresses him disparagingly,

> MR. VENUS: Look, Mr. American Pop Song Maker: if your songs do not critique the hegemony of populist consumption . . .
> SUDABEY: Or if they mimic the phallocentric narrative of verse chorus verse chorus climax fade out smoke a cigarette turn over snore all night and never call me again . . .
> HUGO: Then they are nothing more than tools of the oppressor . . .
> YOUTH: Wait a minute!!! Rock and roll: a tool of the oppressor? What about the Clash? . . .
> HUGO: Punk rock was a marketing strategy. (*PS* 72–73)

At a loss for what he can contribute to the collective, Youth defaults to "exotic" appeal:

> HUGO: Look, let's cut to ze chase scene, ja? Please give us one reason why we should allow you to stay.
> YOUTH: Um . . . because I'm black?
> ALL: What's that?
> YOUTH: (*To* Hugo.) Yeah, Mr. May 68: you know what it's like to be the object of oppression living under police occupation in the ghetto?
> NARRATOR: He did not. . . .
> YOUTH: (*Emboldened, to* Hugo) Well, let me ask you this, Mr. Know-It-All: do you know what it's like to hustle for dimes on the mean streets of South Central?

NARRATOR: Nobody in this play knows what it's like to hustle for dimes on the mean streets of South Central. . . .

YOUTH: NOBODY knows the trouble I've seen! Nobody! I come from hell on earth: illiteracy—guns—drugs—insanity—decay. . . . And I am no mere *popsongmaker*. I am an artist. My work is about re-invention. My work is about . . . transcendence. My work is about . . . the limits of blackness.

(Youth *does James Brown spin, capping it with a . . . hey!* Everyone *except* Desi *flinches . . .*) (*PS* 73–75)

Confirming the ideas in the German texts we have examined thus far, Youth's argument is that his black identity makes him always already revolutionary and rebellious. When he degradingly calls Hugo "Mr. May 68," he refers to the German student movement's interest in the civil rights movement and the Black Panthers and white Germans' idolization of African Americans as the ultimate revolutionary subject.[40] While Ferguson felt oppressed by images of black popular culture in Germany that have been recycled from the past, Youth seeks to take advantage of this past. Once again, the Narrator's Brechtian address to the audience undermines Youth's simulation of an authentic black experience, for he reveals that neither Hugo nor Youth knows the kind of poverty being described.

Youth takes the narrator's advice: "The only way to become your true self" is "you gotta create your true self" (*PS* 64). The "self" that he creates in order to gain the collective's respect is an amalgamation of past performances of black popular culture—a punk-inspired bricolage of past artifacts set to industrial music. He adopts the pseudonym "Mr. Middle Passage," a name that invokes centuries of cross-cultural exchange, including slavery. Singing about the "chains of his identity," Youth dons a metal skirt of bananas. While Ferguson sought to lay Josephine Baker to rest, Youth reawakens her but with a degree of irony. His song "Identity" is followed by "The Black One," which is the narrator's commentary on how Youth is capitalizing on black essentialism.

Youth's insistence that his artwork is about "the limits of blackness" does have some truth. What initiated his journey was his frustration with the limits of *middle-class* black culture, and those are the chains to which his performance *really* refers. While Youth sings "Identity," the voice of his mother can be heard interrogating his life choices:

MOTHER: Why don't you want to be around your own people?

YOUTH: *The key to the real is finally in my hand! And now your expectations are exiting my veins!* (*PS* 77)

The "expectations" to which Youth refers are not the assumptions about black popular culture that plagued Ferguson in Germany, but the expectations of a mother that her son lead an upstanding, middle-class lifestyle. Does the identity Youth creates for himself merely create new limitations, or does his insistence on an identity that is not real but simulated actually *free* him from any expectations? The narrator refuses to answer this question, but leaves it open for the audience to contemplate, *"Is he the post-modern lawn jockey sculpture? . . . Or just a soul on a roll exploding your culture?"* (*PS* 80).

I believe Youth's performance as "Mr. Middle Passage" suggests that he now understands that there is no "real" or authentic black identity. Rather, black identity is constructed from images that have been in circulation for over a century. Youth can access these images to embellish or undermine them as he sees fit. During "The Black One,"[41] Desi suggests that *"he's dancing in a cage,"* to which Youth replies, *"But I'm the one with the key"* (*PS* 80). The narrator then claims that Youth is "the real Voice of America" (*PS* 80). In the film, during this statement, the narrator looks into the camera while shaking his hand by his face and altering his voice to imitate Al Jolson's blackface performance of "Mammy" in *The Jazz Singer*. This act alone has multiple layers. Voice of America (VOA) is the "the U.S. government's international radio agency, broadcasting on shortwave frequencies throughout the world, excluding the United States."[42] Started in 1942, after the United States entered World War II, and broadcasting until the Cold War ended, "the purpose of the VOA was to be America's propaganda arm, disseminating news and information favorable to the US around the world . . . seeking to win allies at the same time that it tried to discredit the Soviet Union and other communist nations."[43] As the Narrator of *Passing Strange* suggests, who better to speak on the subject of freedom than an African American who is often discriminated against in his own country—just like the guard of the *Amerikahaus* in *Slumberland*. But rather than being the "real" VOA, there is nothing real about the black popular culture Youth puts on display. It can only be described as hyperreal.

Youth succeeds in fooling the Nowhaus collective enough that they believe he truly is from the ghetto. They reflect on his performance:

MR. VENUS: Only the slums of America could produce such pain.
HUGO: His ghetto angst is far superior to ours. . . .
MR. VENUS: We love you . . . like an anthropologist loves a tribe.[44]
YOUTH: Tribes must love the attention. I bet it makes them feel like stars!
    (*PS* 79)

In her analysis of the mainstream popularity of gangsta rap, bell hooks—pen name of the American author, feminist, and social activist—argues that consumers desire images of underclass, or more specifically black underclass culture, because it allows them to vicariously engage in black culture, at least in the sensationalist form it takes in the media. But these consumers do not have to experience the physical hardships that normally go along with being poor and black.[45] This thrill is precisely what the Nowhaus collective gets from Youth's performance of ghetto angst. Sudabey even tells Youth, "I envy you so much!!! I want to be re-incarcerated as a black man!!!" (*PS* 80). Her remark points to the privileging of the black male as a model for black popular culture. Furthermore, this play on words (presumably she meant to say reincarnated) reestablishes the physicality of black experience in Lou Reed's "I Wanna Be Black," discussed in chapter 2. If masquerading as a black man gives Sudabey a certain amount of cool, in reality it would also increase her likelihood of being incarcerated.

The Death of the Essential Black Subject

Both Ferguson and Youth attempt to challenge (white) Germans' notions of black popular culture. First of all, by traveling abroad, these characters reclaim a practice that is most often seen as the privilege of whites. Furthermore, these black men reterritorialize what was once "white," through not only their mobility but their musical tastes as well. Once in Germany, Youth explodes the essential black subject by recognizing that identity is a construct and by reclaiming his right to use and/or undermine past images of black popular culture. While Youth embraces the past through citation, Ferguson, in contrast, wishes to be unmarked. But can one say that one or the other of these approaches is more effective for challenging black stereotypes?

Considering Youth's strategy, both he and the members of the Nowhaus simulate their identities, but neither is aware of the other's performance. Aside from Desi, the members of the Nowhaus view Youth's performance as authentic and real. Meanwhile, Youth might reject any essential *black* identity, but he still believes the Nowhaus is the "real." While Youth considers LA fake, plastic, and constructed, he mistakenly thinks Berlin's war-torn streets are more authentic. However, one could argue that the May Day riots are just as much a simulation as Youth's ghetto identity. One sees especially in today's demonstrations that many of these riots have become simulations of past riots—

artificial and lacking meaning; hence, the smooth transition in the musical from riot to spectacle: "The frontline of the uprising became a gilded stage" (*PS* 62). Rather than being a real experience, the May Day riot Youth witnesses is likely a cat-and-mouse game between protestors and police, like the demonstration depicted in *Ich bin ein Elefant, Madame*, discussed in chapter 2. The members of the Nowhaus *perform* the role of the revolutionaries and conceal their bourgeois sensibilities. This becomes clear to Youth on Christmas, when instead of "keeping it real," the members of the Nowhaus abandon him to spend the holidays with their families:

> SUDABEY: No one is here for Christmas.
> HUGO: We all go home for ze holidays.
> YOUTH: Home?
> SUDABEY: To our families in their sleepy West German villages.
> HUGO: I am missing my stupid old friends.
> SUDABEY: I cannot wait to lay around with my teddy bears.
> HUGO: I love the look on my father's face when he serves the blood sausages. He remembers how I loved them as a child. But forgets I'm vegetarian!!! (*Only* Hugo *laughs.*)
> SUDABEY: You know, absence really does make ze heart grow into a state of mind which somehow transforms what you once could not stand about your family into a somehow quaint, pleasure-giving construct. (*PS* 90–91)

Youth assumes that Berlin is the only place for "real" experiences and that the members of the Nowhaus have a stable identity as revolutionaries. These assumptions keep him from truly freeing himself, for he begins to see his artificial identity as real too. When he tells his mother why he won't be joining her for Christmas, he insists it doesn't make sense to return to LA: "Why leave a place where I can be myself to come back to a place where I can't" (*PS* 88). But there is nothing real about his identity in Berlin. It may intentionally consist of citations of past performances of black popular culture, but it is still intended to fulfill the expectations of an audience comprising the Nowhaus collective.

Brandon Woolf argues that Stewart's "real" is a "Real—with a capital 'R'—that is necessarily multiply defined, multiply located, unstable, in motion even."[46] Instead of a complete rejection of anything "real," Stewart's Real is different from narrow notions of an authentic black identity because it is not anchored in one time or place; rather, "For Stew[art], it is the movement between the poles that is productive. It is in and through his refusal to settle, to

stop working, that identity is forged, that music is made, and that the—a—
'Negro problem' is both surpassed and further problematized."[47] So, rather
than finding the Real in Berlin or at home in LA, the Narrator, a now grown
Youth, "*finally f[inds] a home, Between the clicks of a metronome*" (*PS* 95).
The Real exists in the movement between performances, making it impossible
to pin down.

Rather than searching for a "real" identity, Ferguson is more like Oskar in
The Tin Drum, in search of music (and life) that is not determined by preconceived notions. However, while Oskar believed black popular culture was the
key to such freedom, Ferguson rejects the assumption that black culture is
necessarily innovative, and that is why he wants to make "blackness" passé.
After reading a William Faulkner novel Charles Stone gives him for inspiration, Ferguson concludes that, in order to free himself from essentialism, he
must first remove any punctuation from his life and instead commit to fluidity.
Ferguson describes himself as standing at a tri-forked crossroads: three "life-
altering" DJ gigs (*SL* 172). Ironically, the *left* fork is a right-wing, neo-Nazi
rally and the *right* fork is the annual *Bundestreffen* (national meeting) for black
Germans.

Because Ferguson sees himself as unmarked, he finds no problem in
DJing for neo-Nazis, agreeing to DJ at the Nazi rally purely for professional
reasons. Rather than fear for his well-being, he takes the rude comment of one
of the female party guests as a compliment. When a "punky fraulein spat at
[him] and ask[ed] to see his *schwanz*, [he] patted the knot of *deutschmarks* in
[his] pocket and reminded [himself] that [he] knew which 'tail' she *really*
wanted to see" (*SL* 175). Ferguson's remark refers to the double entendre in the
German word *Schwanz* (tail). One could read the white German girl's remark
as a racist suggestion that black men have tails like apes—a rumor that was
actually spread during the immediate postwar to dissuade white German
women from dating black men. However, colloquially *Schwanz* also means
penis. Thus, although Ferguson is aware of the potential for insult, rather than
getting offended, he chooses to reflect on the double entendre as an amusing
testament to white German women's desire for black masculinity.

After his gigs at the neo-Nazi party and the black German picnic, his third
gig, the one representing the path that leads straight ahead, is at the Free University. By the time Ferguson sets up his turntables, the only other person present in the room is a "pretty, vaguely Mediterranean-looking woman" whom he
describes as wearing a "powder-blue dress" (*SL* 181–82). Faced with a sole
audience member, Ferguson reflects on how people often torment him with the
question, "Who is your audience?" This is an especially frustrating question

for someone who does not want to categorize his music. He decides that, on this particular evening, with this woman in blue as his sole audience member, he can craft each track for her as an individual without trying to label her. After Ferguson finished his set, "She stood up, looked at [him] meekly, and asked, 'Are you finished?'" (*SL* 182). When Ferguson nods in response, he realizes that this woman did not come to hear his set; rather she was the cleaning woman, wearing the typical powder-blue uniform, politely waiting to finish her duties. The fact that no one comes to this performance is actually not a disappointment. Ferguson revels in the idea that he literally has no audience, and therefore, no expectations to fulfill.

For Ferguson's final blow to black essentialism, he hangs a banner with the phrase "Black Passé" when he and Charles Stone finally collaborate, performing a Berlin Wall of sound where the original once stood. After their performance, Ferguson asks Stone:

"During that last solo, what were you thinking about?"

"I was thinking about the phrase on the banner, 'Black Passé.' How being passé is freedom. You can do what you want. No demands. No expectations. The only person I have to please is myself." (*SL* 230)

Ferguson and Stone seem to feel they have finally achieved a state of being unmarked, evading anyone's expectations. As L. H. Stallings states, "DJ Darky's journey implicitly symbolizes the desire to make room for indeterminate blackness in terms of cultural production and personal identity."[48] Nonetheless, his and Stone's success in achieving this is brutally contrasted with the suicide of a black German female friend. During his stay in Berlin, Ferguson meets two black German sisters from East Germany, Fatima and Klaudia. Ferguson relays how lonely Klaudia and Fatima felt growing up black in East Germany. Peggy Piesche notes that, in a study of black Germans born in the GDR between 1961 and 1970,

the adolescents in question did not receive any positive support from their social environment during crucial periods of their personal development and identity formation. . . . In the relatively homogenous and closed society of the GDR, Blacks were presumed to be exotic, foreign, and different—patterns of attribution similar to those found in other countries. To be associated with such attributes in the GDR meant also to be regarded as part of "another" society, definitely not as part of the GDR proper, but as a foreigner whose stay is limited.[49]

What further magnified black Germans' feelings of alienation in the GDR was the lack of access to black culture. Piesche continues:

> Eighty percent of those polled acknowledged having had only very limited sources of information with regard to topics of African or Asian history. This was perceived as another lack of possible help in order to come to terms with one's situation and to develop positive self-esteem. In this case, it was the lack of literature, music, media, and travel. Although the books of Kwame Nkrumah, Frantz Fanon, W. E. B. Du Bois, and Alex Haley were available in the GDR, resources for adolescents in the process of individualization and identity-formation were overall rather poor and often ambivalent.[50]

Following reunification, Fatima, the darker-skinned sister, has an especially difficult time adjusting to the brash racial chauvinism she was unaccustomed to in East Germany. While Ferguson and Stone's performance convinces them it is possible to escape black stereotypes, Fatima actually dies trying to achieve an unmarked/featureless existence, when she commits suicide by dousing herself with gasoline and lighting herself on fire. By the time Ferguson arrives on the scene, all that remains of her is a charred corpse. Ferguson cannot bear to look at Fatima's corpse.

> Every now and then, from behind [his] back, [he'd] hear a sharp crack that sounded like a potato chip being snapped in two and [he'd] know that a piece of burnt flesh or tuft of crinkled hair had peeled off [Fatima's] body and was tumbling in the street, being chased down by Klaudia. [He] suppose[d] ultimately that was what Fatima wanted, to be skinless and hairless. Featureless really. (*SL* 185)

The suicide note Fatima leaves behind quotes a poem by black German poet May Ayim entitled, "They're People Like Us."[51] The poem reads:

> We really believe
> That all people are the *same*.
> No one should be discriminated against,
> Just because he's *different*. (*SL* 190)

The irony of these words reflect philosopher Charles Taylor's argument that one of the great challenges of a multicultural society is that "we all [as a society] *recognize* the equal value of different cultures; that we not only let them survive, but acknowledge their *worth*."[52] Fatima's decision to commit suicide testifies to her disbelief that such a society is possible in Germany.

Conclusion

Passing Strange leaves its audience with the idea that, regardless of skin color or gender, all identities are a construction and the "Real" can never be pinned down. While *Slumberland* attempts to make a similar argument, it still constructs a cultural hierarchy. In *Passing Strange*, all of the characters are unmarked and fluid, adopting identities depending on the circumstance. In *Slumberland*, the only characters who *really* achieve an unmarked existence are not only black males, but musicians. With his "Berlin Wall of sound," Ferguson ultimately believes that neo-Nazis can be "cured" of racist thoughts or, at least, become "blind" to color if they encounter the *right* kind of music—music that no one can resist. The fact that this music is played by Ferguson and Charles Stone makes it seem like only a black *male* musician can achieve this. It is entirely possible that Beatty creates a narrative in which postblackness is only accessible to *some*, because he actually rejects the new black aesthetic, as Stallings claims, and therefore Ferguson's character is meant to be a critique of these concepts.[53] This would align with Christian Schmidt's assessment that Beatty purposely makes Ferguson a protagonist who is not socially responsible, and that this is related to the satirical nature of the novel.[54]

Perhaps Beatty's rejection of postblackness and the new black aesthetic is the reason why Ferguson's efforts to make "blackness" passé actually achieve the reverse. Arguably, this happens because "To many, the Schwa [Charles Stone] . . . was a well preserved mummy, a music primitive seemingly unspoiled by commercialism and modernity" (*SL* 212). Germans encountering Stone's music felt like "musical paleontologist[s] and [Ferguson was their] pickax-wielding native assistant" (*SL* 212). Ferguson tries to kill his white friend Lars's essential black subject with his beat, which consists of a diverse range of not only music but everyday sounds. Ferguson and Stone's collaboration is supposed to exemplify music that breaks with all categories—music that is not driven by any preconceptions, does not have a specific audience, and must not fulfill any expectations.

For a brief moment, Ferguson believes his musical efforts have achieved this goal. In the Slumberland bar, as a crowd listens to his beat on the jukebox, a blind white German student approaches him. She tells him, "Today morning[55] in ethnography class my professor played an African chant, a Negro spiritual, a Robert Johnson ballad, some Louis Armstrong, Charlie Parker, Marvin Gaye, and Kool Moe Dee, and asked the class if we could hear the similarities" (*SL* 239). According to Ferguson's thinking, this professor of ethnography made two mistakes: First, she assumed there was a connection between these musical examples just because they were produced by blacks, and she foreclosed any connection between this *black* music and anything else. Despite the shortcomings of her professor, the white German student shows some promise, for she does not necessarily hear any similarities. And when she hears Ferguson's beat, she hears everything from her "grandmother raking the leaves" to black British artist Sade and "her father cheering Borussia Dortmund" (*SL* 239). This student seems to share Ferguson's self-described gift of a phonographic memory that allows a person to hear beyond the racial boundaries that have been constructed around music. As L. H. Stallings points out:

> Because he is able to remember every sound he has ever heard, [Ferguson] can then comprehend the infinite possibilities of any sound based on numerous and varied combinations of the same sound or beat. He can create new sounds, as well as recognize new sounds. This gift makes him weary of the ways in which others cannot do the same.[56]

It initially seems as if Ferguson has at least reached this student with his efforts to become not only an unmarked individual but create music that is neither black nor white. However, Ferguson's hopes are dashed when the ethnography student begins feeling his face with her hands in order to "dissect" his features.

It appears that, in Ferguson's idea of a postunification, postmodern Germany divorced from the notion of the essential black man, not only is the black man not necessarily a rebel or *other* than German, but he can move through Germany freely, from a party for black Germans to a neo-Nazi rally in Marzahn in the eastern part of the city. At the rally, Ferguson questions the neo-Nazi Thorsten about a member of their gang who is clearly of African descent. Thorsten defends his "comrade," claiming: "It's the hate that's important. It doesn't matter who does the hating, but who you hate" (*SL* 175). Thus, in a world where everyone has the freedom to try on identities like clothing, black men can be neo-Nazis and neo-Nazis can idolize black musicians.

However, I find that the lesson Youth learns in Berlin offers a more viable solution for escaping essentialism. I believe Amy Robinson's understanding of "passing" is useful for probing *Passing Strange*'s argument about identity. After all, its title certainly invites a reflection on the practice of passing. One could read the musical's title as referring to Youth's life in Berlin. Youth passes *as* strange; he pretends to be different from Germans and he believes they can only see value in this difference. Pretending to be from the "ghetto," he attempts to hide the middle-class background he has in common with his German friends. Robinson suggests that passing requires a "triangular theater of identity" where "three participants—the passer, the dupe, and a representative of the in-group—enact a complex narrative scenario in which a successful pass is performed in the presence of a literate member of the in-group."[57]

According to Robinson, when a member of the in-group suspects someone is passing, the point is not in the *knowing* whether or not one is correct but in the telling. In that moment, the member of the in-group does not recognize "a stable prepassing identity" but rather "the apparatus of passing that manufactures presumption (of heterosexuality, of whiteness) as the means to a successful performance."[58] By witnessing the passing, the in-group witness realizes that one can never get to the real—there is no truth.

This element of masquerade in *Passing Strange* makes its conclusion a more feasible way of battling the essential black subject in Germany than *Slumberland*'s ending. In *Passing Strange*'s spectorial triangle, Youth is the passer, but he is not passing for white; he is passing for an essentialized notion of an African American. The dupes are the Germans (excluding Desi) who read his performance as authentic, as evidence of his real identity. In this triangulation, the in-group who witnesses the passing is the audience, who knows Youth's middle-class background. From the perspective of the in-group, the audience immediately reads Youth's tales from the ghetto as a performance. Meanwhile the dupes, the Germans, read truth into the performance.

Nevertheless, how might one answer bell hooks's concerns about the shortcomings of this postmodern approach to identity, "Yeah, it's easy to give up identity, when you got one."[59] The concern raised by scholars like hooks, E. Patrick Johnson, and Suzanne Moore is that it is easy to assign power to masquerade when the person who is masquerading already had the power to begin with.[60] Robinson also admits that "as a correlative social practice, identity cannot be divested from a culture that is unrelentingly invested with the value of appearance."[61] Although anyone can masquerade at any time, simulations can go wrong if everyone else insists on reading the scene ontologically.[62]

This question is at the center of one of black German artist Marc Brandenburg's pieces. *Ausländertarnpullover* (*Camouflage Sweater for Foreigners*) addresses the very irony that we accept that identities are fluid enough to be modified by fashion, but yet still hold on to the belief that race is a stable entity that fixes identity. The installation features a series of torsos made from cardboard and a variety of "brightly colored sweaters from thrift stores could be attached to different heads and arms through knitting. Varying colors, such as white, black, yellow and red, matched their imaginary 'races' according to conventional associations of racial identities with colors."[63] According to Jürgen Heinrichs's interpretation, "The sweaters, by virtue of being attachable or removable, highlight how clothes function to constitute, modify, or counteract identities. . . . [The artwork] explores how race is perceived as supposedly 'natural' and stable foundational entity, whereas fashion, by contrast, is seen as functioning to modify or supplement identity."[64]

When Ferguson encounters his first East Germans, his remarks confirm the identity-shaping qualities of fashion. What strikes him most about East Germans is "how incredibly un-eye-catching they [a]re. Not to say they [a]re unappealing" (*SL* 110). The reason why all East Germans look inconspicuous to Ferguson is because they have not had access to the range of self-modifying styles that are available in the capitalist West. With their welcome money, these future citizens of a unified Germany can construct a brand-new identity to help them integrate in their community of choice. But Ferguson laments, "There is no camouflage for being black" (*SL* 188). Only in an art piece, like Brandenburg's *Ausländertarnpullover*, can a black person don a white sweater and thereby become inconspicuous to a potential racist mob. The reality is that a black man *cannot* put on a Lonsdale sweatshirt and attend a neo-Nazi rally in East Berlin intending to "pass" as the majority. And the likelihood that a black man could DJ at such a rally, as in Ferguson's case, is just as poor.

However, Robinson's essay might show how postmodern notions of identity could help black individuals escape the ties of essentialism. Rather than erasing racial differences, the one victory that performance or passing can afford a black person in Germany is undermining essentialist notions of black popular culture—hence, Youth's comment that he might be in a cage, but unlike the blacks on display in the *Völkerschau* or the black security guard at the *Amerikahaus*, *he* has the key. Germans might read authenticity into his performance, but as long as there is a member of the in-group who recognizes his passing, then such a performance is a subversive act that can function as an individual form of resistance to the hegemony, in the sense of Michel de Certeau's tactics.[65]

Ferguson's desire to be unmarked is quite different from Youth's ephemeral passing. Ferguson's aspiration to solve the "Negro problem" of essentialism by achieving an unmarked state seems more naive. He would like for all people to have the luxury of being a blank slate capable of anything. Being unmarked does not require a dupe. It is not about revealing and undermining the apparatus but disregarding it. Thorsten, the neo-Nazi, does not misrecognize Ferguson as white. For Thorsten, Ferguson and Charles Stone remain black men. His acceptance of them is *despite* race and, thus, does not challenge the very notion of race as a stable signifier within a reliable system of knowledge. Ferguson and Charles Stone are seen as "unmarked" because their status as knowledgeable black male musicians gives them a position of authority. Fatima's fate, however, shows how difficult it is to achieve this status. Even if race is disregarded, who achieves an "unmarked" status might still be influenced by tangible factors like gender and class. Fatima, a black German woman, could only achieve her unmarked state of being by literally burning off her features. Though fictional, Fatima's death gives us a glimpse of the real, physical violence at stake in a Germany. If in Germany black culture and race in general continue to be understood as natural, stable entities, then a black person is always in danger of being the target of racist violence, regardless of individual identity.

While it is important that Beatty acknowledges a black German presence in his novel, it is interesting that he chose to represent black Germans with two *female* characters. L. H. Stallings reads DJ Darky as only contributing positively to the black German experience by playing music they can use to help create their identity, but he does not reflect about the ways in which DJ Darky is privileged and allowed a greater degree of fluidity than Fatima.[66] Furthermore, as black German women, Fatima and Katharina might appeal to Ferguson because they are a part of the African diaspora and can understand the problems he faces in Germany. And yet, as Germans, they are still "exotic" to him and represent an additional unknown territory for him to explore and conquer as the quintessential male protagonist abroad. Fatima and Katharina don't pose any *real* threat to Ferguson, whether that means challenging his masculinity, his ideas about blackness, or his ideas about German culture. Fatima and Katharina embody a male, African American fantasy of black German culture—a fantasy devoid of black German men. In the next chapter, I will look more closely at how black German men themselves have voiced their struggles with hegemonic masculinity, national identity, and appropriating African American culture in postwar and postunification Germany.

CHAPTER 5

The Future Is Unwritten

In 1999, German video artist Marcel Odenbach debuted a video installation entitled *Ach, wie gut daß niemand weiß* (*Hal Glad I Am That No One Knows*) at the Museum für Moderne Kunst in Frankfurt am Main. The installation consisted of four screens. On two screens, a white man and a black man jumped on trampolines against a background of footage featuring German and African American historical events. These events were projected on two further screens placed behind them. A few minutes into the videos, the men switch places, jumping into each other's screens for several minutes before returning to their own. Odenbach (b. 1953) explained the concept as follows: "The history of the black person becomes my history, and my history becomes that of the black person."[1]

This work of art demonstrates one of the positive outcomes made possible by global culture and global memory. Like many Germans of his generation, Odenbach had such an emotional investment in African Americans' struggle against racism during the 1960s that he feels the civil rights movement is as much a part of his history as any other event.[2] Nonetheless, something seems to be missing in Odenbach's gesture of cosmopolitical memory. It seems that a real dialogue about race in Germany would have to include a black German perspective.[3] However, in each of the texts by white German authors I examine in the first three chapters of this book, although white protagonists appropriate black popular culture in an act of cross-racial empathy, there is no direct engagement with or acknowledgment of a local black population.

If there is indeed a pattern among postwar German texts to posit black masculinity as an alternative to hegemonic German masculinity, then the absence of any black German men in these texts is quite curious, considering that around five thousand black German children were born in the immediate postwar years. While there is a plethora of depictions of white German males who seek black role models, this chapter discusses how black German men pieced together an identity during the postwar period. To what extent was black German masculinity subjected to stereotypes about African American masculinity? Did white German men longing for rebellion ever consider their black German neighbors potential role models? Or were black German men considered less authentically black than African Americans? And how does all of this impact a contemporary understanding of black German masculinity?

Since the early 2000s, several texts have laid the groundwork for a discussion on black German subjectivity, among them Tina Campt's *Other Germans* and Michelle Wright's *Becoming Black*. But aside from Campt's discussion of Hans Hauck's life surviving Nazi Germany as a black man, much of the scholarship in black German studies has focused on women because of the important role feminist and lesbian artists and activists have played in helping shape a contemporary black German consciousness.[4] Even among the seven black Germans Karin Timm interviews in *Schwarze in Deutschland: Protokolle* (1973), only one, Herbert Gruber, is male.[5] But some scholars, like Fatima El-Tayeb and Alexander Weheliye, have discussed contemporary black German masculinity as it pertains to hip-hop culture.[6]

In my approach to understanding black German masculinity and how black Germans negotiate their identities against German and African American stereotypes, I identify a generational difference between those born decades prior to the solidification of a black German community in the 1980s and those who were relatively young when this happened. Older generations of black German men grew up in relative isolation from any black community, and, therefore, as they constructed identities for themselves, they struggled between appropriating African American culture and striving to be recognized as German according to white hegemonic standards.

Younger generations of black German males have a more diasporic sensibility. In contrast to the isolation experienced by older generations, today's black German men have not only benefited from the politicization and increased visibility of black Germans since the 1980s but also from the benefits of a globalized world. Affordable travel and an increased interest in the African diaspora and the availability of social media technologies have made it easier for black German men to connect with black men across the globe. As a result, they no longer necessarily feel stuck between a binary of hegemonic German masculinity versus a black masculinity composed of stereotypes; nor is their notion of black masculinity tethered to African American culture. These young men do not necessarily feel the need to be seen as German, but they also reject the expectation of others that they should simply adopt African American culture as their own.

In order to demonstrate the generational differences among black German men, in this chapter I will first look at how masculinity is negotiated in several autobiographies of older black German men published in the last twenty years: Hans-Jürgen Massaquoi's *Destined to Witness* (1999), published when he was seventy-three; Theodor Michael's *Deutsch sein und schwarz dazu* (2013), published when he was eighty-eight; Charly Graf's *Kämpfe für dein Leben* (2011), published when he was sixty; and Günther Kaufmann's *Der weiße Neger vom Hasenbergl* (2005), published when he was fifty-eight. When these men came of age, they were isolated from any black community, were often confronted with negative stereotypes about blackness, and were left to construct a form of *black* masculinity mainly from whatever *diasporic resources* happened to be available to them, most of which stemmed from the United States.[7] My discussion is in no way meant to be a comprehensive analysis of these autobiographies. Rather, since no thorough analysis of black German male experiences exists, I introduce a few key themes addressed in these autobiographies in order to provide a brief outline of how these men born before the visible presence of a black German community experienced the intersection of race and gender.

I will then turn to the work of the poet Philipp Khabo Köpsell, who represents a younger generation of black German men. Köpsell was born in 1980 in Marburg to a white German mother and a black South African father. In his youth, he performed in a band, which is how he eventually made the transition from music to spoken word and poetry. Köpsell published his first book of poetry, *Die Akte James Knopf*, in 2010 and has since contributed poetry to edited volumes like *Afro-Shop* and *Arriving in the Future*. Köpsell's critique of identity politics and his interest in Afrofuturism offer a look at what the future might hold for a resistance to hegemonic German masculinity that does not simply reproduce binary thinking. Instead of constructing a black German subject that is diametrically opposed to white German ideals or subjected to African American models, Köpsell experiments with Afrofuturism to explore possibilities for multiple black masculinities that might serve different ends.

Older Self-Perceptions of Black German Masculinity

When trying to locate a specific black German masculinity separate from African American models, it is necessary to consider one of the significant differences between black Germans and African Americans. Fatima El-Tayeb stresses the difference "that points to an important divide between the Americas and continental Europe: the latter's black populations originate not in slavery but in colonialism."[8] As a black person, what does it mean if one's ancestors have not been forcibly brought to Europe, but rather, voluntarily made the journey in a search for economic and educational opportunities? Whether linked by a narrative of slavery or colonialism, what black Germans and African Americans *do* have in common is that their ancestors had to reject the myth of white supremacy taught to them by colonial governments on both sides of the Atlantic. In both the institutions of slavery and colonialism, white men presented themselves as being the most knowledgeable and most powerful. Thus, all men of the African diaspora, regardless of place of origin or settlement, have to find a path to masculinity that does not glorify white masculinity by demonizing black masculinity. What makes the black German condition even more complex is that, for black Germans born in the twentieth century, there has always been a need to position themselves in relation not only to hegemonic German masculinity but to hegemonic African American masculinity as well.

Of the four autobiographies I will discuss, two of the authors, Massaquoi and Michael, were born before World War II, and two after, Kaufmann and Graf. Thus, although these four men are significantly older than Köpsell, one can find in them a multigenerational view of black German masculinity. Massaquoi's and Michael's stories are unique, not only because they were born prior to Hitler's rise to power and had the challenge of surviving Nazi Germany, but also because they had memories of their black fathers. In contrast, and what is more typical of black German men born immediately after the war, is the experience of Graf and Kaufmann, who grew up without contact with their fathers.[9] That being said, Massaquoi and Michael still have very different experiences of coming into a black German masculinity. This might have something to do with their different social circumstances. At the time of Massaquoi's birth, his grandfather, Momulu Massaquoi, was the consul general of Liberia in Germany, and his father, Al-Haj Massaquoi, was a law student in Dublin who visited Germany on occasion. Through witnessing the power and influence his grandfather had, Aija Poikane-Daumke argues, Massaquoi associated black masculinity with superiority.[10] In contrast, Michael had a difficult youth, growing up with foster families and having to work at an early age in *Völkerschauen* (human zoos). Despite their different upbringing, both men relay relatively pleasant early memories of childhood and school, which take a negative turn once Nazis come to power. Likewise, both men turn to African American role models when they suddenly feel rejected by the nation.

For Michael, his inclusive experience at school shifted suddenly when the Nazis came to power and when he attempted, like the other boys in his class, to join the *Jungvolk*[11] in the fourth grade. Rejected because he did not belong to the *Volk*, Michael only found recognition in athletics. Referring to Michael,

"The students in other schools said enviously: 'If you guys bring your Jesse Owens along, we have no chance.'"[12] For Massaquoi, Joe Louis's and Jesse Owens' rise to fame also enabled him a pathway to recognition from his peers and "instilled . . . genuine pride in [his] African heritage at a time when such pride was difficult to come by."[13] Massaquoi could not be acknowledged as a black German, for this was not a recognized identity. But because of his alleged similarities to Louis and Owens, he could be perceived as an African American, as an Other-from-Without.[14] By aligning himself with Louis and Owens, Massaquoi went from a seemingly threatening figure to being perceived as at least similar to African Americans and therefore more acceptable.

Massaquoi also recalls how years of living in terror of persecution under the Nazi regime changed dramatically when Germany was liberated by the Allied forces. With thousands of African American soldiers arriving in Germany, having dark skin was suddenly no longer a stigma but rather symbolized a certain freedom to transgress the strict parameters white Germans were expected to abide by, precisely because he could "pass" as African American. Massaquoi recollects his decision to masquerade as a black GI in order to enjoy certain benefits. As an African American, Massaquoi could take refuge on American ships and share his American friends' rations of food and cigarettes while most white Germans were struggling to make do with much less. Furthermore, it was not even necessary for Massaquoi to pretend to be American to get special treatment. African Americans sympathized with him because he was black, and they pitied him for having lived under Nazi rule. One experience in particular makes clear what kind of cultural capital Massaquoi acquires as a black German man. When two black GIs are seeking out women, Massaquoi facilitates a meeting at a bar. His bilingualism affords him a privileged position as interpreter, a person who inhabits a threshold space and can move between worlds as he negotiates the terms of an encounter between two black GIs and two white German women. Implicitly, this scene reveals that there were times when Massaquoi's black masculinity put him in a position of power in relation to *all* German women. He could survive the difficult postwar years by mere camaraderie with African American soldiers or performance of a black GI, a strategy to which black German women had no access.

Brown Babies

Although Günther Kaufmann and Charly Graf were born after the demise of Nazi Germany, their autobiographies are still marked by a feeling of struggle because of the conditions of their birth to unmarried white women with little income. While some African American men did attempt to financially support their black German children, they made up a minority. And the inability of white German mothers to be with the soldiers who fathered their children was a real problem for German communities regardless of the father's race or nationality. In the postwar years, children born out of wedlock were legally wards of the state, and so-called occupation children were viewed negatively, not only because of a perceived financial burden on the state, but also because their mothers were assumed to be immoral and sexually transgressive. Though one could not simply tell if a child was an "occupation baby" by looking at him or her, this was not the case with black occupation children because their different skin color marked them as fathered by non-Germans.

Even though postwar Germany was eager to distance itself from its racist and fascist past, negative stereotypes about blacks persisted, and black German children commonly suffered from verbal and physical abuse. In *Zwischen Fürsorge und Ausgrenzung*, Yara-Collette Lemke Muniz de Faria discusses how the racist environment in which black German children grew up affected their behavior, and in turn, their perception by others, creating a vicious circle. Muniz de Faria recounts a study conducted by Luise Frankenstein in 1954, which showed that there was nothing inherently wrong with black German children, but the way their environment reacted to them produced problems.[15] This experience is reflected in Herbert Gruber's account of how racism made him fearful and aggressive as a child. As a result, he could not honestly say whether children did not want to play with him because he was black or because of his behavior.[16]

The biographies of Kaufmann and Graf suggest how the racism in their environments contributed to negative life experiences. Unlike Massaquoi and Michael, who had contact with their fathers or fathers' relatives, Kaufmann and Graf came into a world that was much less stable both socially and economically. Both were sons of GIs stationed in Germany during the war. It was common for children in these circumstances to grow up without knowing their father.[17] The relationships between white German women and black GIs varied from prostitution, as discussed in Massaquoi's memoir, to dating and, in some cases, engagements.[18] Marriage was, however, not a given, as the military was not supportive of a black GI returning to a segregated United States with his white German bride. In fact, the U.S. military made it difficult for black GIs to marry German women. And in some cases, black soldiers were relocated by superiors who sought to interfere with their relationships. Kaufmann describes himself as an "accident," stating simply, "My mother got mixed up with a black

GI."[19] Kaufmann also indicates that the U.S. military relocated his father, a paramedic named Jimmy, as soon as his mother became pregnant.[20]

Several familiar tropes about black masculinity are taken up in Kaufmann's autobiography, for example, hypersexuality. Desire and the stages of forming sexual relationships are important parts of an emerging male identity, and, not surprisingly, this process is less present in Michael's and Massaquoi's formative years because of the danger their association with white German women would have created during Nazi rule. Born after the fall of the Third Reich, Kaufmann and Graf had more sexual freedom, but their encounters with white women were not free from racism or racial fetishism. Graf claims to have been desired by many white women thanks to the celebrity of his boxing career. He was once told, for example, that "'women by the ring [get] moist hands,' because I just have 'that special something.'"[21] Nevertheless, he is still rejected by his first wife's parents because he is black.

As an apprentice in a paper factory, Kaufmann was flattered that a woman ten years his senior was sexually interested in him. He brags about how she took his virginity that year. In his description of this pinnacle moment, Kaufmann places himself in the passive role: "She screwed me."[22] Though he claims to have been put off by her insatiable desires, he later claims that he sought her out a second time, "intent on being the 'boss in the ring' this time around."[23] Thus, in addition to being sexually desirable, his identity as a man was also contingent on feeling in control. It is difficult to say to what extent his racial identity played a role in these feelings.

Another familiar trope for black German autobiographies is a foray in the entertainment world and the desire for recognition. At age fourteen, Kaufmann wanted to become a career musician. He was encouraged to pursue art by his ballet teacher; he had benefited from a scholarship for occupation children to take ballet. Like Massaquoi, Kaufmann was drawn to jazz, but these dreams were crushed by his stepfather, who wanted him to learn a practical profession. Kaufmann would finally get his chance to perform when, as a young man a few years out of the navy, a chance encounter with German director Rainer Werner Fassbinder in 1969 on the set of Volker Schlöndorff's film *Baal* led to roles in several of Fassbinder's films, often in the role of an African American. Michael also acted in theater and film following World War II. Not having been allowed to learn a trade under the Nazis, he was trusted only to work in entertainment, including the circus. On the theater stage, he was almost always typecast as the "Neger," Othello or Caliban.[24]

One could argue Graf was encouraged to join an industry that combined athletics and entertainment: professional boxing.[25] While Graf did not experience considerable discrimination thanks to the equalizing status shared by children growing up in the lower-class Mercedes "barracks" of Mannheim in Southwest Germany, he did feel that his corporeality and his athletic talent made him stand out:

> At that time I quickly noticed, that my strength clearly made me superior to the boys my age [seven]. That of course gave me self-confidence, and not only that: my heart weighed less heavily when I boxed. I could put all of my fear and anxiety in those punches and for a short moment, I didn't feel as stressed. I was enamored by other sports, too. That's where I found recognition and wasn't excluded or teased as often about my skin color.[26]

Graf's athletic promise led those around him to express the same hopes for the Olympics that Michael once heard as a boy. In fact, in a Hamburg newspaper from 1969, a reporter expresses disappointment that Germany had not yet been able to turn its "brown babies" into German Olympic hopefuls, and he suggests perhaps Graf would be the saving grace.

Like Massaquoi and Michael, Graf's athletic ability led others to compare him to notable African American stars. For example, at the age of seventeen when he started boxing camp, Graf was proud to be compared to Muhammad Ali because of his light footwork. Graf is, however, discussed in different ways as an individual and when compared to another black fighter. When assessing him as an individual talent, rather than drawing a link between Graf and white German boxers, the press was quick to compare him to an African American boxing star, effectively turning Graf into an "Other-from-without." However, when Graf faced off in a fight against a Nigerian boxer in 1970, he was solely an "Other-from-within." The magazine *Twen* describes Graf as "Germany's first Negro with steel in his fists and a future of gold in sight."[27] The magazine's assessment, that "for the audience, the Nigerian is the 'Negro,' but Charly is just Charly," excellently showcases the Othering that had to take place in order for Graf to be accepted as German.[28] Only in a fight against someone who is even more an "Other" does a white German audience recognize Graf as one of its own. This allows Graf to achieve the recognition all four men discussed in this section have sought. But it seems Graf's recognition as German was only made possible by a particular articulation of factors: a competition involving two black men that pitted nations against each other.

In the case of Michael, Massaquoi, and Kaufmann, acting and music might have brought them some privileges and recognition as entertainers, but not as German entertainers. All three men were always hired to perform an

African or a member of the African diaspora: Michael played an Ethiopian at human zoos; Massaquoi played an African American jazz musician; and Kaufmann played the African American GI in Fassbinder's films. In contrast, Phillip Khabo Köpsell chooses neither to perform generic and recognizable roles of favorable African diasporic subjects, nor to be pitted against other members of the African diaspora in order to be accepted as German.

The End of American Dominance

Black German negotiation with African American culture has not been mono-lithic or static. In *Phonographies*, Alexander Weheliye discusses how earlier black German rappers tried to pass themselves off as African American. With the arrival of the rap group Advanced Chemistry, Weheliye argues, a new gen-eration of black German rappers emerged who no longer tried to "pass" as African American but rather viewed African American identity as the "'detour' through which they establish an black German identity."[29] According to Wehe-liye, this detour was necessary because "there are no precedents for articulat-ing an black German identity, and African American culture serves as the dominant first-world conception of blackness,"[30] a theme that runs throughout this book and is clearly reflected in the biographies in this chapter.

Fatima El-Tayeb has also discussed black German rappers' negotiation between German stereotypes and the dominance of African American culture, specifically in the case of male rappers in the group Brothers Keepers. She claims that the men of the collaborative hip-hop group Brothers Keepers con-struct a black German identity that both demands recognition for German be-longing and asserts independence from American hip-hop. El-Tayeb remarks that minorities are becoming more visible in Germany:

> This presence is still largely restricted to the entertainment sector though, traditionally forcing artists of colour to perform a tightrope-walk between a rare chance to express their point of view and being used to re-enforce racist stereotypes. . . . This strategy has its setbacks, not the least of them a state in which clichés are not used and subverted anymore but taken as the truth—and not only by the audience but by those supposedly subverting them. Black German MCs selling ho-mophobia and sexism as authentic ghetto culture—not only in their songs but on their political agenda—is as far from subverting stereo-types about black machismo as possible.[31]

Thus, according to El-Tayeb, black German hip-hop texts can only be marginally critical of mainstream views on gender because of the tightrope artists must walk in order to keep their music marketable.[32]

By examining the texts of less mainstream, less popular art forms like spoken word and poetry, I reduce the risk of dealing with texts that are meant to fit a specific genre and fulfill stereotypes. Poet Philipp Khabo Köpsell is not concerned with marketability. In fact, in a personal interview in May 2014, he described poetry as the genre with the smallest sales and claimed if he were concerned with making money, he would not be writing poetry.[33] Thus, writing poetry instead of hip-hop lyrics, Köpsell avoids the trap of "black machismo" of which El-Tayeb warns. Indeed, Köpsell negotiates between hegemonic German and African American models by rejecting the idea that he could simply adopt African American models of masculinity. Instead, he explores ways to get beyond these black/white, American/German binaries with the help of Afrofuturism.

Naturally, Köpsell's work has to be considered within the larger history of black German writing, and one must consider to what extent his negotiations with German identity and his use of Afrofuturism represent a shift in this writing. In an article on black German writing from 2012, postcolonial German studies scholar Dirk Göttsche argued that there has been a shift away from victimization in black German writing and that black Germans writing today exhibit "strategies of performative normality."[34] I agree with Göttsche that the tragic mode of past works by an author like May Ayim often does not reflect the work of contemporary black German writing. But I think it is significant that the texts Göttsche discusses stem largely from, in his words, "professionals from the world of arts and media."[35] An actor's, civil servant's, journalist's, or moderator's view on race in Germany will likely be quite different from a poet like Köpsell's. Alexander Weheliye makes a similar observation, commenting that in the early 1990s, black German "public figures choose assimilation, refusing to make race an issue in their work."[36]

In contrast to such public figures, artists often engage with racism in a much different way, reflecting not only on their individual or current experience, but considering how their experience relates to a larger past and proposing how things might change in the future. I see Afrofuturism as offering contemporary black German authors a means of resistance to victimization. While several of Köpsell's poems do deal with him being treated as an Other-from-Without, my discussion of how Afrofuturism influences his work shows a shift from focusing on victimization to hope. Furthermore, I think there is a difference between black Germans saying they feel at home in Germany and white

Germans actually recognizing them as being at home. While I do not argue that all black Germans feel they are Othered, clearly this problem has not just gone away, which Göttsche also admits. However, instead of fighting for white Germans to recognize him as one of their own, Köpsell has oriented himself toward the African diaspora and the cosmos.

Standing outside of Categories

During a performance at the Goethe Institute in New York in August 2012, Köpsell explained that, as is often the case for black Germans, he grew up in isolation, in the absence of any black community. And because he lacked black role models in his immediate environment, he initially turned to American media, specifically Will Smith's popular show *The Fresh Prince of Bel-Air*, in search of an "authentic" model of black masculinity. This experience is addressed in his poem "Outstanding Behavior," which addresses the ambivalent relationship between the words "outstanding" and "stand out" and shows how this ambivalence is reflected in the experiences of black German men. While it is generally understood as something positive to be outstanding, standing out is not necessarily a positive thing, especially if the reason you stand out is because of the color of your skin. The poem attempts to convey the difficult stages of a black German male's experience with a white majority society. The lyrical subject encounters many of the formative experiences relayed by black Germans, many of whom go from just wanting to fit in and not stand out, to feeling compelled to stand out academically in order to counter negative stereotypes, and finally resorting to either succumbing to their exotic status or outright rejecting the norm by intentionally seeking to stand out. In order to articulate the link between the burden of African American culture and the black German's fear of / desire to stand out, it is important to have a more general understanding of the poem. The poem begins,

Stand out from the rest
like the only representative
the way they gon' judge all of you
all of y'all.
remember to be outstanding
stand out like you can't hide
like -shit, they gotcha now
like close eyes quick

until
the fingers fill with blood again
remember to be outstanding
in mathematics, athletics, in ethics
in everything
and quiet
eyes you draw through hallways
always remember
whatever they think of you is
what they will think of you
all.[37]

In the first four lines, Köpsell is able to link the experience of black Germans with those of the larger African diaspora simply in his use of language, and this is reflected more generally in his decision to write the poem in English. While "Stand out from the rest / like the only representative" could very specifically refer to the black German experience of isolation relayed in the four autobiographies discussed in the previous sections, Köpsell's use of African American vernacular for "the way they gon' judge all of you / all of y'all" suggests both that black Germans and African Americans might experience similar racist judgments, and that others might feel entitled to grouping black Germans, African Americans, and other blacks together, to be judged. In terms of masculinity, this poem shows the competing messages black German males receive during their formative years. There is a conflict between wanting to be a strong man who stands up for himself; balling his fists in anger at racist comments; and the need to be quiet and not react, for fear of confirming negative stereotypes or even for fear of physical retaliation or incarceration.[38] This black German male must excel in both mathematics and athletics, the former to prove his mental ability among his white peers, the latter in order to not disappoint the expectation that blacks are especially athletic. Thus, surviving in a white majority society appears to be a dance between consciously embodying certain stereotypes and undermining others.

A threat to the black German's masculinity comes midway through this stanza, as he is addressed as "sweetie" with the request, "don't let that annoy you." Thus, though it may be instinctive for the black German to become upset that he is being stereotyped and categorized, these lines attempt to take away his power and his resistance. Instead, like Ferguson and Youth in chapter 4, he is encouraged to embrace his role as exotic specimen:

Stand out
like a minstrel reference
baggy and shiny
and loud around noon in the cafeteria
act like they do overseas
act like they show on TV
so outstanding like a picaninny pimp
and squeaky with the voice
like the voiceovers
they use over here (*JK* 26–27)

For a black German male, part of accepting a prescribed role of black masculinity is to model other examples found throughout the diaspora, and while
masquerading as Ethiopian might have been strategic for Theodor Michael in
the 1930s when Germans aligned themselves with fascist Italy's interests in
Ethiopia, in a postwar Germany dominated by American culture, one must
adopt examples of black masculinity from the United States. Köpsell describes
a process that could be considered embracing the anti-Tom, similar to the anti-
heroes of the blaxploitation era or the hip-hop artists of today.[39] Köpsell defiantly remarks, "if they want a nigger / they'll get one / one pot smoking penis
to slap them 'round their rosy cheeks / and walk off swinging / like they know
who's the king of the kong now, / bitches!" (*JK* 27). In these lines, Köpsell
conflates several stereotypes about black masculinity (the pronounced phallic
symbol, drug use, violence, and rape). He describes the moment of frustration
when a minority decides to fully embody the projections of the majority society and perform a kind of parody of society's fears.

In these lines, Köpsell also acknowledges that such stereotypes originate
in media images that go back much further than today's TV shows or music, as
he references the film *King Kong* (1933). Regarding models from African
American culture, Köpsell also makes a reference to TV shows overseas like
the squeaky "picaninny pimp," which Köpsell claims is a specific reference to
Will Smith. During his performance at the Goethe Institute in New York City,
Köpsell admitted that part of his own search for an "authentic" black male
voice led him to mimic characters on television, like Smith on *The Fresh Prince
of Bel-Air*. However, Köpsell eventually realized that this mimicry could not
succeed because Smith's voice had been dubbed over by a German, resulting
in a "squeaky" imitation of an African American register. But this potentially
devastating moment can also be read positively. The slippage when Köpsell

mimicked a white German mimicking an African American register in a dubbed show revealed to Köpsell that there is no "authentic" black male voice to be found. The origin of mimesis cannot be recovered.

Another poem that gets at the heart of Köpsell's thoughts about the prominence of African Americans in Germany is in German, "Filmemacher," in which he speaks in first person:

I Black German corpus, bearer of German burdens
stranded goods of the Atlantic, wearer of German masks
I, I accuse, the German media of the masses
who make every black man into a new Negro image. (*JK* 60)[40]

Köpsell's choice of the word "corpus" (*Korpus*) indicates he embodies a black German body but also a black German body of literature and art. Köpsell connects black Germans with other members of the African diaspora, the "stranded goods of the Atlantic," who feel they must wear a mask to be accepted, at least on the surface, by majority white societies, which perhaps could be read as a reference to Du Bois's veil or Fanon's "white masks."[41] The black German may bear the burden of a German identity and wear a white German mask, but he is not afforded the same privileges as a white German. It is significant that, although accusing the German mass media of racism toward black Germans, Köpsell genders this collective black German identity by claiming that the media makes "every black *man* into a new Negro image" (my emphasis). Thus, though all black Germans are affected by the perpetuation of negative stereotypes about blackness in the media, Köpsell places emphasis on the essentialization of black men—they are the origin of the negative stereotypes, and they are the representatives of the black German population.

In the poem's fourth stanza, Köpsell once again addresses the problem of the black German subject being subordinate to African American identities:

Makers want to see something exotic; A job for Jim Knopf!
Champion lover, when the puppet show is on,
and even when he's undercover he's reminded of this.
And he talks so fresh—he's dubbed in German
and he must copy Eddie Murphy, Will Smith and Jamie Foxx. (*JK* 61)[42]

So when the [film]makers want some exotic characters, they rely on Jim Knopf, a black stereotype created by Michael Ende in the children's book *Jim Knopf and Lukas the Engine Driver* (1960). However, it is strange that Jim Knopf would need to be synchronized in German. Here Köpsell perhaps suggests that Jim Knopf is a black character originating in the mind of a white German man. Thus, rather than depicting a self-representation of blackness, Jim Knopf is a puppet ventriloquized by a white German voice. What further complicates Jim Knopf's character in this poem is he is made to align with African American male celebrities: Eddie Murphy, Will Smith, and Jamie Foxx. It is these many layers of representation that make it so difficult to get at a black German articulation of male subjecthood.

Instead of searching for an "authentic" black masculinity among artifacts of African American culture, in his first published collection of poetry, Köpsell chose to confront Germans' perceptions of blackness head-on by embodying Jim Knopf. The beloved childhood figure of Ende's novels is an orphan who mysteriously arrives in a package on the island of Lummerland. There he is raised by one of the island's three inhabitants, Frau Sowas. Jim is as black as coal, which is part of the reason he is able to befriend Lukas the engine driver, whose face is also blackened, but by coal. Because Jim receives no formal schooling, he cannot read. And like a black slave in the United States, he is not even considered a whole subject by the island's king. Interestingly, the whole reason Jim Knopf and Lukas end up leaving Lummerland for their adventures is that, as Jim approaches adulthood and potential status as a full subject, this upsets the balance of the island, and therefore someone must be exiled. In order to save his engine from being cast away, Lukas volunteers, and Jim tags along as the ultimate ethnic sidekick, without family, without an education, and totally dependent.

In 2008, journalist Julia Voss did an interview with Ende, revealing several insights about the story.[43] First, its setting, Lummerland, was based on England. Second, Jim Knopf was based on a Native American foundling named Jemmy Button, whom Charles Darwin discovered on the *Beagle* while en route back to England from South America. Third, the book was not meant as a children's book, but as a surrealist and antiracist treatment of Nazi Germany, ending with Jim Button ruling over a multicultural utopia of children.

While Ende may have had noble intentions for his story, considering that he transformed the Native American, Jemmy, into the black Jim, one can also read the novel's start as an allegory for Germans' fears of black masculinity triggered by the defeats and subsequent occupations by black soldiers following World War II. Similar to lovable "brown babies" like Toxi from R. A. Stemmle's 1952 film and Maxi from the book *Our Little Negro Boy Maxi* (1952) by Alfons Simon, Jim's presence can be tolerated as a child because he is not considered a whole subject.[44] Though Ende rejects the notion of didactic books, *Jim Knopf and Lukas the Engine Driver* is not unlike the colonial novels of the nineteenth century. Ende's story teaches children not only how to assume a superior position toward racial Others—as Lukas conveniently dictates, while the illiterate Jim does most of the dangerous work—but it also teaches children how to colonize. Lukas and Jim are not allowed to return home until Jim affectively colonizes a nearby island, dubbing it Neu Lummerland.

From this brief analysis of Jim Knopf, one can see why Köpsell would be attracted to engaging with this figure and challenging Germans' reading of this story. In an excellent example of mimetic excess, Köpsell's version of Jim Knopf is no longer a childlike sidekick. Rather, Köpsell's embodiment of the character insists on the adult name James Knopf and graces the cover of his book with a baseball bat and a grimace (figure 1).

In the book's first poem, which shares a name with the collection, Jim Knopf is called onto a stage in order to put multiculturalism on display for the audience's amusement. The MC of what appears to be a variety show remarks that the show needs "the funny Negro from the puppet show. Whatshisname . . . / We need Jim Knopf" (*JK* 6).[45] The audience is pleasantly surprised to have this figure from their childhood make an appearance. But Jim Knopf's cameo is made impossible by the questions of whether he's "still serving two years [in jail]? Is he a rap gangster now?"[46] With these remarks, Köpsell suggests that, if the beloved children's figure had been an actual person able to mature as an black male, he would probably be in jail, for as an adult he would lose the benefit of innocence that youthful figures like Jim Knopf and Toxi have.

When translated as "files," the *Akte* in the title of the book possibly refers to Jim Knopf's police record. The notion that black men in Germany are especially in danger of criminality is confirmed not only in the autobiographies of Günther Kaufmann and Charly Graf, both of whom spent time in prison, but also in the documentary film *Dreckfresser* (*Dirt for Dinner*, 2000) by black German director Branwen Okpako about a black German policeman in Leipzig who once became the poster boy for German diversity but whose life took a tragic turn when he became involved with criminals.[47] The MC's question about whether Jim Knopf has become a "rap gangster" references the stereotype that all black men are musically inclined and all rappers are criminal. The MC's last comments about Jim are, "Well, that rascal . . . at least he can't steal anyone's show" (*JK* 6).[48] This remark recalls the stereotype of the black performer as ham *and* thief, a central trope in Ernst Krenek's opera *Jonny spielt auf* (1926), therefore referencing older German ideas about black masculinity. This reference to performance brings up an alternative translation for *Akte*, "acts," such as the acts in a play. Therefore, the title can just as well be a refer-

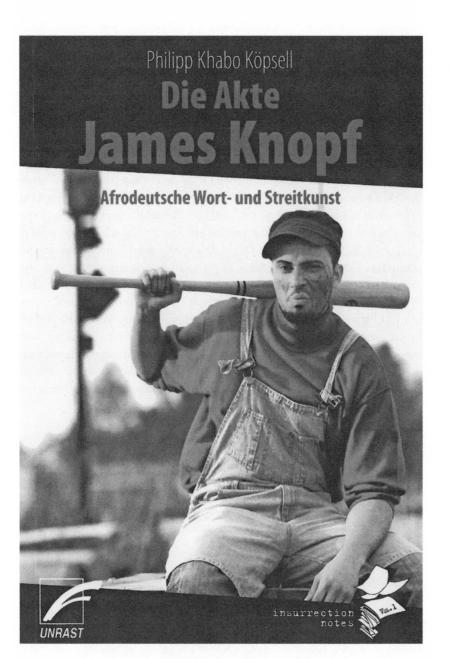

Figure 1. Cover of Köpsell's *Die Akte James Knopf*

ence to the performative aspect of Köpsell's mimicry and blackness more generally. For those reasons, I will only refer to the title in its original German in order to maintain this ambiguity.

Problems with German Masculinity

Considering that Köpsell rejects both African American and fictionalized German models for black masculinity, one might expect him to adopt a German model of masculinity that *includes* him in, rather than excluding him from, the nation. But in Köpsell's poetry, just as Klaus Theweleit asserts in *Male Fantasies*, German masculinity is often tied to chauvinism, violence, and the need to conquer racialized and gendered Others. In *Die Akte James Knopf*, there are two poems in which Köpsell ventriloquizes from a white German male perspective, and neither is flattering. In the poem "Wir lagen vor Madagaskar—in zivilisatorischer Mission" ("We lay before Madagascar—on a Civilizing Mission") Köpsell links his rejection of hegemonic German masculinity to the knowledge-seeking acts of violence associated with German colonialism. Speaking from the position of a white German man, Köpsell seems to equate the German nation with its men and claim that one of the goals of colonialism was to conquer the world by sending men, as representatives of the nation, abroad. The poem begins by boasting about the parameters of the German empire:

> Men!
> We have men in China, men in the South Seas, Samoa, New Guinea,
> Men on the Solomon Islands, men on the Marshall Islands
> Men!
> We have men in Togo, in Cameroon, in German East- and German
>   Southwest . . . and recently even women!
> Men! (*JK* 14)[49]

Aside from listing Germany's colonial territories before they were lost at the end of World War I, including references to German East Africa and German Southwest Africa, what stands out in this poem is the repetition of the word "men," as well as its use framing the information. The statement "Men!" could be meant as an appellative. Perhaps Köpsell is parodying the kind of recruitment ad one might have found in Germany at end of the nineteenth century, trying to convince young men to travel overseas. "Men!" could also be an exclamation remarking at the sheer numbers of men who, on Germany's behalf, were sent to conquer the world. The repetition of "men" also focuses in on how gendered the colonial project was: that white men were meant to explore foreign lands and penetrate foreign cultures both literally and figuratively. Sending white women abroad was initially deemed too risky, until the argument was made that white German women needed to be sent to the colonies to keep the men from marrying and having children with the colonial subjects. What also stands out in this poem is that it consists of a series of statements in first-person plural. "We have ammunition. . . . We've seen the savages in the zoos, we know what they look like" (*JK* 14).[50] These statements attest to a collective mind-set, a collective knowledge of the Other and a collective will to learn more about and control the Other.

In the second half of the poem, Köpsell addresses some of the potential colonizers' fears about the foreign: "Careful men, there's / cannibals and barbarians with bones and sabres in their hair!" (*JK* 14).[51] In parentheses, he lists a series of additional fearful things these white German men might encounter: "human mules, mongrels / Mendelian sensations and some / will hardly be able to keep their zipper closed" (*JK* 14).[52] So in addition to a potentially dangerous foreign culture, white Germans are also afraid of miscegenation, which is represented both by "mongrels" and by "human mules." "Human mules" is simply Köpsell's creative way of saying "mulattoes," a word that stems from the Portuguese word for mule. According to the lyric persona, miscegenation is inevitable because German men cannot keep their zippers closed because of their uncontrollable urges. This stresses the point I made in the introduction, that heterosexual, cross-racial contact often stirs fears of miscegenation. Here the rational stoicism of the white German man is faced with the challenge of a land of transgression and female oddities. The anxiety around miscegenation and genetics is further stressed by the alliteration in the original German: "menschliche Maultiere, Mischlinge, mendelsche Sensationen" (human mules, mongrels, Mendelian sensations) (*JK* 14).

The poem's title is a reference to a German sailor's song, written in 1934 by Just Scheu. The song's lyrics convey a similar tone; German sailors are stranded off of the coast of Madagascar. The conditions are bad and the men are plagued by sickness and dehydration. In 1986, famed German pop singer Heino recorded his own version of the song, which was tellingly included on the album *Die Stimme der Heimat* (*The Voice of the Homeland*). Heino added several strophes and lines to the original. Some of the content Heino added interrupts the homosocial tone of the original song by introducing the sailors' longing for women back home: "Farewell little girl, farewell, farewell." Other lines added by Heino give voice to the sailors' homesickness: "When the accordion is played on board, / then all of the sailors are so quiet, / because each one longs for his homeland, / that he'd so love to see again." The third strophe in Heino's version actually combines the heterosexual element with the longing for one's homeland:

> And his little girl, how he longs for her,
> The one who kisses him so passionately at home!
> And then he looks out onto the wide ocean,
> Across which his homeland lies far away.

Although written fifty-two years after the Nazi-era version, Heino's lyrics are strikingly more heteronormative and nationalist than the original.[53]

While Köpsell's poem "Wir lagen vor Madagascar" is a parody of both versions of the song, the subsequent poem, "Wir lagen vor Madagascar 3," addresses the violent reality of the colonial project. At the start of the poem, Köpsell employs alliteration to stress his point.

> There is blood on the planks in the bureau of the bookkeeper,
> blood on the books,
> blood on the windows,
> on the towels, coffee on the mosquito net
> smoke travels along the molt in the direction of the
> floor. Cracks full of dust
> remaining from the construction of the Usambara railway
> seal of society, outpost of progress (*JK* 15)[54]

In these first few lines, not only does Köpsell insist on the violence of colonialism but also how that violence is linked to bureaucracy and progress, such as his mention of the Usambara railway of Eastern Tanzania. While the preceding poem enthusiastically appeals to men to join the colonial efforts, this poem laments the so-called "white man's burden to bring peace to the world" that "somewhere, somehow got left behind" (*JK* 15).[55] The colonial project has failed, "the endeavor has slipped out of the emperor's control" (*JK* 15).[56] Nevertheless, the lyric persona sarcastically expresses hope that the colonies can be recovered: "But new chancellors will / advocate for the empire / they will rule / new German colonies."[57] Rather than a prediction, this line is more likely a reference to neo-colonialism and Germany's aid and foreign policies with African nations.

In the poem "SchwarzRotGold (. . . a right hand lead)," Köpsell once again ventriloquizes from a white German male's point of view. At first sight, this poem is reminiscent of the rhetorical move made by black German poet May Ayim in "Afrodeutsch I" and "Afrodeutsch II." In these poems, Ayim ventriloquizes from a white German woman's point of view, offering us one side of a conversation between a white German woman and a black German woman. The white woman interpellates the black woman with all of the stereotypes commonly associated with blacks in Germany. She is astonished at the possibility that one can be both African and German. She then inquires about the black German woman's innate African sensibilities and her intimate connections with her African roots. In a paternalist tone, she encourages the black German to return "home" and help her own people, and she is confused by the notion that a black German might lay claim to Germany as home and offended at the suggestion that Germany has problems with racism.[58]

Like Ayim, Köpsell adopts the role of the white German who is insensitive to contemporary problems with racism. However, where Köpsell's poem differs from Ayim's is that the text is not one-sided but a dialogue. Furthermore, the person speaking to the white German is not necessarily a black German because she or he speaks in English. Speaking in English can be strategic, a way to showcase one's cosmopolitanism. But perhaps this speaker is not a black German but an English-speaking member of the African diaspora. Thus, Köpsell might suggest that the task of holding white Germans responsible for past and present racisms lies not only with black Germans but with the African diaspora as a whole. However, one could also argue that this English-speaking interlocutor could be any non-German regardless of race or ethnicity.

At stake in the poem is to what extent Germany's past weighs on its present image. The poem appears to begin in media res, with the English-speaker asking, "Wasn't that Germany with those Nazis and stuff?" (*JK* 13). This question could come as a response to a number of statements. Perhaps the white German has insisted that Germany does not have a problem with racism. Or this is a conversation taking place in a future where some are in danger of forgetting Germany's shameful past. The white German responds, "Don't come at me with the tin drum, that was many moons ago, friend" (*JK* 13).[59] The fact that the white German responds *in German* suggests that, though he might understand the English question, he is not fluent enough in English to respond. This monolingualism is an aspect that Köpsell criticizes in a later poem, "Berlin Westend," in which he discusses controversial German politician Thilo Sarrazin.[60] Furthermore, it is remarkable that the white German equates discussing the Nazi past with a discussion of Grass's novel *The Tin Drum*. This testifies to the important standing this novel has in the history of postwar German *Vergangenheitsbewältigung*.

While the poem may begin with an almost accusatory question, request-
ing that the German-speaker position himself in relation to Germany's fascist
past, the subsequent questions hinge more on stereotypes about what it means
to be German with questions like, "Do you drive a Beamer?" and "What do
you think about the Jews?" (*JK* 13). The white German's response to both of
these questions is silence, indicated by " . . . "; thus he does not feel comfortable answering these questions, perhaps for fear of confirming a stereotype in
the case of his opinions on Jews and, in the case of the BMW, fear of *not* fulfilling the stereotype. The white German tries desperately to offer examples of
what Germany has "contributed to mankind," offering "Ordnung, Atomkraft
und die Aufklärung . . . , oder?" (order, nuclear energy, and the Enlightenment,
right?) (*JK* 13). This statement conveys a degree of insecurity; he questions
whether the things he has been taught as positive were actually positive. But
the English-speaker does not let him off the hook, wondering about the Enlightenment, "Wasn't that when Hegel said that all Africans are savages?" (*JK*
13). The white German tries his best to defend past actions claiming Hegel did
so "aha mit'n edelsten Absichten!" (aha, only with the noblest intentions) and
that Hegel "war halt ôch nur'n Mensch, der Hegel" (Hegel was only human
after all) (*JK* 13). His German is clearly marked by a regional dialect, a device
Köpsell also uses in the poem "Berlin Westend" in order to indicate ignorant
and provincial thinking.

The white German's final act is to try to defend Germany's actions in the
former colonies. When the English-speaker insists that the problem of German
racism preceded Nazi Germany, addressing the concentration camps built in
German Southwest Africa, present-day Namibia, the German responds, "Na,
dafür sprechen die jetzt Deutsch, da" (Yeah, but at least they can now speak
German there) (*JK* 13). The English-speaker's final comment, "and they drive
Beamers" (*JK* 13), intervenes in multiple discourses. First, if driving a
"Beamer" is an indication of a German identity, then not only do Namibians
who do so have a right to a German identity, but they might have more of a
right than this white speaker, who possibly *cannot* afford this German status
symbol. Second, the notion that Namibians can afford such a symbol of cultural and economic capital works against German stereotypes of Africans as
perpetually impoverished. The German's final statement, "kann man stolz
drauf sein," (that's something to be proud of) indicates the absurdity of national
identity and national pride, for the German not only accepts the notion that
driving a BMW makes a German identity, but for him, the fact that Namibians
might drive them is proof of Germany's altruistic improvement of its African
colonies and that is something for which one can be proud.

Asserting/Rejecting a German Identity

Nevertheless, Köpsell's alienation from white German males does not fore-
close a desire to claim a German identity. In several poems, Köpsell follows in
the footsteps of his black German predecessors by laying claim to a German-
speaking position. Throughout the twentieth century, this act of claiming German subjectivity has been an important rhetorical move that demands a more
inclusive definition of German identity that is not based on whiteness. At the
end of "Outstanding Behavior," Köpsell declares one should

> Stand out from the rest
> Like . . . your application form—left box!
> Like I do speak your language. It is mine, too.
> [Dusprichstabergutesdeutsch. Woherkommstdu?
> Ursprünglich?? Kannichmaldeinhaaranfassen???]
> (Youspeakgermanratherwell. Whereareyoufrom?
> Originally?? Canitouchyourhair???) (*JK* 27)

In this stanza, the line "stand out from the rest" does not necessarily mean
one should stand out from other black Germans or other blacks in general but
instead means to stand out compared to those who remain passive. Instead of
resigning himself to a position on the margins, he suggests the black German
male demand recognition of his belonging to the nation, for example, by way
of his confidence in and ownership of the German language. Meanwhile, the
probing questions of his white German interlocutors, reminiscent of the questions Ayim includes in her poems, come across as a jumble of nonsense—
"Youspeakgermanratherwell.   Whereareyoufrom?   Originally?
Canitouchyourhair?"—when faced with a black German who is confident in
his German-speaking position.

Nevertheless, this confident lyric persona is not consistent throughout *Die
Akte James Knopf*. In the poem "Drummer, give the devil some!" Köpsell appears to explain why he so often writes in English:

> why I write in tongues my mother can't speak
> when I stand and speak
> Ich bin schwarz/braun/afrodeutsch
> The judges raise their brows and index fingers
> taking a deep breath in preparation
> for the monologue

painfully equivocating
spinning, juggling facts and foul phantasies
for in dieser sprache here
there is no space for selbstbenennung
without footnotes (*JK* 28)

When Köpsell describes English as "tongues my mother can't speak," this phrase is a play on the word "mother tongue" and therefore questions the assumption that German should be the language he is most comfortable in because it literally comes from his mother's tongue. In *Beyond the Mother Tongue*, Yasemin Yildiz traces the origins of monolingualism and suggests that the idea developed in eighteenth-century Europe, especially among German nationalist thinkers like Gottfried Herder, Wilhelm Humboldt, and Friedrich Schleiermacher. Yildiz suggests that these thinkers viewed the mother tongue as the only language in which one can truly "think, feel and express oneself."[61]

Köpsell's decision to write in English insists on the acceptance of a multilingual reality. Considering that his father is South African and he lived in South Africa for several years, why shouldn't he be as comfortable in English as in German? English is also useful as a tool with which Köpsell can more easily attack *German* assumptions about national identity. The order in which the first two lines are arranged is of significance here. The lyric persona writes English "*when* [he] stand[s] and speak[s]" (my emphasis); these actions take place simultaneously. Thus, the speech act of declaring German belonging with "Ich bin schwarz/braun/afrodeutsch" (I'm black/brown/afrogerman) is best *written in English*, perhaps to capture the attention of a wider audience or to align Köpsell with other members of the African diaspora who have faced similar challenges. Thus, in this reflection on multilingualism, speaking and writing, Köpsell reveals the unique dilemma of black Germans for whom German might be their mother tongue but of whom it is not believed that their fluency in German can be natural. To call the intimate connection between a black German, his or her mother, and the German language into question is the equivalent of denying the black German his or her place in the lineage of German history. This is why, in the second stanza, Köpsell counters this interrogation with a reference to his familial lineage: "But this here path / is straight and simple / dude, I'm just my parent's son. is old as ages" (*JK* 28).

In the first stanza, Köpsell describes the act of articulating his German subject position as if he were standing before a court given the task of determining the validity of such a claim. The actual speech act, "I'm black/braun/afrogerman" is curious in that it suggests at least two different interpretations. The series of adjectives could suggest different phases of identification through which the speaker moves. Perhaps "I am black" is the statement Germans are most willing to accept; "brown" could be considered a shade lighter and therefore indicate the speaker's move away from race and toward a political identity articulated in "afrogerman." His use of a forward slash to separate "black/brown/afrogerman" also suggests that these are not necessarily separate categories, and one identification does not negate the other; rather they can exist simultaneously. Thus these three adjectives indicate how Köpsell's identities are always already multiple; at any given moment he feels black, brown, and/or Afro-German. However, it is "afrogerman" that the imaginary court of Germanness is not willing to accept. Köpsell posits this invalidation as a specifically German problem: "for in dieser sprache here (for in this language here) / there is no space for selbstbenennung (self-naming) / without footnotes." The footnotes to which he refers might be compared to the follow-up questions many people of color living in Germany are asked if they claim a German identity or German origins, for example, "But where are you really from?" Köpsell's ability to shift between English and German in this first stanza demonstrates his confidence in both languages and points to the idea that certain things that might not be possible in German are made possible in English. Köpsell goes on to claim that "switching tongues is mere illusion," which suggests that, although English and German might be considered separate entities, for a bilingual individual like himself they can reside in the same body, in the same tongue; perhaps forming a unique mother tongue belonging solely to Köpsell.

Part of Köpsell's rejection of identifying solely as German has to do with his acknowledgment that one's identity, as it is perceived by others, shifts depending on the interlocutor. In her reading of Ayim's "Afrodeutsch I" and "Afrodeutsch II" poems, Michelle Wright claims that by refusing to write dialogue for the black German voice, Ayim is able to reject "monologic definitions of race and nation," which she contrasts with definitions put forth by male members of the African diaspora, specifically those proposed by W. E. B. Du Bois and Aimé Césaire:

In their use of ventriloquism, both Du Bois and Césaire adhered to the concepts of race and nation that, while not as monologic as its white Western model, nonetheless read the black subject in the West as a synthesis of these two concepts. As a member of a generation that has benefited from the struggles and victories of previous generations of blacks in the West,

Ayim can go further by mocking the white speaking subject as the one who is sadly misguided by outdated and outmoded concepts based on a binary, nationalist understanding of the subject and Other.[62]

Köpsell's articulation of black German subjectivity is similar to May Ayim's rejection of a monologic model. In the poem "Consider One Accordingly," Köpsell progresses from more general identifications, such as human being, twenty-years-old, male, and straight, to the specific racial or ethnic identities projected onto him by others, often depending on location:

Consider one black in the United States
Coloured in South Africa, mixed in Europe
if you ask white people. Consider one white
if you ask Nigerians. Consider one Nigerian
if you are black and ask Germans. (*JK* 24)

This dizzying carousel of identities demonstrates part of the reason why black Germans' identities can be so fluid. The multiplicity of identities that are associated with black Germans in different contexts enables them to avoid being pinned down, labeled and categorized. The punctuation and organization of this stanza conveys significant meaning for Köpsell's argument. By breaking up the lines "Consider one white / if you ask Nigerians," Köpsell challenges assumptions about clear and consistent racial categories, but because he leaves some moment for reflection of "Consider one white" before he introduces the qualifier, he forces the reader to entertain the notion that he be considered white. Furthermore, those who identify as white might be made insecure by the qualifier "if you ask Nigerians," because it opens up the possibility that one might *not* be white in another context. In this way, the poem "Consider One Accordingly" disrupts seemingly neat, fixed binaries that associate white with German and set these identities against everything else.

It is the acceptance of this fluidity that enables Köpsell to eventually reject the need for recognition as *only* German. In the preface to *Afro-Shop*, a collection of poems featuring several black German authors, Köpsell speaks collectively, stating, "Yes, we [black Germans] can be German—but we don't have to be . . . this break is unavoidable—and it's a liberating moment."[63] What sets today's black Germans apart from previous generations is the ability to claim a German identity but the lack of a necessity to do so. Though Köpsell might be critical of looking to African American cultural models to help form an identity, that does not mean he does not align himself with African diasporic culture. Part of the reason Köpsell might want to orient himself toward a more diasporic community, rather than one that is specifically African American or German, is because of the sheer diversity among black Germans who can have one or more parents from anywhere in Africa and the African diaspora (including North America, South America, the Caribbean, and Europe).

What Lies in the Future for Black Germans? A Look at the Potential of Afrofuturism

So what is the solution for a black German artist who feels alienated both by hegemonic German culture and by an African diasporic culture dominated by the United States? For Köpsell, the answer seems to be using Afrofuturism as a platform for imagining alternative origins as well as focusing on the future. Afrofuturism is a recurring theme not only in Köpsell's work but more generally among contemporary black German artists; from the Afronaut painting cycle of artist Daniel Kojo Schrade to recent Ingeborg Bachmann Prize winner Sharon Dodua Otoo's Afrofuturist works *Synchronicity* and "Herr Gröttrup setzt sich hin" and finally the recent series on blackness at the Ballhaus Naunynstrasse Theater in Berlin entitled "We are Tomorrow."

The term "Afrofuturism" was coined in 1994 by Mark Dery in order to retroactively describe a cultural and theoretical phenomenon that reached back decades and spanned several countries in the African diaspora.[64] From the space fantasies of jazz artist Sun Ra to the science fiction novels of Samuel Delaney, Afrofuturism describes African diasporic artists' engagement with science, science fiction, speculative fiction, and fantasy. In the last twenty years, a handful of conferences on Afrofuturism have taken place in Germany including "Loving the Alien: Science Fiction, Diaspora, Multikultur" at Volksbühne in Berlin in November 1997; in 2011, the Bayreuth International Graduate School of African Studies held a conference entitled "Remembering Flash Forward"; in May 2012, the conference "Apocalypse Now (and Then): The End of the World in Pop Culture" took place at the Hebbel Am Ufer Theater in Berlin; and in June 2015, the African Languages Association held a conference titled "African Futures and Beyond" in Bayreuth.

Though Afrofuturism is partly influenced by African American science fiction writers like Samuel Delaney, Octavia Butler, and Ishmael Reed, who have used the genre to tackle racism, it is the connection to jazz, funk, reggae, and techno that presents Afrofuturism as another example of how ideas in the African diaspora are transmitted through music. John Akomfrah, English artist and cofounder of the Black Audio Film Collective, suggests it is white Germans' love of techno and techno's roots in African American music circles, specifically in Detroit, that stirred their interest in Afrofuturism. He claims that "there were these elective affinities between musical tastes that Afrofuturism seemed to enact."[65] African American author Greg Tate adds that the key artists associated with Afrofuturism—Sun Ra, George Clinton, and Lee "Scratch" Perry—have long been celebrated in Germany.[66]

According to Tate, in Germany, fans are "attracted to this dialectic of mind body and soul, for example, in the person and concept of someone like Sun Ra—to be as interested in what Sun Ra is actually saying as thought [as a theorist of sound], as in what he presents with his artistry."[67] Finally, Tate suggests one could link white German interest in Afrofuturism to older German movements and celebrations of modernity, more specifically, Weimar's "presentation of or curiosity about black performance, of the advocacy of Jazz music as the copy background to a certain kind of social, sexual kind of emancipatory moment in German culture."[68] While these reasons, especially the last one, support the claims made throughout this book regarding why white Germans are attracted to black popular music, including Afrofuturism, they do not address the question of why black Germans in particular would be drawn to this art form.

In order to understand the potential Afrofuturism holds for black German artists, it is necessary to consider why African diasporic peoples would be interested in science fiction in the first place. Mark Dery has suggested that, considering the strangeness of the African diasporic experience, science fiction seems the most suitable genre for discussing it:

> African Americans, in a very real sense, are the descendants of alien abductees; they inhabit a sci-fi nightmare in which unseen but not less impassable force fields of intolerance frustrate their movements; official histories undo what has been done; and technology is too often brought to bear on black bodies (branding, forced sterilization, the Tuskegee experiment, and tasers come readily to mind).[69]

For Dery, articulating the African diasporic experience through science fiction allows one to highlight how alienating, inhumane, and otherworldly the treatment of black people has been throughout history. But this way of reinterpreting the past and the present is only one part of Afrofuturism's potential. A second aspect is the Afrofuturist's imagination of time travel, something that imbues black people with the agency to take control of their past, present, *and* future. In the Afrofuturist film *The Last Angel of History* (1996), black British actor Edward George defines the Afrofuturist as a data thief, someone who is "surfing across the Internet of black culture, breaking into the vaults, breaking into the ruins, stealing fragments, fragments from cyber culture, techno culture, narrative culture."[70] By taking control of the goods and the narrative of African diasporic peoples, Afrofuturism provides a form of resistance to hegemonic discourses on black culture.

African American scholar Michelle Wright invokes the concept of time travel in her most recent book, *The Physics of Blackness*:

> Our constructs of blackness are largely historical and more specifically based on a notion of spacetime that is commonly fitted into a linear progress narrative, while our phenomenological manifestations of blackness happen in what I term Epiphenomenal time, or the "now," through which the past, present, and future are always interpreted. . . . In other words, the current moment, or "now," can certainly correlate with other moments, but one cannot argue that it is always already the effect of a specific, previous moment.[71]

Wright introduces the concept of epiphenomenal blackness in order to expand the definition of blackness and make it more inclusive. One of the main arguments of her book is that, instead of relying on a Middle Passage epistemology, relating everything back to slavery, scholars of black culture should instead consider a postwar epistemology. For example, in Köpsell's case, relating his work to postwar migration or even to colonialism makes more sense than relating it to the history of slavery. By viewing blackness as a phenomenon at the intersection of the historical and the epiphenomenal, Wright argues, we can "produce a definition of blackness that is wholly inclusive and nonhierarchical."[72]

Wright's concept of the epiphenomenal can help us further unlock Afrofuturism's potential. First of all, by engaging with time travel and embracing epiphenomenal time, Afrofuturism can achieve the more inclusive, nonhierarchical definition of blackness to which Wright appeals. This is indicative in the kinds of Afrofuturist volumes Köpsell has produced: *Arriving in the Future* and *The Afropean Contemporary*. Both volumes feature a variety of texts, from the past, present, and future, by black authors from all over the world. And neither book attempts to categorize authors by country of origin, language, genre, or time. Second, time travel unchains Afrofuturism from previous artistic and theoretical movements. While movements like Pan-Africanism and negritude positioned themselves in relation to Western

European theories and adapted European concepts of subjectivity and state-hood, Afrofuturism need not position itself in the same way, for it is past, present, and future simultaneously.

From a linear, progressive understanding of time, Afrofuturism follows futurism, which was an Italian avant-garde movement whose founding members initially came from the Left. The futurists were led by artist Tommaso Marinetti, who published the founding manifesto of futurism in *Le Figaro* in 1909.[73] Futurism appealed to artists because of its desire to deregulate society and release individual creativity. Futurism was especially concerned with destroying the past and focusing on scientific discoveries and technological innovation. Another futuristic element was an interest in releasing "the self from human limitations."[74] In a posthumanist era this could be interpreted as embracing cyborgs and technological enhancements for humans. However, the movement soon became associated with Mussolini's brand of fascism because of its political views.[75] Some of the problematic positions the futurists supported included the insistence on Italian supremacy, support of colonialism, "scorn for women," a cult of youth, embracing violence and war, and subjecting nature to man.[76]

Futurism's problematic positions show how different it is from Afrofuturism. As a diasporic undertaking, Afrofuturism is decolonial, not nationalist. Afrofuturism embraces the past as well as the future and therefore does not prefer youth. Afrofuturism is not inherently violent, nor interested in the biopolitical rhetoric of "cleansing" populations. Rather, Afrofuturist artists embrace a diversity of opinions and ways of existing.[77] Scholars have questioned whether Afrofuturism tends to be discussed as a particularly male undertaking. Greg Tate, however, points out we cannot discount the influence of female writer Octavia Butler. Furthermore, many black female authors have emerged since Butler, like Nalo Hopkinson, N. K. Jemisin, Nnedi Okorafor, and Helen Oyeyemi.[78] Finally, Afrofuturism is receptive of indigenous African relationships with nature, and therefore does not conform to the modernist belief that man must control nature. Thus, aside from its name and the goal of freeing humans from limitations, Afrofuturism is nothing like futurism. By existing in epiphenomenal time, Afrofuturism can be *like* futurism, in that it is forward-looking, but without inheriting futurism's problems or having to position itself against it.

The third and final asset of Afrofuturism is that it is a symbolic answer to the nihilist atmosphere of postwar, black ghetto culture. Afrofuturism was an important influence for early house music artists living in Detroit. These musicians found inspiration in innovative artists both at home (George Clinton) and abroad (Kraftwerk), and they were surrounded by a destitute urban environment linked to the deterioration of the auto industry. According to Mark Dery, techno and Afrofuturism go so well together because some of techno's first artists repurposed found objects of industrial garbage in order to create a minimalist sound that was reminiscent of machines.[79] Dery argues this resonated with what it meant to be poor and black in the postindustrial United States. This ingenuity gave urban youth hope for the future.

Part of Köpsell's engagement with Afrofuturism is the act of imagining an alternative history of Africa that counters a racist refusal to acknowledge the depths of African history and African cultures' contributions to human development. In the middle of the poem "A Rumble in the Petri Dish," the text takes an unusual detour from the topic of scientific racism toward Afrofuturism:

There are lasers in the jungle and wires in the bible
And a distant culture parallel to yours
That—distilled to its meagre essence—could explain why you exist
Except it's not and it doesn't.[80]

The notion that there are "wires in the bible" suggests that the Bible is not the old text that we believe but a text from the future. The "wires in the bible" could also suggest that we think of the Bible, religion, and missionary work as kinds of technologies and in so doing consider their positive *and* negative effects on societies. Likewise, the phrase "there are lasers in the jungle" could have multiple meanings. Köpsell might be connecting to Dery's comparison between the transatlantic slave trade and alien abduction. Instead of Hegel's notion of Africa as a place "outside of history," Köpsell presents Africa as an alternative planet with advanced technologies of which we might be unaware. This might possibly be the "distant culture" that, "distilled to its meagre essence, could explain why [black people] exist." When Köpsell immediately negates this claim with the line, "except it's not and it doesn't," he suggests that (1) this is perhaps all fantasy or (2) even if it were true, the evidence has been buried and denied. This ambivalence is part of the power of Afrofuturism. Africa's history as a space of scientific exploration and knowledge production prior to colonialism receives little attention in the West. By imagining Africa to be a different planet, Köpsell not only frees it from Afropessimist narratives but also suggests that, rather than Africa lacking technologies, either we are incapable of understanding or appreciating them, or their traces have been lost.[81] This idea seems to be reinforced by two artworks that immediately follow the poem.

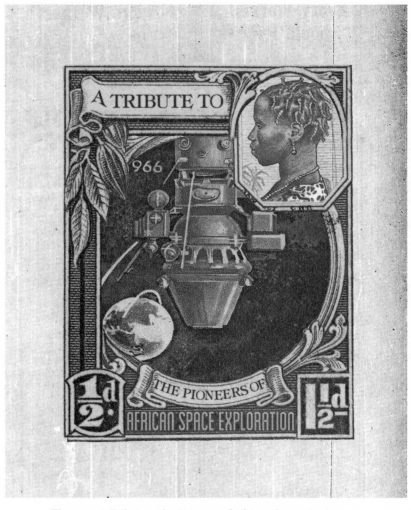

Figure 2. *A Tribute to the Pioneers of African Space Exploration*

These two images recall the commemorative stamps and postcards produced to celebrate the world's fairs. Figure 2 presents a black woman with braided hair in the upper right-hand corner, in a position one would expect a head of state or some other prominent person. In the middle of the image is what appears to be part of a spaceship. Below the spaceship and to the left is a miniature of the world. The heading on the "stamp" reads "A Tribute to the Pioneers of African Space Exploration." While there was an attempt in Zambia to create a space

Figure 3. Transcontinental trains, Accra-Hamburg

program in 1964, led by science teacher Edward Festus Mukuka Nkoloso, it never came to fruition, and there has not been a space program in Africa since.[82] This fact and the lack of any dates on the "stamp" suggest this is an object from an imagined future. Likewise, figure 3 seems to make similarly positive predictions about Africa's future with the suggestion that there will one day be a train line from Accra to Hamburg with state-of-the-art trains. Once again, a black woman with braided hair is positioned in the upper right-hand corner, this time overlooking an image of an impressive train station. These kinds of positive predictions about Africa's future, which often flip the hierarchy of power between Africa and the West, can be compared to the art intervention *Africa Is the Future*, which consists of fake magazine covers created by Nicolas Premier and Patrick Ayamam between 2004 and 2014.

Köpsell's resistance to Afropessimism is also clear in the poem "Dein Afrika und Albtraum (ein besseres Spendengesuch)" ("Your Africa and Nightmare (a better charity)"). Here, Köpsell ventriloquizes for the stereotypical campaigns in Germany that seek to raise money for African aid. Köpsell's play with stereotypes is reflected in a line that informs us the poem was "*translated from a dialect with monosyllabic clicking sounds*" (*JK* 18).[83] This "translator's note" invokes the assumptions about African languages and feigns a degree of authenticity that would make the poem a believable account of African life. Speaking for the images of African children looking destitute, Köpsell addresses the white German who is not used to engaging with blacks so directly: not the well-meaning white German academic, whom Köpsell criticizes in a poem like "The Brainage," but the working-class white German with tacky taste (nail extensions) who is international only in terms of consumerism (Reeboks) and not political consciousness. Köpsell writes, "I see you / with your three bags of groceries from Edeka / Reeboks and nail extensions."[84] This line not only remarks on a certain class of white German, but also a pervasive ignorance about Germany's colonial past. It is significant that of all the German supermarkets, Köpsell mentions Edeka, a store entangled with Germany's colonial past. Founded in 1898 by Fritz Borrmann, Edeka was originally named Einkaufsgenossenschaft der Kolonialwarenhändler im Hallschen Torbezirk zu Berlin (EdK), roughly translated, Shopping Cooperative of the Colonial Goods Merchants in the Hallschen Tor District of Berlin.[85] The name Edeka is a vocalization of the abbreviation EdK. Thus, it was originally a colonial goods' store, much like the ones I discuss in chapter 1. With Edeka bags in tow, the white shopper in Köpsell's poem is not only guilty of believing the racist stereotypes about Africans perpetuated in aid campaigns, but also oblivious to Germany's past colonial entanglements, which are often hidden in plain sight.

After addressing the white German "you," the lyric persona positions himself as a stereotypical image of Africa:

I squat silently between Accra and Addis Abeba
in the dust of squeaking mines
next to steaming rubber and Russian helicopters
flies drink the salt of my tears. (JK 18)[86]

Though these lines at first appear to merely reproduce Afropessimist images of Africa, Köpsell's engagement with Afropessimism in the entirety of the poem seems to agree that Africa is misrepresented in the media. However, Köpsell does more than attack racist images in the media. Rather, he complicates them by both including more positive images and presenting an African subject who is not just the object of the gaze but has the power to look himself. It is quite powerful that the lyric persona in Köpsell's poem not only directly addresses the German who would rather look away, but it is the *African* who is looking *through* the German. In the second part of the poem, the lyric persona counters these negative images of Africa with an acknowledgment of the continent's diversity and varied individuals:

Your Africa. I sit
between Accra and Addis Abeba. I play
with the shards of old lighters. . . .
Maybe I'll be in Joburg tomorrow
in the East Gate Mall™
Let myself be advised about the advantages of a Blackberry
Maybe even in Lagos
sitting at a pedicure and drinking Gin Fizz
But today
just for this moment
I chew spit
and stare down from your blank street corner. (*JK* 18–19)[87]

Rather than being stuck in an impoverished state, the lyric persona demonstrates that this is one of many roles he can play. He has the ability to change subject positions. He describes Africa not as a giant, faceless continent, but composed of major cities where Africans are consumers not unlike their white German counterparts.

This brings me to the second way Afrofuturism is used in Köpsell's poetry: to create a utopian imagination of what a more positive future might hold for Africa and for African diasporic peoples. This is a point explored by Kodwo Eshun in *The Last Angel of History*:

> The connection between the architects of Afrofuturism, between Sun Ra, Lee Perry and George Clinton and between techno and jungle later on in the 80s and 90s is simply that they hold nothing in common with the common idea of black music which is that it belongs to the street or to the stage . . . they are studio musics, they are impossible imaginary musics and yet because they're imaginary, they're even more powerful, because they suggest the future. They don't reflect the past. They imagine the future. . . .
>
> In the eighteenth century, slaves like Phyllis Wheatley read poetry to prove that they were human, to prove that they weren't furniture, to prove that they weren't robots and to prove that they weren't animals. In that sense, a certain idea of cybernetics has already been applied to black subjects ever since the 18th century. I think what we get at the end of the 20th century in music technology is a point where producers kind of willingly take on the role of the cyborg, willingly take on that man machine interface just to explore the mutation that's already happened to them and to accelerate them some more. Now the question is, cyborgs for what? And the reason is, to get out of here. To get out of this time here, this space now.

The desire of black German artists to "get out of this time here, this space now" resonates throughout their work. In Sharon Otoo's novel *Synchronicity*, she creates a world where one can lose the capability of seeing color. The protagonist's inability to see color makes her all the more grateful when she is slowly able to appreciate color through sense. In Olumide Popoola's play *Also by Mail*, a deceased Nigerian character is able to come back from the beyond in order to give his black German children a glance into the future and reassure them that there will be a day when racial profiling is no longer acceptable in Germany. The futures imagined by Otoo and Popoola are defined by a move toward eradicating racism.

The optimism of black German Afrofuturism presents a stark contrast to how the future is discussed in the autobiographies of the older generations.[88] In these autobiographies, one repeatedly encounters the assumption that black Germans will have no future or a bleak one, either through discrimination or some inherent character flaw. In *Kämpfe für dein Leben*, Charly Graf describes the bleak circumstances of his childhood neighborhood, the so-called Benz-Baracken.

The scum of society lived here; the people with whom no one wanted anything to do, the antisocial people. But even then the streets bore names that sounded much different, names that didn't have anything to do with the daily life in Waldhof: "Good Profess," "Light Cell," "Strong Hope," "Your Own Place," "Good Confidence," "Strong Will," "Good Endurance," and even "New Life," which was the street that led to my house. On the one hand you had the misery of the barracks, and on the other you had these street names. Today I can only shake my head over the cynicism of the people who thought of that.[89]

Günther Kaufmann addresses a similar topic when he recalls a story his mother told him about a wealthy couple with no children of their own who offered to adopt him when he was a baby. The woman "made it clear to my mother that I would have a rather difficult future. With my skin color."[90] Remarkably, Kaufmann wishes that he had been adopted:

In glowing colors, the woman described what kind of future I would have as the only child of a factory owner: the best education, protected from any attacks by the reputation and standing of the family. Yes, and eventually I would inherit the factory.

In a nutshell—brilliant prospects.

I'm not blaming my mother. But it was actually pretty egotistical of her. I would have had a much better life if the couple with the factory had adopted me. I regret that it didn't happen that way.[91]

This nihilistic tone and assumption that black Germans have a bleak future results from multiple causes. There were sociohistorical issues: many of the mothers of these children were single parents and had low income, and there was often a housing shortage immediately after the war. And these sociohistorical issues were compounded by the fact that, as "illegitimate" children of mothers who were seen as degenerate, black German children were assumed to have no future because of their lack of means, inherent character flaws, and the challenges they would face in a racist society.

This nihilism is in stark contrast to Köpsell's Afrofuturist work. Köpsell's experimentation with Afrofuturism seems like a clear attempt to be hopeful for the future of the black German community. For example, in the brochure for "We Are Tomorrow," a series of events that commemorated the 130th anniversary of the Berlin Conference at the Ballhaus Naunynstrasse Theater in Berlin, Köpsell adopted a fictional persona, Batho ba rena ba lefase, who lives in the year 2084 and presumably travels back in time to 2014. He ponders, "and if Babylon does fall—how do we receive tomorrow? / In the dust of fallen walls, in the rust of old fences, /let us approach our dreams clearly and ask the new day to dance."[92] Babylon is not only a reference to the Old Testament but also to the Rastafarian use of the term, which refers to oppressive governments rooted in slavery and colonialism. Thus, Köpsell's futurist persona encourages black Germans to be prepared for a day when the evils of society *will* succumb and to be optimistic about what tomorrow will bring.

Köpsell's optimism is also articulated in the poem "A Futurist's Manifesto," which is included in an anthology of black German writing with the telling title *Arriving in the Future*. The poem's epigraph announces, "this poem is from the future but since you have been good you get it early." More than three-quarters of the text is spent preparing us for what to expect from the poem, which consists of three sentences. This preparation is necessary because we must first get acquainted with the society from which this poem hails, if we are to understand it. We must also adjust ourselves to the notion that this is no ordinary poem, but one that can time-travel and change the past. We are told, "This poem got sent back in time to kill Hitler." Here Köpsell asks us to imagine a future in which the horrors of the Third Reich never happened because Hitler has been assassinated.

Despite its misleading title, what makes "A Futurist's Manifesto" an *Afrofuturist* poem is it is not a *prediction* of the future. Rather it is a poem that knows more than we, that knows better than we. This poem comes from the future to give us an alternative view of our present. Instead of stagnating in the face of current problems that may seem unconquerable, this poem asks us, imagine that there already *is* a different reality we could be living at any moment if we embrace the potential. The Germany of the future may not be free of racism, but it is a place where "poets of color write about their loved ones' ear lobes, dealing with life, death, health and healing . . . in the future we love too much."[93] Köpsell's "Futurist's Manifesto" ends with the hope that, in the future, black artists can write about anything, including love. Thus, a part of countering the nihilism haunting older generations of black Germans is imagining a future in which they are not limited to writing about racism and are not valued only for their commentary on racism. In the future Köpsell imagines, black subjectivity is not created as a counter to whiteness, but, instead, black subjects *can* identify as German, without the need to do so. In fact, in Köpsell's future, there is no single way of being black, nor is a person limited to a single identity. In this way, Köpsell's poetry unhinges blackness from a perpetual state of rebellion and a constant orbiting around an alienating center.

Conclusion

My goal in this book was to demonstrate that in fiction, nonfiction, poetry, and films, blackness has been discursively employed to signify male rebellion against hegemonic German culture throughout the long postwar. By progressively covering a different decade in each chapter and by largely organizing the book chronologically, I have chosen this interdisciplinary body of works to convey that certain notions about blackness and its value for white male rebellion in Germany persist throughout history, while also providing the context necessary to understand why these notions might have changed over time.

I began this book with an analysis of *The Tin Drum* because, as a text that spans the period of the Third Reich and the immediate postwar years, it provides an excellent opportunity to see how blackness and white male rebellion are invoked to shape Oskar's embodied resistance to fascism over time. Despite the privilege of Oskar's whiteness, his middle-class status, and his national belonging, he considers himself an outsider, and his self-fashioning as such relies on an imagined proximity to blackness and knowledge of black culture, both embodied by rhythm and jazz. Nevertheless, because Oskar's interest in black culture is completely self-serving and does not exempt him from participating in the Nazi regime, he is plagued by a feeling of concern that his farce will be revealed. His guilt is embodied by the figure of the Black Cook, who haunts him until the very end.

As a mammoth of the German canon, *The Tin Drum* has been discussed by many scholars, who have taken countless approaches to the work. Some have read it as an engagement with *Vergangenheitsbewältigung*, while some have read it as a picaresque novel or an example of magical realism. One also finds differing understandings of Oskar as a protagonist. He has been discussed as a resister to Nazism or a Hitler figure, either a critic of religion or a Jesus figure. Smaller details of the novel have also been analyzed, from Grass's portrayal of gender to the trope of eating and the Black Cook. I am the first scholar, however, to focus on blackness and how it intersects with Oskar's rebellion and his fear of femininity—the Black Cook, in this context, signifies both physical blackness and metaphorical blackness. While I still read the novel as largely about coming to terms with the past, I highlight what Oskar's relationship to black culture has to do with his relationship to the country's fascist past. I am the first to propose that Grass's memoir underscores an interest in blackness as rebellious and non-German, ideas that are prevalent in the novel. Engaging with the memoir also helps me show that his own thoughts about race reflect the naive way in which blackness is constructed by the narrator. I would, however, not suggest that Grass and his protagonist are one and the same. Like Oskar, Grass unproblematically aligns himself with black culture in his memoir. However, in the novel, Grass does not allow his protagonist to get away with this identification; for in the end, Oskar must answer to the Black Cook, who does not let him forget his whiteness or his own culpability in Germany's Nazi past.

A thread that consistently runs through the book is bringing texts into conversation that people would not necessarily think to combine. In chapter 2, I demonstrate this by discussing Thoman Valentin's novel *Die Unberatenen* in combination with Peter Zadek's film *Ich bin ein Elefant, Madame*. This combination is not unorthodox in that Zadek's film is adapted from Valentin's novel. Nevertheless, no one has bothered to look at these works together. In fact, there is very little scholarship on either text. Valentin's novel tends to be appreciated as a *Schulroman* (school novel) that offers insight into the generational conflicts of West Germany in the 1960s. Zadek's film maintains a cult status as a radical depiction of the 1968 student movement. I look at these texts together to demonstrate a German interest in black culture that continues on through the 1950s and 1960s and associates blackness with difference and rebellion.

While the protagonist of Valentin's novel is of a younger generation than Oskar, and therefore too young to have participated in the Nazi regime, the notions about blackness in Valentin's novel are just as naive and reductive as Oskar's in *The Tin Drum*. For Valentin's rebellious white protagonist, Jochen Rull, black culture signifies a certain innocence, a culture and a people who are unscathed by the hypocrisies of West German culture. However, when Zadek adapts the material for a film, he does not simply replicate this West German romantic desire to flee one's origins by adopting a foreign culture. Instead, Zadek creates distance between the white German rebel and the black culture he admires by introducing a mediator—the Velvet Underground, a white American band influenced by black culture. Zadek also asks whether a white German rebel really can and should disengage with his cultural legacy in order to identify with American culture.

I bring these texts into conversation to highlight the artists' differing approaches to *Vergangenheitsbewältigung* and cultural appropriation. Valentin's novel is sympathetic toward its students, especially its protagonist. But Zadek employs alienation techniques that make it difficult to identify with Rull, perhaps because Zadek wants us to be critical, not just of the authoritarian German teachers, but also of the idealistic students. If in Valentin's novel appropriation of black culture is treated unproblematically, Zadek's film asks us to question, not only whether it's possible for young Germans to disassociate with their past and choose new cultural father figures, but also what problems might be swept under the rug if they do.

In chapter 3, I introduce two East German texts, Ulrich Plenzdorf's *The New Sufferings of Young W,* and Michael Schorr's film *Schultze Gets the Blues,* to demonstrate the similarities and differences between appropriation of black culture in West and East Germany. Compared to the other German works I discuss, scholars have indeed commented on the role that race plays in *Schultze Gets the Blues*. This film more obviously engages with issues of race and appropriating black culture because Schultze's newfound interest in zydeco drives the plot. Furthermore, unlike the other German texts by white authors discussed in this book, in *Schultze Gets the Blues* the protagonist has an actual encounter with black people, specifically African Americans. Thus, it is not surprising that scholars would comment on these aspects.

However, bringing *Schultze Gets the Blues* into dialogue with Plenzdorf's *The New Sufferings of Young W* leads to new revelations. These works are separated by at least thirty years, and they have differing sociohistorical contexts; Plenzdorf's text takes place in East Germany, Schorr's film takes place after reunification. Furthermore, despite the vast commentary on Plenzdorf's text, scholars have not addressed the trope of black culture. As I mentioned in the introduction, this is likely because Edgar's interest in blues and black artists seems marginal to the book's themes. However, a focus on how black culture is constructed and employed supports theories about Edgar's outsider status. When one looks at both Plenzdorf's text and Schorr's film through the lens of race, numerous similarities emerge: the characters' outsider status, their problems with hegemonic masculinity and modernity, and finally their rebellion. Discussing these texts together also stresses continuities between East Germany prior to and after reunification. When one views these texts together, postunification problems with race in the East no longer seem to come out of nowhere but rather have roots in East Germany's persistent Othering of blackness.

The texts I bring together in chapter 4, Paul Beatty's *Slumberland* and Mark Stewart's *Passing Strange*, really seem made for each other. They are

both written by African American male artists who have spent time in Germany
and who have sought to engage with white German appropriation and valorization of black culture. Furthermore, both of these artists challenge assumptions
about black culture and propose that black culture and black individuals are
more complex and diverse than they have typically been represented in Germany. As I demonstrated in chapter 4, most scholars who have written about
Slumberland and *Passing Strange* separately have discussed the themes of race
and identity. And Alisa Roost brings *Passing Strange* into dialogue with other
musicals that do not necessarily thematize race or blackness, but do highlight
their protagonists' lack of connection to others in postmodern society.[1] My
analysis is not meant to contradict this previous work, but to suggest that even
more insight is possible if one discusses them together.

Both *Slumberland* and *Passing Strange* take us into the 1980s; by then the
presence of African Americans (particularly soldiers) and black culture had
become quite commonplace in German cities. And it is the stories circulated
among African American men who had been to Germany that make it seem
like a desirable place for young African American men, like the protagonists
Ferguson and Youth, to go to and rebel. Thus the sociohistorical context of
these texts allows me to pose the question, if black people go to Germany to
rebel and if certain black bodies have been "normalized" in Germany, can
black culture really be inherently rebellious, or has it become passé, as is
claimed by Ferguson? This chapter is also important because it allows me to
reverse the gaze and inquire what black artists think about German notions of
blackness. Scholarly works that engage with Afro-Americanophilia, like
Moritz Ege's *Schwarz werden*, tend to focus on what white Germans think
about this phenomenon. However, to move the conversation forward, black
people have to be included in it.

Nevertheless, including African American voices is not enough. While
some African American students, scholars, and artists might have firsthand experience with German racism and the essentialization of black culture there,
these individuals are usually in Germany for a limited time and, in many ways,
are shielded by their privilege as American citizens. Black Germans are the
ones who either have to deal with the daily struggles of racism more perma-
nently or decide to leave their home country because of these struggles. Black
Germans also have a unique experience, having to position themselves against
both German culture and African American culture, as they are, in Michelle
Wright's words, often seen as "Others-from-Without." This is why the book
concludes with black German perspectives in chapter 5.

What is most innovative about chapter 5 is the texts in the conversation.

Autobiographical texts by prominent, older, black German men—*Destined to Witness, Deutsch sein und schwarz dazu, Kämpfe für dein Leben,* and *Der weisse Neger vom Hasenbergl*—are juxtaposed with the poetry of the young, black German Philipp Khabo Köpsell. Within the field of black German studies, much important work has been done on autobiographies, and the autobiography has been an essential genre that gave black Germans a space to tell their stories and claim a German identity. But a lot has changed in the black German community since these first autobiographies began to be published. As I state in chapter 5, black Germans of a younger generation often have a more diasporic sense of self and do not necessarily feel the need to claim a German identity. This is what comes across in Köpsell's poetry, where he criticizes stereotypes of "Germanness" but also interrogates the dominance of African American culture in German society. By turning to Afrofuturism, Köpsell rejects the narrowness imposed by national categories.

"Ick bin ein Obama"

Another important question I raised in the introduction was whether the white German association between blacks and rebellion was disrupted with the arrival of America's first black president. On the one hand, Barack Obama could be seen as an underdog who, for the length of his two terms as president, fought off critiques from the Republican Party, many of which were outrageous and often racist, such as the attacks on his citizenship. Interestingly, it seems white German politicians chose to see Obama as simply a successful, charismatic politician to be envied. If one were to compare Obama's life experiences to those of one of the many black GIs present in Germany immediately after the war, the most obvious difference is how much *American* society has changed. Not only is racial discrimination no longer written into the army's policies, but Americans are prepared to and did vote for a black president, twice. If in Germany from the 1950s until the 1990s, the image of a black man evoked associations with oppression, suffering, struggle, and rebellion, how might these associations have changed in an age where a black man led the most powerful nation in the world for eight years? Some prominent African American critics have argued that not only did Obama's presidency *not* change much about the lives of black people around the world (including in the United States), but that the election of Donald Trump as America's forty-fifth president is symbolic of a backlash against Obama's presidency and of the continuing power of white supremacy.[2] Trump's victory could be read as an indication of white male insecurity, white Americans' reluctance to rescind privilege, and their desire to return to a romanticized past, in the 1950s, when America was allegedly "great." And considering that this populist trend is visible both in the United States and in Germany, perhaps it is too optimistic and naive to believe *that* much has changed in either country's understandings of race.

Nevertheless, it is still important to consider to what extent Obama's presidency might have influenced discourses on race in Germany. On July 24, 2008, sixty years after Truman's executive order to desegregate the U.S. Army, Obama delivered a speech to an audience of one hundred thousand people in Berlin while he was still a presidential candidate. Although he followed in their footsteps, Obama certainly gathered a much larger crowd than such African American predecessors as Martin Luther King Jr. and Paul Robeson—both of whom also attracted impressive crowds during the 1960s in East and West Berlin.[3] At the time of the speech, Obama's American critics were confused and even upset that a U.S. presidential candidate felt it necessary to address a foreign audience abroad instead of focusing solely on Americans' opinions of him. They were even more puzzled at the Obama fever that seemed to captivate Germany. From those present at his speech to the teens and tweens that proudly hung his poster on their wall courtesy of the youth magazine *Bravo*, Germans were enthralled by this young, smart, handsome black presidential candidate. The fact that Americans had already been comparing Obama to John F. Kennedy, perhaps the most beloved American president in German history, only strengthened this love affair with Obama.

In his article about Obama's visit to Berlin, "Citizenship and the Obama Moment in Berlin," African American cultural anthropologist Damani Partridge recounts discussions with several people of color in Berlin about their reactions to Obama's speech. Some felt that if Obama won the presidency, it would open up opportunities for them, because second-generation immigrants could ask the white German majority, why can't they be allowed to contribute more to German politics? But others were more skeptical, like Turkish German filmmaker Neco Celik, who tells Partridge, "*Du bist exot. Ich sehe Fremd aus*" (You are exotic. I look like a stranger).[4] Partridge reflects, "His statement perfectly dissected the widespread ambivalence about the Turkish presence within Germany and the simultaneous desire for American and even African American culture."[5] The ambivalence people of color felt about whether Obama's win could positively affect their experience in Germany once again reveals the special status of African American culture in postwar Germany.

On a similarly critical note, in September 2008, Turkish German journalist Mely Kiyak skeptically responded to white Germans' love for Obama and their desire for an "Obama" of their own. According to Kiyak, the few Germans with a migrant background who had actually made it into the high ranks of the political system had been ignored. "No, we in Germany would rather recognize the social accomplishments in other countries. Recognize the civil rights movements, protest marches and the wild unrest about inequality outside of our own borders."[6] Now, ten years later, it seems Kiyak's claims still ring true. In 2012, German comedian Martin Sonneborn created a controversy with a satirical campaign poster (he was a candidate for the European Parliament) that featured him in blackface under the headline, "Ick bin ein Obama" (I am an Obama). By purposefully misspelling "Ich" (I) as "Ick," Sonneborn was both mimicking Berlin dialect and referencing John F. Kennedy's blunder during a speech in 1963, when he mistakenly announced "Ich bin ein Berliner," whereas the correct sentence leaves out the indefinite article.[7] Though done in poor taste, Sonneborn's poster poked fun at white German politicians' persistent desire to embody the African American president and white German voters' gullibility.

But white Germans' love affair with Obama is not just about their failure to recognize the accomplishments of minorities in their own country. Additionally, white Germans have long preferred to identify with minorities abroad rather than at home. American studies scholar Sabine Broeck has claimed that white Germans prefer to identify with African Americans because they are oppressed bodies against whom white Germans *did not* transgress.[8] Thus, by identifying with African Americans, white Germans can condemn American racism and imagine themselves in the role of the oppressed without having to interrogate their own racism and white privilege. However, this unreflective cross-racial identification has become increasingly difficult, in part because the larger and more public presence of a black German community pushes back against white Germans' claims of colorblindness and uncovers the many forms of racism present in German society.

Sonneborn's staging is just one of several recent blackface scandals in Germany, particularly on the German stage. It is astonishing that, even today, in the German theater, white German actors seem to consider themselves racial chameleons, able to adopt black subjectivities (such as perform as black asylum seekers in Dea Loher's play *Innocence*) without engaging in any critical discussions about race.[9] Meanwhile, journalist Nele Obermueller states sarcastically, blacks are only convincing in theater as "DJs, asylum seekers, criminals and servants."[10] Some of the discussions surrounding these issues might offer a clue to this persistent insensitivity toward race, blackface, and the right or ability to appropriate black culture.

In response to criticism of the blackface performance in Schlosspark Theater's production of Herb Gardner's *I'm Not Rappaport*, one journalist rhetorically asked, "If only black actors should be allowed to play black roles, does that mean only Danish princes can play Hamlet?"[11]a question that conflates race with cultural or national difference. One online commentator responding to an article on Germany's first black mayor, John Ehret, even suggested that white Germans are exempt from critically discussing antiblack racism because Germany "had no need for slaves."[12] Thus, despite black Germans' presence in the German public, and the fact that African American culture is no longer synonymous with suffering and rebellion, these developments have not changed white Germans' insistence on standing on "the right side of history" and having the freedom to uncritically appropriate black culture. As Sabine Broeck suggests, it appears, in order to really interrogate white German cross-racial identification, more work will have to be done to uncover Germany's entanglements with the slave trade.[13]

Some of that work has already started, with publications like the recent volume edited by Eve Rosenhaft and Felix Brahm, *Slavery Hinterland*, which documents German companies' involvement in and benefit from the slave trade, as well as the presence of individual slaves in Germany who were bought at foreign ports by noblemen. The African slave bought by Prussian nobleman Joachim Erdmann von Arnim, whom I mentioned in the introduction, is an example of the fact that white Germans did have to make the choice between protecting the rights of human beings or the rights of property. And in the case against von Arnim's slave, Friedrich the Great chose property over a black man's life, a life that was seen as being animalistic and less than human. Thus, the argument that Germany's problems with racism cannot be compared to the United States because it was not implicated in slavery no longer works. This is why it is even more important to interrogate white German identification with African Americans.

I'd like to close with one final question first raised in my introduction. I asked, if appropriating black popular culture is so potentially problematic, what is the answer? This book does not take issue with *all* appropriation of black culture in texts by white German artists, but specifically with unreflectively associating black culture with rebellion. Reading blackness as always already rebellious strips black culture and black people of their complexity. Moreover, if blackness is always already coded as Other, then it is impossible for individuals to be both black and German. So what is the solution? It *is* possible for white artists to at least problematize these notions. And I believe that Grass, Zadek, and Schorr *do* problematize them, either by having their protagonists fail at "becoming minor," like Oskar and the students in Zadek's film, or by recognizing their characters' whiteness, as in Schultze's case when he disrobes and reveals his white protruding stomach to the African American woman in the hot tub. In this way, these authors are able to discuss white German valorization of blackness and what it means for the construction of white Germans without essentializing blackness and without denying the physicality and threat that comes along with being a black person. But it is equally important that as scholars we recognize when white German authors are or are not problematizing the appropriation of black culture. When we brush over the use of jazz in *The Tin Drum*, the significance of Louis Armstrong in *Die Unberatenen*, and the trope of the blues in *The New Sufferings of Young W*, we are not doing our job as scholars to think critically about how these texts and their characters are constructed. When a white artist includes references to black music or black culture more generally, it is not accidental. So if white German artists choose to engage with black culture in their works, it is our job to interrogate what those choices are trying to tell us about the characters and the texts. Finally, I think the best way to get away from the association of blackness with Otherness and rebellion is if white Germans recognize their intimate kinship with the African diaspora, and part of that means recognizing white German involvement in the slave trade and in colonialism. Only when white Germans recognize that blackness has long been a part of German history, rather than outside of it, will black characters and cultures in artistic works cease to be shorthand for difference and rebellion, *and* black Germans cease to be seen as Other and always just arriving.

Notes

INTRODUCTION

1. For essential readings on critical race theory see Richard Delgado and Jean Stefancic, *Critical Race Theory: An Introduction* (New York: New York University Press, 2012); Daniel G. Solóranzo, "Critical Race Theory, Race and Gender, and the Experience of Chicana and Chicano Scholars," *Qualitative Studies in Education* 11, no. 1 (1998): 121–36; Gloria Ladson-Billings, "Just What Is Critical Race Theory and What Is It Doing in a Nice Field Like Education?," *International Journal of Qualitative Studies in Education* 11, no. 1 (1998): 7–24.

2. Peter Martin, *Schwarze Teufel, edle Mohren: Afrikaner in Geschichte und Bewußtsein der Deutschen* (Hamburg: Hamburger Edition, 2001), 11.

3. Martin, *Schwarze Teufel, edle Mohren*, 11.

4. Martin, *Schwarze Teufel, edle Mohren*, 12–13.

5. Tia DeNora discusses the importance of music as "part of how individuals are involved in constituting themselves as social agents" in *Music in Everyday Life* (Cambridge: Cambridge University Press, 2000), 47.

6. Katrin Sieg, *Ethnic Drag: Performing Race, Nation, Sexuality in West Germany* (Ann Arbor: University of Michigan Press, 2009), 187.

7. Uta Poiger, *Jazz, Rock, and Rebels: Cold War Politics and American Culture in a Divided Germany* (Berkeley: University of California Press, 2000), 89.

8. While the discipline of whiteness studies is relatively well established in the United States, it is only starting to gain traction in German academia. Some of the first volumes to discuss the issue of whiteness in a German context are Martina Tißberger, Gabriele Dietze, Daniela Hrzán, and Jana Husmann-Kastein, eds., *Weiß—Weißsein—Whiteness: kritische Studien zu Gender und Rassismus* (Frankfurt am Main: Peter Lang, 2006) and Maureen Maisha Eggers, Grada Kilomba, Peggy Piesche, and Susan Arndt, eds., *Mythen, Masken und Subjekte: kritische Weißseinforschung in Deutschland* (Münster: Unrast, 2009).

9. Timothy L. Schroer, *Recasting Race after World Word II: Germans and African Americans in American-Occupied Germany* (Boulder: University of Colorado Press, 2007), 33.

10. Quoted in Moritz Ege, *Schwarz werden: "Afroamerikanophilie" in den 1960er und 1970er Jahren* (Bielefeld: Transcript, 2007), 154. The term "white Negro" comes from Norman Mailer's essay *The White Negro*, published in 1957. Mailer argues that

postwar white American jazz fans, or hipsters, can relate to African Americans because they share their sense of living under the constant threat of punishment or death if they don't conform to mainstream society. I will discuss Mailer's text at greater length in chapter 2. Norman Mailer, *The White Negro* (San Francisco: City Lights, 1957).

11. Ege, *Schwarz werden*, 163.

12. See Poiger, *Jazz, Rock, and Rebels* and Yara-Collette Lemke Muniz de Faria, *Zwischen Fürsorge und Ausgrenzung: afrodeutsche "Bezatzungskinder" im Nachkriegsdeutschland* (Berlin: Metropol, 2002).

13. Ege, *Schwarz werden*, 159.

14. Ege, *Schwarz werden*, 158.

15. Similar to my claim, in *Schwarz werden* Ege also remarks that during the 1960s and 1970s specifically, black was read as always already rebellious; it functioned as a sign of rebellion. Nevertheless, there are several ways in which this book departs from Ege's project. While I am primarily examining aesthetic texts—literature, film, a musical, and poetry—Ege bases his discussion on journalistic media (magazines and newspapers), advertisements, and interviews. He also limits his discussion to contemporary objects from the time frame of 1967–1975, which he describes as a unique historical conjuncture. However, one can expand this moment of Afro-Americanophilia in either direction to include the immediate postwar up until the present, albeit taking into consideration changing sociohistorical circumstances. The contemporary media Ege examines show us snapshots of what blackness meant at a given moment in time, but not what it meant in a particular person's lifespan. The interviews he conducts with white people who at one time appropriated black culture might give us a better idea of how this moment of Afro-Americanophilia functioned in their own personal lives, but their statements are of course influenced by the limits of their memories and personal desires to present themselves in a certain way. However, in a fictional text such as a novel or film, we can see how blackness functioned within a character's life trajectory and there is no issue of fidelity or truth, because we know the real question is what is this author telling us about blackness through this fictional life story.

16. Dick Hebdige borrows the term "bricolage" from Lévi-Strauss. According to Hebdige, in the hands of a subcultural *bricoleur*, "prominent forms of discourse (particularly fashion) are radically adapted, subverted and extended." Dick Hebdige, *Subculture: The Meaning of Style* (London: Routledge, 1979), 104. Ella Shohat and Robert Stam define cultural syncretism as "a conflictual yet creative intermingling of cultures" in *Unthinking Eurocentrism: Multiculturalism and the Media* (London: Routledge, 1994), 237.

17. James O. Young, *Cultural Appropriation and the Arts* (Malden, MA: Blackwell, 2008), 5.

18. Young, *Cultural Appropriation*, 5.

19. Young, *Cultural Appropriation*, 6.

20. Young, *Cultural Appropriation*, 7.

21. Young, *Cultural Appropriation*, 9.

22. This is by no means a comprehensive list, but see, for example, Susan Arndt, ed., *Afrika Bilder: Studien zu Rassismus in Deutschland* (Münster: Unrast, 2011); Angelica Fenner, *Race under Reconstruction in German Cinema: Robert Stemmle's*

"*Toxi*" (Toronto: University of Toronto Press, 2011); Sander Gilman, *On Blackness without Blacks: Essays on the Image of the Black in Germany* (Boston: G.K. Hall, 1982); Dirk Göttsche, *Remembering Africa: The Rediscovery of Colonialism in Contemporary German Literature* (Rochester, NY: Camden House, 2013); Reinhold Grimm and Amadou Booker Sadji, eds., *Dunkle Reflexe: Schwarzafrikaner und Afro-Amerikaner in der deutschen Erzählkunst des 18. und 19. Jahrhunderts* (Bern: Peter Lang, 1992); Sara Lennox, ed., *Remapping Black Germany: New Perspectives on Afro-German History, Politics and Culture* (Amherst: University of Massachusetts Press, 2016); Sara Lennox, "Claiming Blackness in Germany," in *The Meaning of Culture: German Studies in the 21st Century*, ed. Martin Kagel and Laura Tate Kagel (Hannover: Werhahn, 2009), 177–92; Sara Lennox, "Reading Transnationally: The GDR and Black American Writers," *German Monitor* 74 (2011): 111–29; Paul Lützeler, *Schriftsteller und "Dritte Welt": Studien zum postkolonialen Blick* (Tübingen: Stauffenberg, 1998); and Susanne Zantop, *Colonial Fantasies: Conquest, Family, and Nation in Precolonial Germany, 1770–1870* (Durham, NC: Duke University Press, 1997).

23. Martin, *Schwarze Teufel, edle Mohren*, 11.

24. Loretta Todd, "Notes on Appropriation," *Parallelogramme* 16, no. 1 (1990): 24–26.

25. Todd, "Notes on Appropriation," 26.

26. See Jeff Bowersox, *Raising Germans in the Age of Empire: Youth and Colonial Culture, 1871–1914* (Oxford: Oxford University Press, 2013).

27. Todd, "Notes on Appropriation," 26.

28. Todd, "Notes on Appropriation," 30.

29. Martin, *Schwarze Teufel, edle Mohren*, 85.

30. Beth Kolko, Lisa Nakamura, and Gilbert B. Rodman, eds., *Race in Cyberspace* (New York: Routledge, 2000), 2.

31. Kolko, Nakamura, and Rodman, *Race in Cyberspace*, 2.

32. Charles Mills, *Blackness Visible: Essays on Philosophy and Race* (Ithaca, NY: Cornell University Press, 1998), xiv.

33. Stuart Hall, "What Is This 'Black' in Black Popular Culture?," in *Stuart Hall: Critical Dialogues in Cultural Studies*, ed. David Morley and Kaun-Hsing Chen (London: Routledge, 1996), 471.

34. Hall, "What Is This Black," 471.

35. It is important to note that Broyard was of a very light complexion and had passed as white as an adult. See Bliss Broyard, *One Drop: My Father's Hidden Life—a Story of Race and Family Secrets* (New York: Little, Brown, 2007).

36. Mark Greif, "Positions," in *What Was the Hipster? A Sociological Investigation*, ed. Mark Greif, Kathleen Ross, and Dayna Tortorici (New York: n+1 Foundation, 2010), 7.

37. Greif, "Positions," 8.

38. Hall, "What Is This Black," 472.

39. In fact, Peter Martin argues that the "black" more generally functions as a kind of head of Janus in the white German imaginary, which is what creates whites' ambivalent fascination and rejection of blacks: "he [the black] looks two-faced, facing forward

and backward simultaneously, cleverly looking toward the future full of promise, and looking toward the losses meaningfully and threateningly." Martin, *Schwarze Teufel, edle Mohren*, 11.

40. See Achille Mbembe, *On the Postcolony* (Berkeley: University of California Press, 2001).

41. For some discussion of the political and personal experience of African students in postwar Germany, see Quinn Slobodian, *Foreign Front: Third World Politics in Sixties West Germany* (Durham, NC: Duke University Press, 2012).

42. See Michelle Wright, "Others-from-Within from Without: Black German Subject Formation and the Challenge of a Counter-discourse," *Callaloo* 26, no. 2 (2003): 296–305.

43. See Jacqueline Nassy Brown, "Black Liverpool, Black America, and the Gendering of Diasporic Space," *Cultural Anthropology* 13, no. 2 (1998): 291–325.

44. There is a wealth of research on the early German reception of jazz. See, for example, Clarence Lusane, *Hitler's Black Victims: The Historical Experiences of Black Germans, European Blacks, Africans, and African Americans in the Nazi Era* (New York: Routledge, 2002); Michael H. Kater, *Different Drummers: Jazz in the Culture of Nazi Germany* (Oxford: Oxford University Press, 1992); and Michael J. Budds, ed., *Jazz and the Germans: Essays on the Influence of "Hot" American Idioms on 20th-Century German Music* (Hillsdale, NY: Pendragon Press, 2002). Prior to the arrival of jazz, white Germans had already encountered African Americans performing other kinds of music. The Fisk Jubilee Singers famously toured Europe, including Germany in 1877, performing Negro spirituals. In *Black People*, Rainer Lotz documents African American ragtime musicians who performed in Germany in the late nineteenth century. See Rainer Lotz, *Black People: Entertainers of African Descent in Europe and Germany* (Bonn: Birgit Lotz Verlag, 1997). Furthermore, in her dissertation, Kira Thurman also documents African American and Afro-Caribbean artists who performed classical music and lieder in Germany and Austria as early as the 1870s. Thurman's dissertation looks at how these African American and Afro-Caribbean artists' performance of what was considered "German" classical music challenged both ideas about hegemonic German *and* black culture. See Kira Thurman, "A History of Black Musicians in Germany and Austria, 1870–1961: Race, Performance, and Reception" (PhD diss., University of Rochester, 2013).

45. In her dissertation, Kira Thurman also discusses the Fisk Jubilee Singers' ten-month tour of Germany, as well as an encounter between Afro-Cuban musicians, a group called the Jimenez Trio, and white Germans during the 1870s. Thurman, "History of Black Musicians," 17–18. The Trio's patriarch, Jose Julian Jimenez, had studied music in Leipzig from 1853 until 1863. And in 1869 he was joined by his two sons, who would make up the remaining members of the trio. Thurman, "History of Black Musicians," 50–51.

46. Andrew Ward, *Dark Midnight When I Rise: The Story of the Jubilee Singers, Who Introduced the World to the Music of Black America* (New York: Farrar, Straus and Giroux, 2000), 349.

47. Thurman, "History of Black Musicians," 58.

48. Thurman, "History of Black Musicians," 58.

49. Ward, *Dark Midnight*, 355.

50. Thurman, "History of Black Musicians," 61.

51. For a catalog of African American musicians who traveled to Germany in the late nineteenth century and early twentieth century see Lotz, *Black People*. I take the term "black cultural traffic" from Harry Elam Jr. and Kennell Jackson, *Black Cultural Traffic: Crossroads in Global Performance and Popular Culture* (Ann Arbor: University of Michigan Press, 2005). In the book's introduction, Jackson defines black cultural traffic as "actual movements of black cultural material from place to place, rather than in a conceptual sense. . . . Between black performances and the viewers looking in on those performances, there occurs trade in ideas, styles, impressions, body language, and gestures." Kennell Jackson, "Introduction: Travelling While Black," in Elam and Jackson, *Black Cultural Traffic*, 8.

52. By using the term "black music," I do not intend to generalize the various genres of African diasporic music. Rather, I wish to point out that African American musical genres are most often influenced by other locations in the African diaspora, i.e., the Caribbean or the UK. Furthermore, "black music" is a term used in Germany to designate genres that have been pioneered by African Americans. It can include genres ranging from R & B and soul to funk and hip-hop. The label "black music" is used by concert venues, clubs, and music stores. Partly because of the intense circulation of musical ideas within the African diaspora, a white German fan of hip-hop or reggae is more likely to refer to her taste as "black music" rather than specifically "African American" or "Jamaican" music respectively.

53. Paul Gilroy, *Small Acts: Thoughts on the Politics of Black Culture* (Essex: Serpent's Tail, 1993), 35.

54. James Snead, "On Repetition in Black Culture," in *Racist Traces and Other Writings: European Pedigrees / African Contagions*, ed. Kara Keeling, Colin MacCabe, and Cornel West (New York: Palgrave Macmillan, 2003), 21.

55. Peter Wicke, *Rock Music: Culture, Aesthetics and Sociology* (Cambridge: Cambridge University Press, 1990).

56. In the essay "The Traffic in Women" (1975), Gayle Rubin suggested that "sex was about biology, gender about the attribution of meaning to sexual bodies. . . Judith Butler ([Gender Trouble] 1990) deconstructed the sex/gender opposition. . . If gender established the meanings of sex, then physical bodies were not the matter of sexed identities. Butler moved the analysis in another direction, suggesting that these identities were achieved through repetitive performances." Joan W. Scott, "'Entre braguette'—Notes on the Translation of Gender," in *Border Crossings: Translation Studies and Other Disciples*, edited by Yves Hambier and Luc van Doorslaer. Amsterdam: Philadelphia John Benjamins Publishing, 2016), 355–56. Butler's *Gender Trouble* was first published in Germany in 1991 as *Das Unbehagen der Geschlechter*.

57. A special issue of *Freiburger Geschlechter Studien* from 2007 dedicated to the topic "Männer und Geschlecht" (men and gender) includes lectures by Theweleit and Andrea Maihofer, followed by a conversation with the audience. See Andrea Maihofer, Klaus Theweleit, and Nina Degele, "Das moderne männliche Subjekt im Anschluss an Adorno, Horkheimer und Foucault," *Freiburger GeschlechterStudien* 21 (2007): 329–67.

58. Some earlier texts are Wolfgang Rath, *Not am Mann: zum Bild des Mannes im deutschen Gegenwartsroman* (Heidelberg: C. Winter, 1987) and Thomas Lacquer, *Auf*

den Leib geschrieben: Die Inszenierung der Geschlechter von der Antike bis Freud (Frankfurt am Main: Campus, 1992). For a history of men's studies from the perspective of *Germanistik* see Walter Erhart, "Das zweite Geschlecht: 'Männlichkeit,' interdisziplinär," *Internationales Archiv für Sozialgeschichte der deutschen Literatur* 30, no. 2 (2005): 156–232. For more recent texts see Claudia Benthien and Inge Stephan, eds., *Männlichkeit als Maskerade: kulturelle Inszenierungen vom Mittelalter bis zur Gegenwart* (Cologne: Böhlau, 2003); Walter Ehrhart, *Familienmänner: über den literarischen Ursprung moderner Männlichkeit* (Munich: Wilhelm Fink, 2001); Roy Jerome, ed., *Conceptions of Postwar German Masculinity* (Albany: State University of New York Press, 2001).

59. R. W. Connell, *Masculinities* (Berkeley: University of California, 2005), 77.

60. Connell, *Masculinities*, 55.

61. Connell says of race and masculinity specifically: "It is now common to say that gender 'intersects'—better, interacts—with race and class. We might add that it constantly interacts with nationality or position in the world order. . . . White men's masculinities, for instance, are constructed not only in relation to white women but also in relation to black men." *Masculinities*, 75.

62. Connell, *Masculinities*, 164.

63. One example of how black men's "wild nature" could be used not only to subordinate them under white men, but to deny them their freedom, is a case from Prussia in the eighteenth century. In 1780 an African slave who had been bought from a Dutchman by the German Joachim Erdmann von Arnim wrote a petition to Frederick the Great of Prussia, arguing that he should be set free because his original contract stated he must work for seven years and von Arnim had kept him much longer. The slave also argued that von Arnim was cruel and had denied him the right to learn Christian doctrine. As the slave's owner, according to Prussian law von Arnim was responsible for his soul and his religious education. But as a counterargument, von Arnim claimed the slave was much too animalistic and wild to even understand Christianity, even if he had allowed the slave to convert. Frederick ruled in favor of von Arnim. See Rebekka von Mallinckrodt, "There Are No Slaves in Prussia?," in *Slavery Hinterland: Transatlantic Slavery and Continental Europe, 1680–1850*, ed. Felix Brahm and Eve Rosenhaft (Woodbridge, Suffolk, UK: Boydell Press, 2016).

64. Isabel Karremann, "Männlichkeitsforschung und Literatur(wissenschaft) in Deutschland," *Jahrbuch für finnisch-deutsche Literaturbeziehungen* 36 (2004): 35.

65. Toni Tholen, "Perspektiven der Erforschung des Zusammenhangs von literarischen Männlichkeiten und Emotionen," in *Literarische Männlichkeiten und Emotionen*, ed. Toni Tholen and Jennifer Clare (Heidelberg: Winter, 2013), 9.

66. Connell, *Masculinities*, 77.

67. Connell, *Masculinities*, 90.

68. See Klaus Bogdal, "Hard-Cold-Fast: Imagining Masculinity in the German Academy, Literature, and the Media," in *Conceptions of Postwar Masculinity*, ed. Roy Jerome (Albany: State University of New York Press, 2001), 13–42.

69. Some examples of fictional representations of relationships between black men and white German women after World War II are novels like William Gardner Smith's *The Last of the Conquerors* (1948) and Willi Heinrich's *Gottes zweite Garnitur* (1962). Examples of films are Rainer Werner Fassbinder's *Die Ehe der Maria Braun* (1979) and *Die Sehnsucht der Veronika Voss* (1981). Annette von Brauerhoch's *Fräuleins und GIs:*

Geschichte und Filmgeschichte discusses these representations in films. Some of the history texts that have addressed this topic are Maria Höhn, *GIs and Fräuleins: The German American Encounter in 1950s West Germany* (Chapel Hill: University of North Carolina Press, 2002); Heide Fehrenbach, *Race after Hitler: Black Occupation Children in Postwar Germany and America* (Princeton, NJ: Princeton University Press, 2005); and Schroer, *Recasting Race*.

70. For example, in the historical analyses of relationships between African Americans and white Germans following World War II, the focus is primarily on black male soldiers and white German women, and there is little if any discussion about African American women's experience in Germany. This is an issue I will address in greater detail in chapter 4.

71. Eric Lott, *Love and Theft: Blackface Minstrelsy and the American Working Class* (New York: Oxford University Press, 1995), 49. See also Robert Reid-Pharr, *Once You Go Black: Choice, Desire, and the Black American Intellectual* (New York: New York University Press, 2007).

72. Richard Dyer, *White* (London: Routledge, 1997), 25.

73. Detlef Siegfried, *Time Is on My Side: Konsum und Politik in der westdeutschen Jugendkultur der 60er Jahre* (Göttingen: Wallstein Verlag, 2006), 380.

74. Sieg, *Ethnic Drag*, 25.

CHAPTER 1

1. See Patricia Pollock Brodsky, "The Black Cook as Mater Gloriosa: Grass' *Faust* Parodies in *Die Blechtrommel*," *Colloquia Germanica* 29 (1996): 235–47; Elisabeth Krimmer, "Ein Volk von Opfern? Germans as Victims in Günter Grass's *Die Blechtrommel*," *Seminar* 44, no. 2 (2008): 272–90; Siegfried Mews, *Günter Grass and His Critics: From "The Tin Drum" to "Crabwalk"* (Cambridge: Camden House), 2008; Nathalie Kónya-Jobs, "'Ist die Schwarze Köchin da?': Angst und Raum in Günter Grass' 'Die Blechtrommel,'" *Transcarpathica* 9 (2010): 249–59.

2. Barbara Becker-Cantarino, "'The Black Witch': Gender, Sexuality, and Violence in the Tin Drum," in *Approaches to Teaching Grass's "The Tin Drum*," ed. Monika Shafi (New York: Modern Language Association of America, 2008), 177.

3. The first article to revisit a reading of *The Tin Drum* with regard to Grass's autobiography is Matthias N. Lorenz, "'von Katz und Maus und mea culpa'." Uber Günter Grass' Waffen-SS-Vergangenheit und 'Die Blechtrommel' als moralische Zäsur in *Wendejahr 1959*, ed. Matthias N. Lorenz (Bielefeld: Aisthesis-Verlag, 2011), 281–305. Lorenz's main premise for discussing the two texts together is to defend Grass against accusations that he concealed his participation in the Waffen-SS so that he would be taken seriously as the moral conscience of postwar Germany. Lorenz makes two claims in defense of Grass. First of all, one could read his autobiography as a supplementary text to the *Danziger Trilogy*, and, depending on how you read *Cat and Mouse*, one could argue that Grass already confessed this part of his life in that text. Second, the Waffen-SS were by 1943 no longer volunteers. "In order to cover the need on the front, recruits liable for military service were enlisted and forcibly drafted" (285). Ulrich Bergmann argues similarly that Grass dealt with his military past in *Cat and Mouse*. See Ulrich Bergmann, ". . . und fürchte mich immer noch vor der Schwarzen Köchin," *Matrix* 36,

no. 2 (2014): 129. Gunter Pakendorf suggests reading *Peeling the Onion* as a "metatextual picaresque novel based on Grass' experiences in the period 1939–1959." Here he sees a significant influence from Grimmelshausen's *Simplicissimus*. Gunter Pakendorf, "Die gehäutete Zwiebel oder Dichtung und Wahrheit bei Günter Grass," *Acta Germanica* 35 (2007): 53–66.

4. Oskar's claim to have been born with a fully matured mental capacity is why some read the novel as an anti-bildungsroman. Mews, *Günter Grass and His Critics*, 23–26.

5. Günter Grass, *The Tin Drum*, trans. Breon Mitchell (New York: Mariner Books, 2010), 3. This text will hereafter be cited as *TD*.

6. Dagmar Herzog points out that a lot of the ideas about sex that the Nazis associated with Weimar were also ones they themselves promoted. Dagmar Herzog, *Sex after Fascism: Memory and Morality in Twentieth Century Germany* (Princeton, NJ: Princeton University Press, 2007).

7. See, for example, Oliver Kohns, "An Aesthetics of the Unbearable: The Cult of Masculinity and the Sublime in Ernst Jünger's *Der Kampf als inneres Erlebnis* (Battle as an Inner Experience)," *Image and Narrative* 14, no. 3 (2013): 141–50; Horst Nitschack, "Modernisierung als Bedrohung der Männlichkeit bei E. Jünger, J.M. Arguedas, und J.L. Borges," *Brückenschlag* (2002): 232–40; Thorsten Voss, "Schmerz und seine stoisch-heroische Kompensation als Konstrukt soldatischer Maskulinität bei Alfred de Vigny, Ernst Jünger und Céline," in *Schmerzdifferenzen: physisches Leid und Gender in kultur- und literaturwissenschaftlicher Perspektive*, ed. Iris Hermann and Anne-Rose Meyer (Königstein am Taunus: U. Helmer, 2006), 169–89.

8. David James Prickett, "The Acceleration of the Masculine in Early-Twentieth-Century Berlin," *German Life and Letters* 65, no. 1 (2012): 20.

9. Herzog, *Sex after Fascism*, 64–68.

10. This is more accurately translated as "Perhaps there may have been."

11. For example, Europeans marveled at the physical attributes of Saartije Baartman, whom they called the "Hottentot Venus," and who was exhibited in nineteenth-century *Völkerschauen*. See Brandi Wilkins Cantanese, "Remembering Saartjie Baartman," *Atlantic Studies* 7, no. 1 (2010): 47–62. Until this day, her preserved genitals, which were taken off display in 1985, still belong to the French Museum of Man. See Lusane, *Hitler's Black Victims*, 59.

12. Stacey Olster, "Inconstant Harmony in *The Tin Drum*," *Studies in the Novel* 73, no. 1 (1982): 73.

13. Olster, "Inconstant Harmony," 74.

14. Budds, *Jazz and the Germans*, 77–78.

15. Coincidentally, during Nazi dictatorship there was a "black drummer named Jimmy from South-West Africa" who performed in Berlin "as late as the summer of 1939." Kater, *Different Drummers*, 70.

16. Lusane, *Hitler's Black Victims*, 204.

17. Olster, "Inconstant Harmony," 73.

18. The term *Kolonialwarengeschäft* is simply translated into English as "grocery store."

19. Paul Kretschmer, *Wortgeographie der hochdeutschen Umgangssprache* (Göttingen: Vandenhoeck & Ruprecht, 1969), 267.

20. John Phillip Short, *Magic Lantern Empire: Colonialism and Society in Germany* (Ithaca, NY: Cornell University Press, 2012), 38.

21. Monika Albrecht understands the use of the term as evidence of that colonialism was more present in postwar German society than scholars have argued until now: "Terms like *Kolonialwarenladen* . . . were still in use in the 1950s. Apparently in the case of such phenomena we are not dealing with hard-to-understand remnants of a long-forgotten time; rather, they are signs of a presence that one still recognizes today. But they have been left widely unidentified because they are taken for granted." Monika Albrecht, *"Europa ist nicht die Welt": (Post)Kolonialismus in der Literatur und Geschichte der westdeutschen Nachkriegszeit* (Bielefeld: Aisthesis Verlag, 2008), 139.

22. German colonies prior to World War I included German Southwest Africa, German East Africa, Togo, Cameroon, Kiautschou in China, and parts of the Marshall Islands.

23. Short, *Magic Lantern Empire*, 39.

24. Walter Benjamin, "On the Mimetic Faculty," in *Walter Benjamin: Selected Writings*, ed. Howard Eiland and Michael Jennings vol. 2, pt. 2 (Cambridge, MA: Harvard University Press, 1999), 720.

25. "Until the mid-1950s, they [*Amerikahäuser*] rarely sponsored jazz events, because most American elites themselves considered jazz low culture. . . . But American popular culture found its way into East and West Germany through other channels: American soldiers; Allied radio stations, especially the American and British Forces Networks; the increasing efforts of the American movie industry to gain access to the West German market and German musicians and music fans who now shared their enthusiasm for music." Poiger, *Jazz, Rock, and Rebels*, 39. According to Timothy Schroer, however, the U.S. government did attempt to use jazz in democratizing and denazifying the Germans, but with little success. So-called Negro spirituals proved to be more popular with Germans of all ages. Schroer, *Recasting Race*, 158–63.

26. Budds, *Jazz and the Germans*, 16.

27. Poiger, *Jazz, Rock, and Rebels*, 56.

28. Poiger, *Jazz, Rock, and Rebels*, 56. An example of such an attitude is reflected in the film *Die Frühreifen* (*The Premature*, 1957), which depicts the *Halbstarke* youth culture. In the film, the bourgeois former *Halbstarke* Freddy expresses his disgust for the youth culture, comparing the teenagers' wild dancing to the primitivism of "prehistoric people." During one music sequence, his voice is heard offscreen accompanied by images of white German youth dancing erratically to drum beats, knocking over glasses and behaving in a sexual manner.

29. See Rita Chin and Heide Fehrenbach, eds., *After the Nazi Racial State: Difference and Democracy in Germany and Europe* (Ann Arbor: University of Michigan Press, 2009).

30. Siegfried, *Time Is on My Side*, 358.

31. Ben Sidran, *Black Talk* (New York: Da Capo Press, 1983), 137.

32. Theodor Adorno, "On Lyric Poetry and Society," in *Notes to Literature*, ed. Rolf Tiedemann, trans. Shierry Weber Nicholsen (New York: Columbia University Press, 1957).

33. While Sinti and Roma are not part of the African diaspora, they have sometimes

been associated with black culture because of their marginalization and Otherness. Django Reinhardt was a prominent jazz musician and Romani.

34. Schroer, *Recasting Race*, 7–8.

35. Krimmer, "Ein Volk von Opfern," 277.

36. Psychoanalysts Alexander and Margarete Mitscherlich eventually make this claim in *Die Unfähigkeit zu trauern* (*The Inability to Mourn*), published in 1967, eight years after *The Tin Drum*. The Mitscherlichs argued that white Germans were unwilling to confront the past and therefore unable to mourn. White Germans' preoccupation with industry, modernization, and building a successful economy in the postwar years made it possible for them to forget the past. In the debate that followed, some white Germans argued it was necessary to maintain a certain silence around National Socialism in order to build a functioning society (Herman Lübbe), while others believed the German public needed to come to terms with the past more explicitly and there was otherwise a danger that Germans would see themselves as victims. Klaus Pezold connects this chapter in *The Tin Drum* to the Mitscherlichs' work. Pezold, "Günter Grass' *Blechtrommel* in der Literaturgeschichte," *Germanica Wratislaviensia* 81 (1990): 11. Furthermore in *On the Natural History of Destruction* (1999), W. G. Sebald warns that if Germans are not able to discuss the pain of the firebombings during World War II, they will never be able to work through their fascist past. Nevertheless, any attempt to discuss Germans as victims of World War II, whether those killed during the firebombings or those driven out of Eastern Europe, is controversial.

37. Sidran, *Black Talk*, 37.

38. Günter Grass, *Peeling the Onion*, trans. Michael Henry Heim (Orlando, FL: Harcourt, 2007), 197. Henceforth this text is referred to as PTO.

39. Timothy Schroer also documents that Germans took note of the hypocrisy of American racism during the early postwar years and questioned how a nation with laws discriminating against blacks could be in charge of teaching them how to be more democratic and tolerant. Schroer, *Recasting Race*, 38.

40. Because Grass frequently switches between first and third person in *Peeling the Onion*, Matthias N. Lorenz refers to his writing style as *Autofiktion*: "Grass demands that the reader repeatedly question his testimony. This points out the hidden character of every anecdote-heavy memoir . . . and the style makes it obvious through the constant switch between first and third person that he is *narrating* and not just reporting facts." Lorenz, "von Katz und Maus," 287.

41. Grass's rejection of Germans' so-called inability to mourn is a reference the Mitscherlichs' *The Inability to Mourn*. Grass' portrayal of The Onion Cellar is interesting because he stresses white Germans' desire *and* ability to mourn during the immediate postwar years. Nevertheless, Oskar might help Germans come to terms with the past, but he still sees himself as a victim of Nazism. I will explore the issue of Germans seeing themselves as victims in the conclusion of this chapter.

42. Interestingly, the theme of force feeding and abusive cooks is also present in one of the few texts Grass wrote before *The Tin Drum*, namely the play *Die bösen Köche* (*The Evil Cooks*, 1956). The play is about a cook's apprentice, Vasco, who is suspected of knowing the secret recipe to a cabbage soup that a group of other cooks seeks to find out. In order to punish him, they decide to force-feed him a strange con-

coction. Günter Grass, *Die bösen Köche* in *Theaterstücke* (Neuwield: Luchterhand, 1970), 181–82.

43. See David Coury, "Transformational Considerations in the Filmic Adaptation of Günter Grass' 'Die Blechtrommel,'" *New German Review* 8 (1992): 74–84.

44. Otto Kampmüller, *Oberösterreichische Kinderspiele* (Linz: Oberösterreichischer Landesverlag in Komission, 1965), 90.

45. "Black Cook Rhyme" (K XC 75), V 9/5885, (A 114332), (1928) Deutsches Volksliedarchiv Freiburg.

46. Lotz, *Black People*. For a more recent discussion on blackface in Germany, see also Jonathan Wipplinger, "The Racial Ruse: On Blackness and Blackface Comedy in *Fin-de-Siècle* Germany," *German Quarterly* 84, no. 4 (2011): 457–76.

47. Lott, *Love and Theft*, 159.

48. Lott, *Love and Theft*, 159.

49. Annemarie Bean, James V. Hatch, and Brooks McNamara, eds., *Inside the Minstrel Mask: Readings in Nineteenth-Century Blackface Minstrelsy* (Middletown, CT: Wesleyan University Press, 1996), 165.

50. Quoted in Mews, *Günter Grass and His Critics*, 33. Likewise, Barbara Becker-Cantarino claims that the female characters in the novel are solely portrayed in an objectifying way. Becker-Cantarino, "The Black Witch," 182.

51. Gilman, *On Blackness without Blacks*, 96. Peter Martin discusses an even earlier example of the trope of the black woman as sexual threat in Grimmelshausen's *Simplicissimus* (1668). Simplicissimus encounters an Abyssinian Christian woman on an island where he is shipwrecked. Simplicissimus refers to her as a "Black Cook" because she offers to cook food for him and his companion. Grimmelshausen's Black Cook is characterized by stereotypical attributes associated with black women at the time the text was written. She is deceptive; she offers to be a slave to Simplicissimus and his traveling companion in exchange for protection. However, she soon attempts to manipulate the two men, using her sexuality to gain control. As Martin writes, "She reveals herself to be a true she-devil and spreads bloodlust and disharmony among the friends." Martin, *Schwarze Teufel, edle Mohren*, 76. Her association with the devil is underscored when Simplicissimus's act of signing the cross before a meal makes her disappear. He remarks, "Both our cook and her box disappeared, including whatever was in the aforementioned box, and she left behind her a smell so horrible that it made my comrade faint." Grimmelshausen, *Simplicissimus* (Stuttgart: Reclam, 1996), 686.

52. Dyer, *White*, 27–28.

53. Jana Husmann-Kastein also refers to the "black witch" as a common Christian figure. See Jana Husmann-Kastein, "Schwarz-Weiß. Farb- und Geschlechtssymbolik in den Anfängen der Rassenkonstruktionen," in Tißberger et al., *Weiß—Weißsein—Whiteness*, 48.

54. Becker-Cantarino, "The Black Witch," 184.

55. Becker-Cantarino, "The Black Witch," 177.

56. Peter Martin also discusses this in *Schwarze Teufel, edle Mohren*, 23–24.

57. Husmann-Kastein, "Schwarz-Weiß," 44–45.

58. Chima Oji, *Unter die Deutschen gefallen* (Wuppertal: Peter Hammer Verlag, 1992), 282.

59. Peter Unbehauen, *Daß ihr euch ja nich' schietig macht: 111 Lieder und Spiele von Hamburger Straßen und Höfen* (Hamburg: Dölling & Galitz, 2000), 105.

60. Is the Black Cook there?
No, no, no!
I have to march around three times
The fourth time I lose my head
The fifth time: come with (Frau Schmidt)
Is the Black Cook there?
Yes, yes, yes!
She's standing there
She's standing there
The cook from America!
Zisch, zisch, zisch!
"Ist die schwarze Köchin da?," *Volksliederarchiv*, http://www.volksliederar chiv.de/ist-die-schwarze-koechin-da-kreisspiel/

61. Antoinette T. Delaney, *Metaphors in Grass' "Die Blechtrommel"* (New York: Peter Lang, 2004), 119.

62. Krimmer, "Ein Volk von Opfern," 282.

63. By refusing to speak for the most of his childhood, Oskar refuses to enter the realm of the symbolic which reflects a desire to remain close to his mother. This insistence on existing in a prelingual state associates him with primitivity and an additional racist belief about blacks. See Laurence A. Rickels, *"Die Blechtrommel*: zwischen Shelmen- und Bildungsroman," *Amsterdamer Beiträge zur neueren Germanistik* 20 (1986): 115.

64. Krimmer, "Ein Volk von Opfern," 275.

65. Krimmer, "Ein Volk von Opfern," 277.

66. Lott, *Love and Theft*, 122.

67. Rickels, *"Die Blechtrommel*," 130.

68. Peter Michelsen, "Oskar oder das Monstrum: Reflexionen über die 'Blechtrommel' von Günter Grass," *Neue Rundschau* 84 (1972): 738.

69. Michelsen, "Oskar oder das Monstrum," 738.

70. In yet another variation of the nursery rhyme, the children sing of traveling to Paris and taking the Black Cook with them. "Wir reisen durch die Stadt Paris, wer reist mit? Die Köchin mit dem langen Schwanz, sie reist mit" (We travel through the city of Paris, who's coming along? The cook with the long tail, she's coming along). Deutsches Volksliedarchiv (A 114332), 1928. The reference to the cook having a tail is another example of the connection made between the cook and the devil.

71. Greta Horak, *Tiroler Kinderleben in Reim und Spiel, Volksmusik in Tirol* (Innsbruck: Innsbruck Eigenverl. d. Inst. für Tiroler Musikforschung, 1986), 65. This version from Tirol has a slightly different text. "Is the Black Cook there? No, no, no. You have to march around three times. The fourth time you lose your head, the fifth time say: you are beautiful, you are beautiful, you are most beautiful! Tell me a color! (Green) And so I put on my veil. Or (Green) Turn around, laugh, and look for a better one" (69). There are apparently also different rules to the game in the Tirolian version. The final child left

"is made fun of by everyone else and tries to catch one of the taunters. The taunter who is caught is the next Black Cook; otherwise she has to be the Black Cook again" (67).

72. Armstrong is one of several specific black musicians whose music was banned under the Nazis. He will also play a prominent role in chapter 3, for the main character of Ulrich Plenzdorf's *The New Sufferings of Young W* not only listens to "Satchmo" but likens his singing voice to his as well.

CHAPTER 2

1. Prior to writing *Die Unberatenen*, Valentin also published the novels *Hölle für Kinder* (*Hell for Children*, 1961) and *Die Fahndung* (*The Manhunt*, 1962). However, Valentin never garnered much attention from the public as a writer. *Die Unberatenen* was successful in East Germany, largely because of its intense critique of West Germany. See Michael Westdickenberg, "'Es ist zu empfehlen, dem Buch ein Nachwort über die Alternative beizugeben': Veröffentlichungsstrategien und Literaturzensur westdeutscher belletristischer Literatur in der DDR am Beispiel von Thomas Valentins Roman *Die Unberatenen*," *Internationales Archiv für Sozialgeschichte der deutschen Literatur* 28, no. 1 (2003): 88–110.

2. Daniel Rellstab, "Jugendsprache verstehen in den 1960er Jahren: Thomas Valentins Schulroman 'Die Unberatenen' (1963)," in *Kannitverstan: Bausteine zu einer nachbabylonischen Herme(neu)tik: Akten einer germanistischen Tagung vom Oktober 2012*, ed. André Schnyder (Munich: Iudicium, 2013), 404.

3. Although the city is not named in the novel, Heinz Schlüter claims the characters in the novel are modeled after residents in Lippstadt. Heinz Schlüter, ed., *Thomas-Valentin-Lesebuch* (Paderborn: Igel Verlag Literatur, 1997), 261.

4. This time shift is very fitting, considering that *Die Unberatenen* gained Valentin a reputation as the "prophet of the student unrests of 1968." Schlüter, ed., *Thomas-Valentin-Lesebuch*, 261.

5. Several historians have investigated the importance of the civil rights movement and African American struggles for the German student movement. See, for example, Martin Klimke, *The Other Alliance: Student Protest in West Germany and the United States* (Princeton, NJ: Princeton University Press, 2010) and Katharina Gerund, *Transatlantic Cultural Exchange: African American Women's Art and Activism in West Germany* (Bielefeld: Transcript, 2013).

6. According to Atina Grossmann, "The numbers reported for these rapes vary wildly, from as few as 20,000 to almost one million or even two million altogether as the Red Army pounded westward. A conservative estimate might be about 110,000 women raped, many more than once, of whom up to 10,000 died during or as a result of the assaults." Atina Grossmann, "The 'Big Rape': Sex and Sexual Violence, War, and Occupation in German Post–World War II Memory and Imagination," in *Gender and the Long Postwar: The United States and the Two Germanys, 1945–1989*, ed. Karen Hagemann and Sonya Michel (Baltimore: Johns Hopkins University Press, 2014), 31–32. Though charges of rape against American soldiers were not nearly as frequent, there are incidents of rape accusations in the American zones in southern Germany (40).

7. Hagemann and Michel, *Gender and the Long Postwar,* 5.

8. Hagemann and Michel, *Gender and the Long Postwar,* 3.

9. Erik H. Erikson, "The Problem of Ego Identity," *Journal of the American Psychoanalytic Association* 4, no. 1 (1956): 56–121.

10. Paradoxically, while the parents of *Halbstarke* viewed them as emasculated and feeble, these youths were actually wreaking havoc in the streets. Parents felt teenage violence was worsened by the screening of certain American films like *The Wild One*, *Rebel Without a Cause*, and *Blackboard Jungle*.

11. Poiger, *Jazz, Rock, and Rebels*, 89 and 172–75. Poiger quotes the West German youth magazine *Bravo*, which describes rock and roll as "rooted in the ritual music of 'Africa's Negroes'" and refers to rioting white British rock fans as "white Negroes." Poiger also notes that rock and roll icon Elvis Presley was portrayed with African American features in the German press. White Germans felt his effeminate, oversexualized hip swinging and his pronounced lips suggested he had "black blood." Rock and roll was seen as both overly aggressive and too feminine. This paradox makes complete sense when one contextualizes it in racist discourses that described black men in the same ways: at once the oversexed, violent brute and the submissive, effeminate servant. In *Bravo Amerika*, Kasper Maase argues that the negative association between black popular culture and rock and roll was just a continuation of earlier prejudices against black culture. "The culture shock since the end of the nineteenth century that had been caused by the 'American tempo,' skyscrapers, impulse-arousing dances, and 'Nigger-Jazz' had not yet been overcome." Kasper Maase, *BRAVO Amerika. Erkundungen zur Jugendkultur der Bundesrepublik in den fünfziger Jahren* (Hamburg: Junius, 1992), 11.

12. Maase, *BRAVO Amerika*, 83.

13. Jennifer Clare, "Der 'männliche' Weg zur Revolte? Andreas Baader als denkende, fühlende und handelnde Figur in retrospektiver Literatur," in *Literarische Männlichkeiten und Emotionen*, ed. Toni Tholen and Jennifer Clare (Heidelberg: Winter, 2013), 206.

14. See Slobodian, *Foreign Front.*

15. Rellstab, "Jugendsprache verstehen," 405; Hartmut Steinecke, "Nachwort," in *Die Unberatenen* (Oldenberg: Igel Verlag, 1999), 291.

16. Steinecke, "Nachwort," 291.

17. The German secondary school system is three-tiered, a system that has existed since the nineteenth century. Following elementary school, in fifth grade students go to a *Hauptschule*, a *Realschule*, or a *Gymnasium*.

18. Maase, *BRAVO Amerika*, 177.

19. Maase, *BRAVO Amerika*, 178.

20. R. C. Andrews, "The German School-Story: Some Observations on Paul Schalluck and Thomas Valentin," *German Life and Letters* 23 (1970): 107–8.

21. Thomas Valentin, *Die Unberatenen* (Oldenburg: Igel Verlag, 1999), 74. I will henceforth cite the novel as *DU*.

22. R. C. Andrews claims the title of the novel was taken from a remark in one of Franz Kafka's letters regarding his upbringing. Andrews, "German School-Story," 107.

23. A 1946 poll showed that the ratio of German men to women was 100:126. Mark Fenemore, *Sex, Thugs and Rock 'n' Roll: Teenage Rebels in Cold-War East Germany* (New York: Berghahn, 2009), 48.

24. Fenemore, *Sex, Thugs and Rock 'n' Roll*, 43. This scenario is portrayed in the film *Die Halbstarken* (1957). In *Die Halbstarken* the leader of a teenage gang, Freddy, refuses to recognize his father as the head of the family. He accuses his father of being a weak role model who is indebted to his in-laws and cannot properly provide for his family.

25. Frank Biess, "Survivors of Totalitarianism: Returning POWs and the Reconstruction of Masculine Citizenship in West Germany, 1945–1955," in *The Miracle Years: A Cultural History of West Germany, 1959–1968*, ed. Hanna Schissler (Princeton, NJ: Princeton University Press, 2001), 59–61.

26. Heinz Schlüter, *Thomas-Valentin-Lesebuch*, 261.

27. Biess, "Survivors of Totalitarianism," 63.

28. The "John Brown Song" was actually also recorded by Paul Robeson, whose spirituals were quite popular in both East and West Germany.

29. The popularity of this song in Germany is reflected in its publication in a children's songbook first published in 1974. See Martin Ketels, ed., *Liederbuch* (Ulm: J. Ebner, 1984), 84.

30. According to Michael Westdickenberg, the character of Groenewold was an "homage to an editor by the same name at Claassen Verlag," where his first three books were published. Westdickenberg, "Es ist zu empfehlen," 90.

31. Rull's suggestion that economic wealth has added to the corrupt state of West German society might echo the Mitscherlichs' claims mentioned in the last chapter.

32. The song first gained popularity in Europe when the Fisk Jubilee Singers toured there in 1873 and 1874. Paul Gilroy suggests that "the Fisk Singers have a profound historical importance because they were the first group to perform spirituals on a public platform, offering this form of black music as popular culture" (Gilroy, *Small Acts*, 88). Until then, white Europeans were mostly familiar with black popular culture through blackface minstrel performances. Those who saw the Fisk Singers considered them their first encounter with authentic Negro performers (Gilroy, *Small Acts*, 88–89). Of their private performance for Queen Victoria, Gilroy suggests that "seeing and hearing the Fisk Jubilee Singers presented liberal white British patrons an 'opportunity to feel closer to God and to redemption'" (Gilroy quoted in Paul Allen Anderson, *Deep River: Music and Memory in Harlem Renaissance Thought* [Durham, NC: Duke University Press, 2001], 21). Louis Armstrong recorded his rendition of the song in 1958.

33. Michael Rogin argues that Jewish immigrants' performance of blackface was a way for them to assimilate. They became white by participating in America's age-old pastime of representing black popular culture on the stage. Michael Rogin, *Blackface, White Noise: Jewish Immigrants in the Hollywood Melting Pot* (Berkeley: University of California Press, 1996).

34. Linda Williams, *Playing the Race Card: Melodramas of Black and White from Uncle Tom to O.J. Simpson* (Princeton, NJ: Princeton University Press, 2001), 137.

35. Slobodian, *Foreign Front*, 15. See also Richard Langston, "Roll Over Beethoven! Chuck Berry! Mick Jagger! 1960s Rock, the Myth of Progress, and the Burden of National Identity in West Germany," in *Sound Matters: Essays on the Acoustics of Modern German Culture*, ed. Nora M. Alter and Lutz Koepnick (New York: Berghahn, 2004), 183.

36. Günter Ehnert, ed., *Hit-Bilanz: deutsche Chart Singles, 1956–1980* (Norderstedt: Tarus Press, 2000).

37. In the play, the song plays again in a scene in the café where the students, and the teachers, Herr Violat and Herr Groenewald, are present.

38. Valentin, *Die Unberatenen*, 48.

39. All dialogue excerpts are based on the German-language dialogue as it is heard in the DVD release of the film (the author's translation).

40. *If* features a group of rebellious students who are referred to as "Crusaders" and who lead a bloody revolt at a British boarding school.

41. Peter Zadek, *My Way: eine Autobiographie 1926–1969* (Cologne: Kiepenheuer & Witsch, 1998), 522.

42. Esther Fischer-Homberger, "Ich bin ein Elefant, Madame," *Reformatio* 19, no. 2 (1970): 145.

43. Fischer-Homberger, "Ich bin ein Elefant," 145.

44. Fischer-Homberger, "Ich bin ein Elefant," 145.

45. Zadek, *My Way*, 468–69.

46. Zadek, *My Way*, 469.

47. In the play version of *Die Unberatenen*, Zadek does not use the motif of the "John Brown Song" or Armstrong's "Go Down Moses," but Rull still listens to jazz.

48. Joseph Vilsmaier, *Comedian Harmonists: eine Legende kehrt zurück. Der Film* (Leipzig: Gustav Kiepenheuer Verlag, 1998), 23.

49. After 1933, the Comedian Harmonists were unable to perform in Germany because its Jewish members could not become members of the national organization for musicians, the Reichsmusikkammer. Because of this hindrance, the group split, forming two new groups that continued to perform under the name Comedian Harmonists: one abroad and one in Germany. The group that remained in Germany was forced to change its name to the Meistersextett and remove from its repertoire all songs written by Jewish composers. In 1941, the Meistersextett was also banned because its music was judged unfit for supporting "den Wehrgedanken des deutschen Vokes" (the military ideas of the German people). Vilsmaier, *Comedian Harmonists*, 35.

50. Joe Harvard, *The Velvet Underground and Nico* (New York: Continuum, 2004), 1–2.

51. Langston, "Roll Over, Beethoven," 184.

52. Langston, "Roll Over, Beethoven," 184.

53. These pioneers are artists such as Bo Diddley, Chuck Berry, and Little Richard. In the volume *Cross the Water Blues*, several essays discuss the influence of blues on British rock and roll bands of the 1960s. See Neil A. Wynn, ed., *Cross the Water Blues: African American Music in Europe* (Jackson: University of Mississippi Press, 2007).

54. Mailer, *The White Negro*, 4.

55. Albin Zak and Albin Zak III, *The Velvet Underground Companion: Four Decades of Commentary* (New York: Schirmer Trade Books, 2000), 186.

56. Zak and Zak, *The Velvet Underground Companion*, 164.

57. Kobena Mercer, "Skin Head Sex Thing: Racial Difference and the Homoerotic Imaginary," in *Masculine Studies Reader*, ed. Rachel Adams and David Savran (Malden, MA: Blackwell, 2002), 197.

58. The black drug pusher has long been a mythological figure of cool for white Americans. See Eithne Quinn, "'Tryin' to Get Over': *Super Fly*, Black Politics, and Post-Civil Rights Film Enterprise," *Cinema Journal* 49, no. 2 (2010): 86–105.

59. Richard Witts, *The Velvet Underground* (Bloomington: Indiana University Press, 2006), 46.

60. See Rupert Till, "The Blues Blueprint: The Blues in the Music of the Beatles, the Rolling Stones, and Led Zepplin," in Wynn, *Cross the Water Blues*, 183–201.

61. For more information on the British explosion and black music see Rupert Till and Leighton Grist's essays in Wynn, *Cross the Water Blues*.

62. Clinton Heylin, ed., *All Yesterdays' Parties: The Velvet Underground in Print: 1966–1971* (Cambridge, MA: Da Capo Press, 2005), xiv–xvi.

63. Harvard, *The Velvet Underground*, 1–2.

64. See *Nico Icon*, dir. Susanne Ofteringer, Bluehorse Films, 1995.

65. Witts, *Velvet Underground*, 38.

66. Jon Stratton, "Jews, Punk and the Holocaust: From the Velvet Underground to the Ramones—the Jewish-American Story," *Popular Music* 24, no. 1 (2005): 96.

67. Erikson, "The Problem of Ego Identity," 86.

68. Witts, *Velvet Underground*, 49.

69. Zadek, *My Way*, 473–74.

70. Valentin, *Die Unberatenen*, 284.

71. Gustav Ernst, *Sprache im Film* (Vienna: Wespennest, 1994), 41.

72. Erik H. Erikson, "Reflections on the Dissent of Contemporary Youth," *International Journal of Psycho-Analysis* 51, no. 11 (1970): 12.

73. Erikson, "Reflections on Dissent," 13.

74. Barbara Kosta, "*Väterliteratur*, Masculinity, and History: The Melancholic Texts of the 1980s," in *Conceptions of Postwar German Masculinity*, ed. Roy Jerome (Albany: State University of New York Press, 2001), 225.

CHAPTER 3

1. Reiner Kunze, *Die wunderbaren Jahre: Lyrik, Prosa, Dokumente*, ed. Karl Corino (Frankfurt am Main: Büchergilde Gutenberg, 1978), 206.

2. For the reception of Richard Hildreth's abolitionist novel *The White Slave* (1852) in East Germany see Heike Paul, "Cultural Mobility between Boston and Berlin: How Germans Have Read and Reread Narratives of American Slavery," in *Cultural Mobility: A Manifesto*, ed. Stephen Greenblatt (Cambridge: Cambridge University Press, 2005), 122–71. For more information on African American theater in East Germany see Astrid Haas, "A Raisin in the East: African American Civil Rights Drama in GDR Scholarship and Theater Practice," in *Germans and African Americans: Two Centuries of Exchange*, ed. Larry Greene and Anke Ortlepp (Jackson: University Press of Mississippi, 2010), 166–84. For more information on the *Indianerfilme* see Gerd Gemünden, "Between Karl May and Karl Marx: The DEFA Indianerfilme," in *Germans and Indians: Fantasies, Encounters, Projections*, ed. Gerd Gemünden, Colin G. Calloway, and Susanne Zantop (Lincoln: University of Nebraska Press, 2002), 243–56.

3. Among those African Americans who were championed in the GDR were Paul Robeson, W. E. B. Du Bois, Martin Luther King Jr., and Angela Davis. The campaign on Angela Davis's behalf while she was still imprisoned in 1971 ranged from a rally of seven hundred students from Humboldt University and a celebration honoring her

twenty-seventh birthday with two thousand Berliners in attendance, to having school-children write solidarity postcards to her and protest letters to President Richard Nixon and California governor Ronald Reagan. Maria Höhn and Martin Klimke, *A Breath of Freedom: The Civil Rights Struggle, African American GIs and Germany* (New York: Palgrave Macmillan, 2010), 134–35. Sara Lennox also writes about how African American literature was promoted in East Germany in her essay "Reading Transnationally."

4. Quinn Slobodian, "Socialist Chromatism: Race, Racism, and the Racial Rainbow in East Germany," in *Comrades of Color: East Germany in the Cold War World*, ed. Quinn Slobodian (New York: Berghahn, 2015), 25–26.

5. Slobodian, "Socialist Chromatism," 27. Slobodian refers to the visual representation of race in East Germany as "socialist chromatism," suggesting that although many colors were represented, "the white man appeared as the first among equals" (23).

6. For more general information on East German policies toward foreign workers see Deniz Göktürk, David Gramling, and Anton Kaes, eds., *Germany in Transit: Nation and Migration, 1955–2005* (Berkeley: University of California Press, 2007) and Peggy Piesche, "Black and German? East German Adolescents before 1989: A Retrospective View of a 'Non-existent Issue' in the GDR," in *The Cultural After-Life of East Germany: New Transnational Perspectives*, ed. Leslie A. Adelson (Washington, DC: American Institute for Contemporary German Studies, 2002), 38. Piesche lists the few academic studies that have been published on the topic of blacks in East Germany.

7. See, for example, the documentary about Namibian children who spent their childhoods in East German orphanages during Namibia's war with South Africa, *Omulaule heißt schwarz* directed by Beatrice Möller, Nicola Hens, and Susanne Radelhof. For information on the interaction between East Germans and foreign workers see Mike Dennis and Norman LaPorte, *State and Minorities in Communist East Germany* (New York: Berghahn, 2011), 87–123.

8. Höhn and Klimke, *Breath of Freedom*, 127.

9. Quoted in Slobodian, "Socialist Chromatism," 32.

10. Slobodian, "Socialist Chromatism," 31.

11. Piesche, "Black and German," 39. Piesche also notes differences between East German policies toward African students and African workers. Students were more likely admitted to East German universities if their home countries "lean[ed] towards a Western market-based economy" because they could pay with foreign currency, more specifically U.S. dollars. In contrast, "The GDR bore all related costs for workers from socialist countries, which could be used for propaganda purposes as an expression of solidarity" (41). An example of racist government policies is that in the cases of female workers from Cuba, Vietnam, Mozambique, and Zambia, if they happened to become pregnant during their stay in the GDR, they would be immediately deported, a passage that was not revoked until 1989 (42).

12. Höhn and Klimke, *Breath of Freedom*, 141.

13. The SED was the Sozialistische Einheitspartei (Socialist Unity Party), the sole ruling party throughout the GDR's forty-year existence.

14. Höhn and Klimke, *Breath of Freedom*, 141.

15. Fenemore, *Sex, Thugs and Rock 'n' Roll*, 100.

16. Fenemore, *Sex, Thugs and Rock 'n' Roll*, 102.

17. Fenemore, *Sex, Thugs and Rock 'n' Roll*, 184.

18. The GDR even boasted that its army uniform was based on Prussian tradition, while the Bundeswehr modeled its uniforms after "alien" American culture. Fenemore, *Sex, Thugs and Rock 'n' Roll*, 186.

19. Fenemore, *Sex, Thugs and Rock 'n' Roll*, 195.

20. Fenemore, *Sex, Thugs and Rock 'n' Roll*, 127.

21. Holger Brandes, "Hegemonic Masculinities in East and West Germany (German Democratic Republic and Federal Republic of Germany)," *Men and Masculinities* 10, no. 2 (2007): 182.

22. Brandes, "Hegemonic Masculinities," 190.

23. Heike Trappe, Rachel A. Rosenfeld, and Janet C. Gornick, "Gender and Work in Germany: Before and after Reunification," *Annual Review of Sociology* 30 (2004): 103–24.

24. Fenemore, *Sex, Thugs and Rock 'n' Roll*, 45.

25. Brandes, "Hegemonic Masculinities," 188–89.

26. Fenemore, *Sex, Thugs and Rock 'n' Roll*, 123.

27. Fenemore, *Sex, Thugs and Rock 'n' Roll*, 136.

28. Fenemore, *Sex, Thugs and Rock 'n' Roll*, 139.

29. Poiger, *Jazz, Rock, and Rebels*, 158.

30. Michael Rauhut, "Lass es bluten: Blues-Diskurse in West und Ost," in *Ich hab' den Blues schon etwas länger: Spuren einer Musik in Deutschland*, ed. Michael Rauhut and Reinhart Lorenz (Berlin: Christoph Links Verlag, 2008), 108.

31. Rauhut, "Lass es bluten," 116–17.

32. Detlef Siegfried, "Authentisch schwarz: Blues in der Gegenkultur um 1970," in Rauhut and Lorenz, *Ich hab' den Blues*, 217.

33. Rauhut, "Lass es bluten," 121.

34. Ulrich Plenzdorf, *The New Sufferings of Young W*, trans. Kenneth P. Wilcox (Long Grove, IL: Waveland Press, 1996), 13. This will be referred to as *NS*.

35. As for the title of this section: Plenzdorf's protagonist Edgar enjoys listening to the Modern Soul Band, an East German jazz and soul band. One of their hits was "Child of Bitterfeld." Mittenberg is Edgar's fictional hometown.

36. D. G. John, "Ulrich Plenzdorf's *Die neuen Leiden des jungen W.*: The Death of a Fool," *Modern Drama* 23 (1980): 34.

37. Peter Hutchinson, "Plenzdorf, *Die neuen Leiden des jungen W.*," in *Landmarks in the German Novel*, ed. Peter Hutchinson and Michael Minden (Bern: Peter Lang, 2010), 64.

38. John, "Ulrich Plenzdorf's *Die neuen Leiden*," 34.

39. Hutchinson, "Plenzdorf," 63.

40. Hutchinson, "Plenzdorf," 68.

41. Plenzdorf quoted in Susan E. Hunnicutt, "'The Werther-Pistol Killed Me!' Understanding Ulrich Plenzdorf's Novel Die neuen Leiden des jungen W. as a Cult Book," *Focus on Literatur* 5, no. 1 (1998): 19.

42. Ute Brandes and Ann Clark Fehn, "Werther's Children: The Experience of the Second Generation in Ulrich Plenzdorf's Die neuen Leiden des jungen W. and Volker Braun's 'Unvollendete Geschichte,'" *German Quarterly* 56, no. 4 (1983): 622 n. 15.

43. Brandes and Fehn, "Werther's Children," 619.

44. Barbara Currie, "Diverging Attitudes in Literary Criticism: The 'Plenzdorf Debate' in the Early 1970s in East and West Germany," *Neophilologus* 79, no. 2 (1995): 288.

45. Hutchinson, "Plenzdorf," 63.

46. Hunnicutt, "Werther-Pistol Killed Me," 20.

47. There was a close link between the East German blues scene and a culture of wayfarers. See Michael Rauhut and Thomas Kochan, eds., *Bye Bye, Lübben City: Bluesfreaks, Tramps und Hippies in der DDR* (Berlin: Schwarzkopf & Schwarzkopf, 2004).

48. Karl von Eckartshausen, "Isogin und Celia, eine Geschichte von einem unsrer schwarzen Brüder aus Afrika, von einem Mohren (1787)," in *Die edlen Wilden: Die Verklärung von Indianern, Negern und Südseeinsulanern auf dem Hintergrund der kolonialen Greuel. vom 16. bis zum 20. Jahrhundert*, ed. Gerd Stein (Frankfurt am Main: Fischer, 1984), 157.

49. Mailer, *The White Negro*, 2.

50. In *On the Road*, Jack Kerouac writes, "[I wish] I were a Negro, feeling that the best the white world had offered was not enough ecstasy for me, not enough life, joy, kicks, darkness, music, not enough night." Quoted in Penny Vlagopoulos, "Rewriting America: Kerouac's Nation of *Underground Monsters*," in *On the Road: The Original Scroll*, ed. Howard Cunnel (New York: Viking, 2007), 59.

51. Hutchinson, "Plenzdorf," 70.

52. Hutchinson, "Plenzdorf," 70.

53. In one scene, Edgar watches a film at school that is clearly propaganda for the military. Edgar confronts the director about making such persuasive films that are not entertaining. The director, with whom Edgar speaks, is actually supposed to be Plenzdorf. This was Plenzdorf's way of criticizing artists who conform to the censor's rules, himself included.

54. In the film, Edgar's father confesses to Charlie that he was once a painter but stopped after he left Edgar and his mother.

55. Barner quoted in Slavija Kabić and Eldi Grubišić Pulišelić, "'Ich Idiot wollte immer der Sieger sein': Der Anti-Held Edgar Wibeau aus Ulrich Plenzdorfs Erzählung Die neuen Leiden des jungen W.," *Zagreber Germanistische Beiträge: Jahrbuch für Literatur- und Sprachwissenschaft* 16 (2007): 53.

56. While in Plenzdorf's text Edgar primarily listens to blues, in the film he alternately listens to blues, contemporary rock (Santana, Cat Stevens, and Iron Butterfly) and 1950s rock and roll.

57. Kabić and Pulišelić, "Ich Idiot wollte," 65.

58. Frank Schäfer et al., eds., *Kultbücher: von "Schatzinsel" bis "Pooh's Corner": eine Auswahl* (Berlin: Schwarzkopf & Schwarzkopf, 2000), 96. MSB eventually became the well-known East German band Die Puhdys, for whom Plenzdorf wrote the songs "Geh zu ihr" ("Go to Her") and "Wenn ein Mensch lebt" ("If a Person Lives"), which were both featured in *The Legend of Paul and Paula*.

59. Currie, "Diverging Attitudes," 286.

60. Siegfried, "Authentisch schwarz," 221–22. See also Siegfried, *Time Is on My Side*, 366–67.

61. In the film this scene proceeds slightly differently. While they are still in the

boat, Charlie lays her head on Edgar's shoulder. Then she begins kissing him. During the boat trip, nondiegetic drumming is heard and intensifies when Charlie kisses Edgar. The director's use of the drumming in this scene suggests a link between drumming, carnal desire, and Edgar, which relates well to Edgar's subsequent comparison between the experience of kissing Charlie and a black man who kisses his first white woman.

62. Interestingly, in the film Edgar does not correct himself; rather he unapologetically uses the word "Neger."

63. Frantz Fanon, *Black Skin, White Masks*, translated by Charles Lam Markmann (New York: Grove Press, 1967), 45.

64. The film takes things a bit further, implying sex between Edgar and Charlie. After relieving herself on the island, Charlie asks Edgar if he wants to go skinny-dipping. He agrees and the two strip down and slowly walk toward each other. This scene cuts to the camera panning across the forest, before settling on a half-naked Edgar and a fully clothed Charlie lying next to each other in the grass. The pastoral setting and the rain have a biblical effect, linking the two to Adam and Eve. This scene may be shot from the naive perspective of Edgar, who at the time believes he has a future with Charlie.

65. Hunnicutt, "Werther-Pistol Killed Me," 23.

66. Georg Kaiser, "From Morning to Midnight," in *German Expressionist Plays*, ed. Ernst Schürner (New York: Continuum, 2002), 197.

67. Kaiser, "From Morning to Midnight," 197.

68. The quotation in the title of this section is what Schultze's friend Manfred says when the two contemplate how to react to their forced retirement.

69. The GDR's economic stability in the 1970s made it possible for the government to roll back restrictions pertaining to the arts. Currie, "Diverging Attitudes," 283.

70. Annette Erler, "Von Spielmannszügen und Bergsängern im Harz: Musikalische Aktivitäten in einer geteilten Region," in *Musikalische Volkskultur als soziale Chance: Laienmusik und Singtradition als sozialintegratives Feld. Tagungsbericht Hildesheim 94 der Kommission für Lied-, Musik- und Tanzforschung in der Deutschen Gesellschaft für Volkskunde*, ed. Günther Noll and Helga Stein (Essen: Verlag die blaue Eule, 1996), 341.

71. All dialogue excerpts are based on the German-language dialogue as it is heard in the DVD release of the film (based on subtitles and the author's translation).

72. Robert Pirro, "Tragedy, Surrogation and the Significance of African-American Culture in Postunification Germany: An Interpretation of *Schultze Gets the Blues*," *German Politics and Society* 26, no. 88 (2008): 69.

73. Emily Hauze, "Keyed Fantasies: Music, the Accordion and the American Dream in *Stroszek* and *Schultze Gets the Blues*," *German Life and Letters* 62, no. 1 (2009): 93.

74. Teutschenthal has held competitive motocross competitions since 1966.

75. Pirro claims that "periodic episodes of labored breathing and coughing depicted throughout the film suggest the cause of [Schultze's] death is congestive heart failure." Pirro, "Tragedy, Surrogation and the Significance," 70. However, as Emily Hauze rightly suggests, Schultze's reaction to this news report leads one to believe that he has lung cancer, or fears he does.

76. Martin Stokes, "Introduction: Ethnicity, Identity and Music," in *Ethnicity, Identity and Music*, ed. Martin Stokes (Oxford: Berg, 1994), 12.

77. Philip V. Bohlman, "Landscape—Region—Nation—Reich: German Folk Song in the Nexus of National Identity," in *Music and German National Identity*, ed. Celia Applegate and Pamela Potter (Chicago: University of Chicago Press, 2002), 108.

78. Bruce Campbell, "*Kein schöner Land*: The Spielschar Ekkehard and the Struggle to Define German National Identity in the Weimar Republic," in Applegate and Potter, *Music and German National Identity*, 128.

79. Pirro, "Tragedy, Surrogation and the Significance," 70.

80. Bohlman, "Landscape—Region—Nation," 110.

81. Campbell, "*Kein schöner Land*," 139.

82. Erler, "Von Spielmannszügen und Bergsängern im Harz," 347.

83. Erler, "Von Spielmannszügen und Bergsängern im Harz," 362.

84. This was the major form of agricultural collective in the GDR.

85. Schroer, *Recasting Race*, 7.

86. Martin, *Schwarze Teufel, edle Mohren*, 85.

87. Martin, *Schwarze Teufel, edle Mohren*, 83.

88. Hauze, "Keyed Fantasies," 84.

89. One claim about the word "zydeco" is that it is merely the Creole pronunciation of the French word for snap beans, *les haricots*, and that the first zydeco song had to do with expressing frustration over poverty and the lack of money to buy meat to add to a pot of beans. Hence a common line in Zydeco tunes, "The beans aren't salty." Hauze reiterates this myth as the origin of the name. "Keyed Fantasies," 92. According to Michael Tisserand, however, "For black Creoles in Louisiana, the word 'zydeco' may have a similar blended history, resulting from the French *les haricots* converging with words from several languages of West African tribes, including the Yula, where *a zaré* means 'I dance.' Support for this theory, which was put forth in 1986 by folklorist Nicholas Spitzer, and further developed by Barry Ancelet in his essay 'Zydeco/Zarico: The Term and the Tradition,' can be found in the remarkable existence of some musical cousins to zydeco located on a number of Indian Ocean islands, especially Rodrigues. . . . A dance called *séga* includes a pantomime of the planting of beans. . . . Ancelet reports that the traditional *séga* connects beans, fertility, and sex in a symbolic dance." Michael Tisserand, *The Kingdom of Zydeco* (New York: Arcade Publishing, 1998), 17.

90. Pirro, "Tragedy, Surrogation and the Significance," 77.

91. Chester Rosson, "Some Thoughts on the Survival of German Music in Texas," in *Musikalische Volkskultur als soziale Chance*, ed. Günther Noll (Essen: Die blaue Eule, 1996), 161.

92. Rosson, "Survival of German Music," 163.

93. Hauze, "Keyed Fantasies," 95.

94. Rauhut, "Lass es bluten," 15. Peter Wicke, "Die Leiden des weißen Mannes: Konstruktionen von Authenzität in der Geschichte des Blues," in Rauhut and Lorenz, *Ich hab' den Blues*, 243–53.

95. Middleton quoted in Wicke, "Die Leiden des weißen Mannes," 249.

96. Middleton quoted in Wicke, "Die Leiden des weißen Mannes," 249.

97. Wicke, "Die Leiden des weißen Mannes," 244.

98. Siegfried, "Authentisch schwarz," 390 n. 9.

99. Hendrix quoted in Siegfried, "Authentisch schwarz," 226.

100. Amiri Baraka, *Blues People: Negro Music in White America* (New York: Harper Perennial, 2002), 61.
101. Baraka, *Blues People*, 61.
102. Baraka, *Blues People*, 51.
103. Baraka, *Blues People*, 64.
104. Baraka, *Blues People*, 54–55.
105. Baraka, *Blues People*, 55.
106. Baraka, *Blues People*, 64.
107. Pirro, "Tragedy, Surrogation," 78.
108. Pirro, "Tragedy, Surrogation," 82.

CHAPTER 4

1. Saul Austerlitz, "DJ Darky's Deutschland Daze," *Village Voice*, July 9, 2008.
2. Höhn and Klimke, *Breath of Freedom*, 83.
3. Werner Sollors, *The Temptation of Despair: Tales of the 1940s* (Cambridge, MA: Harvard University Press, 2014), 191.
4. Mark Anthony Neal uses the term "postsoul" to describe "political, social, and cultural experiences of the African-American community since the end of the civil rights and Black Power movements." Mark Anthony Neal, *Soul Babies: Black Popular Culture and the Post-soul Aesthetic* (New York: Routledge, 2002), 3.
5. Mark Anthony Neal, *What the Music Said: Black Popular Music and Black Public Culture* (New York: Routledge, 1999), 105.
6. Paul Beatty, *Slumberland* (New York: Bloomsbury, 2008), 43. The text will be here forth quoted as *SL*.
7. The term "crossover" designates music that appeals to black and white audiences.
8. Alice Echols, *Shaky Ground: The '60s and Its Aftershocks* (New York: Columbia University Press, 2002), 166–67.
9. Neal, *What the Music Said*, 62.
10. Trey Ellis, "The New Black Aesthetic," *Callaloo* 38 (1989): 235.
11. Richard Dyer remarks that tanning is usually associated with healthiness, "the outdoor life, fresh air, exercise," and leisure. He suggests that the desire to tan demonstrates white people's disposition for incorporating "into themselves features of other peoples." Dyer, *White*, 49. The association between tanning and visiting exotic lands is exemplified in the coupon Ferguson uses at the salon, which features "a glossy aerial photo of a Caribbean coastline" and the different tanning specials "*Malibu, Waikiki,* or *Ibiza*" (*SL* 4).
12. Höhn and Klimke reported that many black GIs criticized the army's practice of tokenism. As one soldier remarks, "Whenever we got a parade or something, you got the black man out front to show equal rights of man or something. It's bullshit." Höhn and Klimke, *Breath of Freedom*, 147.
13. In fact, while first studying abroad in Germany in 2001, I was equally shocked to see this used as a legitimate musical category.

14. This title of this section is a play on the slogan of German unification, "Wir sind ein Volk" (We are one people).

15. Even today, East Germans feel they are openly discriminated against. In 2006, the first case to be tried under Germany's new antidiscrimination law, which was ratified in 2005, involved a white East German woman who claimed she was turned down for a position because she was an "Ossi." "Ossi" is a degrading term for an East German. When the woman received her application back, she observed that the company had written "kein Ossi" (No Easterner) on her papers. The Stuttgart Labor Court ruled against her, reasoning that East Germans are not a separate ethnicity and therefore could not use the General Equal Treatment Act in such cases. "Frau erhält Jobabsage wegen 'Ossi'-Herkunft," *Der Spiegel*, April 8, 2010, http://www.spiegel.de/wirtschaft/soziales/0,1518,687929,00.html

16. George Blaustein, "Flight to Germany: Paul Beatty, the Color Line, and the Berlin Wall," *Amerikastudien* 55, no. 4 (2010): 730.

17. Elisa Schweinfurth, "'They looked German, Albeit with Even Tighter Pants and Uglier Shoes, but There Was Something Different about Them': The Function of East and West Germany and the Fall of the Berlin Wall in Paul Beatty's *Slumberland*," *COPAS: Current Objectives of Postgraduate American Studies* 11 (2010), http://copas.uniregensburg.de/article/view/123/147

18. With the phrase "touch tales," I am borrowing the language Leslie Adelson used to describe how German, Turkish, and Jewish histories and narratives intersect in the work of Turkish German authors. See Leslie Adelson, *The Turkish Turn in Contemporary German Literature: Toward a New Critical Grammar of Migration* (New York: Palgrave Macmillan, 2005).

19. See Damani Partridge, *Hypersexuality and Headscarves: Race, Sex and Citizenship in the New Germany* (Bloomington: Indiana University Press, 2012), 17–19.

20. May Ayim, "The Year 1990: Homeland and Unity from a Black German Perspective," in Göktürk, Gramling, and Kaes, *Germany in Transit*, 126–28.

21. L. H. Stallings, "Sampling the Sonics of Sex (Funk) in Paul Beatty's *Slumberland*," in *Contemporary African American Literature: The Living Canon*, ed. Lovalerie King and Shirley Moody-Turner (Bloomington: Indiana University Press, 2013), 204.

22. The title of this section is taken from a photomontage by Marc Brandenburg entitled *Punk and Circumstance along the Yellow Brick Road*. Brandenburg is a black German artist, born in Berlin in 1965 to a white German mother and an African American father who was stationed in Germany. He spent his childhood in Texas with his parents; however, when they divorced in 1977, he returned to Berlin with his mother. In the late 1970s, he was involved in Berlin's punk scene. And during the 1990s, when he lived in London, he became involved with the group Young British Artists (YBAs). He is currently based in Berlin. Jürgen Heinrichs, "Mixed Media, Mixed Identities: The Universal Aesthetics of Marc Brandenburg," in *From Black to Schwarz: Cultural Crossovers between African America and Germany*, ed. Maria I. Diedrich and Jürgen Heinrichs (Münster: LIT Verlag, 2010), 309–31.

23. In Spike Lee's film of the musical's final performance at the Belasco Theater on July 20, 2008, in the final scenes of the musical Stewart's wardrobe mirrors that of

Youth's, which further suggests the musical can be read as Stewart's reflections on his younger self.

24. Mark Stewart, *Passing Strange: The Complete Book and Lyrics of the Broadway Musical* (New York: Applause Theatre and Cinema Books, 2008), 2. The text will be henceforth referred to as *PS*.

25. Brandon Woolf, "Negotiating the 'Negro Problem': Stew's Passing (Made) Strange," *Theater Journal* 62, no. 2 (2010): 194.

26. Neal, *Soul Babies*, 9.

27. There is a suggestion that Mr. Franklin might be hiding his homosexuality when during his monologue to Youth about the freedoms of Europe, he makes a reference to James Baldwin's *Giovanni's Room*.

28. Mark Anthony Neal argues that black soul artists' "willingness to use their 'sacred' [musical] gifts in the service of the secular desires" is what made them the target of black middle-class critique. Neal, *Soul Babies*, 15. Youth's choices of punk over spirituals and his garage band over the church choir can be understood in relation to this history. In *Soul Babies*, Neal relates Al Green's description of the pain he experienced "of having the choice between lifting up your voice for God or taking a bow for your third encore" (16). This pain is articulated throughout *Passing Strange*.

29. Woolf, "Negotiating the Negro Problem," 202.

30. Woolf, "Negotiating the Negro Problem," 202.

31. Stephen Lamb and Anthony Phelan, "Weimar Culture: The Birth of Modernism," in *German Cultural Studies: An Introduction*, ed. Rob Burns (Oxford: Oxford University Press, 1995), 76.

32. Jean Baudrillard, *Simulations*, trans. Paul Foss, Paul Patton, and Philip Beitchman (New York: Semiotext(e), 1983), 2.

33. Baudrillard, *Simulations*, 5.

34. Baudrillard, *Simulations*, 50.

35. Baudrillard, *Simulations*, 50.

36. Tobias Nagl, *Die unheimliche Maschine: Rasse und Repräsentation im Weimarer Kino* (Munich: Edition Text und Kritik, 2009), 9–10.

37. Stiftung der Geschichte der Bundesrepublik in Deutschland und Bundeszentrale für politische Bildung, *Rock! Jugend und Musik in Deutschland* (Berlin: Ch. Links Verlag, 2005), 63.

38. If one recalls Richard Langston's arguments in chapter 2, it would have been unthinkable for the '68 generation to *prefer* German-language songs. In the late 1960s, Anglophone music and lyrics were embraced as revolutionary, in part because they were not German. Music by black artists, in particular soul, brought white Germans closer to their African American brothers and sisters who were struggling for civil rights. Thus, the German new wave's turn away from English and embrace of the German language is a direct reaction to previous musical developments.

39. Ferguson claims the jukebox he programs in Berlin does not have hip-hop because it does not fit the mood of a bar or a café. Hip-hop needs "spatial intimacy with the listener" (*SL* 87) and is best heard on headphones or in the privacy of one's room.

40. Höhn and Klimke address these views in chapter 6 of *A Breath of Freedom*.

41. This song is set to the music of "One" from the musical *A Chorus Line* (1975);

this underlines the connections between Youth's performance, cabaret, and Berlin's historical underground cultures reaching back to the 1920s.

42. David F. Krugler, *The Voice of America and the Domestic Propaganda Battles, 1945–1953* (Columbia: University of Missouri Press, 2000), 1.

43. Krugler, *The Voice of America*, 1.

44. According to Baudrillard, anthropology is the death of a "tribe" because it seeks to preserve people and culture and artificially shelter culture from modern influences. One could equate this practice with the white jazz fan's desire to "mummify" the genre and keep it from evolving in order for it to remain "authentic." See Krin Gabbard, *Black Magic: White Hollywood and African American Culture* (New Brunswick, NJ: Rutgers University Press, 2004).

45. bell hooks, *Outlaw Culture: Resisting Representations* (New York: Routledge, 2006), 152.

46. Woolf, "Negotiating the Negro Problem," 194.

47. Woolf, "Negotiating the Negro Problem," 195.

48. Stallings, "Sampling the Sonics, 191.

49. Piesche, "Black and German," 39.

50. Piesche, "Black and German," 45.

51. Ayim, born in Hamburg in 1960, wrote both poetry and essays that addressed racism in Germany. She committed suicide in 1996.

52. Charles Taylor, ed., *Multiculturalism: Examining the Politics of Recognition* (Princeton, NJ: Princeton University Press, 1994), 64.

53. Stallings, "Sampling the Sonics," 197.

54. Christian Schmidt, "Dissimulating Blackness: The Degenerative Satires of Paul Beatty and Percival Everett," in *Post-soul Satire: Black Identity after Civil Rights*, ed. Derek C. Maus and James J. Donahue (Jackson: University of Mississippi Press, 2014), 158.

55. Beatty purposely uses the awkward formulation "today morning" in order to mimic the kinds of mistakes a German speaking English might make. In this case, "today morning" would be a direct translation of the German *Heute morgen*.

56. Stallings, "Sampling the Sonics," 192.

57. Amy Robinson, "It Takes One to Know One: Passing and Communities of Common Interest," *Critical Inquiry* 20, no. 4 (1994): 723.

58. Robinson, "It Takes One," 721–22.

59. bell hooks, *Yearning: Race, Gender and Cultural Politics* (New York: Routledge, 2015), 28.

60. "As a discursive practice [postmodernism] is dominated primarily by the voices of white male intellectuals and/or academic elites who speak to and about one another with coded familiarity" (hooks, *Yearning*, 24).

61. Robinson, "It Takes One," 735.

62. Baudrillard, *Simulations*, 39.

63. Heinrichs, "Mixed Media," 324.

64. Heinrichs, "Mixed Media," 325.

65. See Michel de Certeau, *The Practice of Everyday Life*, trans. Steven Rendall (Berkeley: University of California Press, 1984).

66. Stallings, "Sampling the Sonics," 202.

CHAPTER 5

1. Hans Belting, "Interview: 5. Februar 1999 / February 5, 1999," in *Marcel Odenbach: ach, wie gut, daß niemand weiß*, ed. Udo Kittlemann (Cologne: Verlag der Buchhalter Walther König, 1999), 54.

2. Three texts that address white German '68ers' unique interest in African American politics and culture are Moritz Ege's *Schwarz werden*; Katharina Gerund's *Transatlantic Cultural Exchange*; and Nils Seibert, *Vergessene Proteste: Internationalismus und Antirassismus 1964–1983* (Münster: Unrast, 2008).

3. The term "Afro-Deutsch" was coined by African American feminist author Audre Lorde together with black German women when she taught a poetry workshop in English at the Freie Universität in Berlin in the spring of 1984. In the foreword to *Showing Our Colors*, a foundational text for documenting the history and experience of black Germans, Lorde explains the term as a positive label that unites black Germans with other "hyphenated people of the Diaspora." Audre Lorde, foreword to *Showing Our Colors: Afro-German Women Speak Out*, ed. Katharina Oguntoye, May Opitz, and Dagmar Schultz (Amherst: University of Massachusetts Press, 1992), viii. Another term that came into use during this time was *schwarze Deutsche*, or black Germans, such as in the name of the organization Initiative Schwarze Deutsche (Initiative of Black Germans), founded in 1986. Today, some are critical of the term "Afro-German" because it is often used to designate people with one white German parent and one parent who is either African, African American, Afro-European, or Caribbean. "Black German" is meant to refer to a broad community that also incorporates people with two black parents, as well as non-German citizens. I have decided to use the term "black German" exclusively because of its inclusivity.

4. Fatima El-Tayeb, "'If You Can't Pronounce My Name, You Can Just Call Me Pride': Black German Activism, Gender and Hip Hop," *Gender History* 15, no. 3 (2003): 460–86.

5. Gruber is a black German born in 1952 to a white German mother and an African American soldier who, at the time of Timm's interview, sent him 150 DM per month. Karin Timm and DuRell Echols, *Schwarze in Deutschland: Protokolle* (Munich: Piper & Co. Verlag, 1973), 120.

6. See El-Tayeb, "If You Can't"; Alexander Weheliye, "My Volk to Come: Peoplehood in Recent Diaspora Discourse and Black German Popular Music," in *Black Europe and the African Diaspora*, ed. Darlene Hine Clark, Trica Danielle Keaton, and Stephen Small (Urbana: University of Illinois Press, 2009), 161–79; and Alexander Weheliye, *Phonographies: Grooves in Sonic Afro-Modernity* (Durham, NC: Duke University Press, 2005).

7. According to Jaqueline Nassy Brown, diasporic resources "may include not just cultural productions such as music, but also people and places, as well as iconography, ideas, and ideologies associated with them." Brown, "Black Liverpool," 298.

8. El-Tayeb, "If You Can't," 461.

9. Massaquoi's father, Al-Haj Massaquoi, was the son of Liberian ambassador Momulu Massaquoi. Michael's father was Theophilius Wonja Michael, a Cameroonian performer who frequented circuses and *Völkerschauen*.

10. Aija Poikane-Daumke, *African Diasporas: Black German Literature in the Context of the African American Experience* (Berlin: LIT Verlag, 2006), 64.

11. The Jungvolk was an organization for boys aged ten to fourteen within the larger organization of the Hitler Youth.

12. Theodor Michael, *Deutsch sein und schwarz dazu: Erinnerungen eines Afro-Deutschen* (Munich: Deutscher Taschenbuchverlag, 2013), 41.

13. Hans Jürgen Massaquoi, *Destined to Witness: Growing up Black in Nazi Germany* (New York: Perennial, 1999), 114.

14. Wright, "Others-from-Within."

15. Muniz de Faria, *Zwischen Fürsorge und Ausgrenzung*, 65.

16. Timm and Echols, *Schwarze in Deutschland*, 125.

17. See Fehrenbach, *Race after Hitler.*

18. See Höhn, *GIs and Fräuleins.*

19. Günther Kaufmann and Gabriele Droste, *Der weiße Neger vom Hasenbergl* (Munich: Diana, 2004), 37.

20. Kaufmann and Droste, *Der weiße Neger*, 37.

21. Charly Graf and Armin Himmelrath, *Kämpfe für dein Leben: Der Boxer und die Kinder vom Waldhof* (Ostfildern: Patmos, 2011), 42.

22. Kaufmann and Droste, *Der weiße Neger*, 44.

23. Kaufmann and Droste, *Der weiße Neger*, 45.

24. Michael, *Deutsch sein*, 134.

25. Theodor Michael also turned to boxing shortly after World War II to build his confidence and give him skills with which he could defend himself. Michael, *Deutsch sein*, 117.

26. Graf, *Kämpfe für dein Leben*, 25.

27. Graf, *Kämpfe für dein Leben*, 39.

28. Graf, *Kämpfe für dein Leben*, 39.

29. Weheliye, *Phonographies*, 169.

30. Weheliye, *Phonographies*, 169.

31. El-Tayeb, "If You Can't," 480–81.

32. Alexander Weheliye also remarks that global hip-hop is highly influenced by a form of blackness that is specifically American, masculine, and combative. Weheliye, *Phonographies*, 148.

33. Philipp Khabo Köpsell, in discussion with the author, 2014.

34. Dirk Göttsche, "Self-Assertion, Intervention and Achievement: Black German Writing in Postcolonial Perspective," *Orbis Litterarum* 67, no. 2 (2012): 116.

35. Göttsche, "Self-Assertion," 103.

36. Weheliye, *Phonographies*, 165.

37. Philipp Khabo Köpsell, *Die Akte James Knopf* (Münster: Unrast, 2010), 26. This will subsequently be referenced as *JK.* Because Köpsell writes in both German and English and sometimes mixes the two languages, if I have translated anything I will include the original quotes in footnotes so that it is clear what I have translated.

38. Ta-Nehisi Coates describes a similar experience in his award-winning book *Between the World and Me*, where he relates an incident when he speaks up to a white woman for pushing his young son, only to eventually back down to a white man who

comes to her defense and threatens to call the police. Coates argues that blacks in America must always be aware that at any moment, whether or not they behave aggressively, repressive state apparatuses have the right to take their bodies and justify their deaths. Ta-Nehisi Coates, *Between the World and Me* (New York: Spiegel and Grau, 2015).

39. In contrast to the figure Uncle Tom from Harriet Beecher Stowe's novel *Uncle Tom's Cabin*, who is known for his docile and passive nature, whites used the term "anti-Tom" during Reconstruction to symbolize the violent black man who rapes white women.

40. "Ich afrodeutscher Korpus, Träger deutscher Lasten / Strandgut des Atlantiks, Träger deutscher Masken / Ich, ich klage an, die deutschen Medien der Massen, / die aus jedem Schwarzen Mann nen neues Negerimage machen."

41. In *The Souls of Black Folk* (1903), W. E. B. Du Bois uses the "veil" as a metaphor to describe how African Americans' reality is vastly different from that of white Americans. But to function within white society, African Americans must hide their true feelings and emotions behind the veil. Fanon's title *Black Skin, White Masks* (1952) asserts that black people must adopt the norms of white society in order to succeed.

42. "Macher wollen Exotik sehen; Ein Job für Jim Knopf! / Championlover, wenn die Puppenkiste flimmert, / und auch undercover wird er immer daran erinnert. / Und er labert nicht so fresh—er wird deutsch synchronisiert / und wird auf Eddie Murphy, Will Smith und Jamie Foxx kopiert."

43. Julia Voss, "Jim Knopf rettet die Evolutionstheorie," *Frankfurter Allgemeine Zeitung*, December 16, 2008, http://www.faz.net/aktuell/wissen/darwin/wirkung/darwin-jahr-2009-jim-knopf-rettet-die-evolutionstheorie-1741253.html

44. For an analysis of the film *Toxi* and the function of blackness in West German society, see Angelica Fenner, *Race under Reconstruction*.

45. "den lustigen Neger vonne Puppenkiste. Wieheißter . . . / Wir brauchen Jim Knopf!"

46. "Wie, der sitzt noch zwei Jahre ab? Is der jetz Rapgangster?"

47. The films *1 Berlin Harlem* (1974) and *Otomo* (1999), which was actually based on a true story, also perpetuate this link between black men and criminality.

48. "Na, der Halunke . . . Kanna wenigstens keinem die Show stehlen."

49. "Männer! / Wir ham Männer in China, Männer inna Südsee, Samoa, Neu-Guinea, / Männer auf den Solomon-, Männer auf den Marshall-Inseln. / Männer! / Wir ham Männer in Togoland, in Kamerun, in Deutsch-Ost und Deutsch- / Südwest . . . und neuerdings auch Frauen! / Männer!"

50. "Wir haben Munition . . . Wir ham die Wilden in den Zoos gesehen, wir wissen wie die aussehen."

51. "Vorsicht Männer, da gibt's / Kannibalen und Barbaren mit Knochen und Säbeln in den Haaren!"

52. ". . . menschliche Maultiere, Mischlinge, / mendelsche Sensationen und manch einer / wird kaum seine Hose zuhalten können."

53. Heino actually recently recorded a remake of the song in the style of heavy metal that he entitled "Wir lagen vor Madagascar 2014" and included on the album *Schwarz blüht der Ezian* (*The Bavarian Gentian Blossoms in Black*).

54. "Da ist Blut auf den Bohlen im Bureau des Buchhalters, / Blut auf den Büchern,

/ Blut auf den Fenstern, / an den Tüchern, Kaffee am Moskitonetz / Rauch läuft am Lauf der Mauser Richtung / Boden. Ritzen voller Staub / noch vom Bau der Usambara-Bahn Siegel der Gesellschaft, Vorposten des Fortschritts."

55. "die Bürde des Weißen, die Welt zu befrieden / ist irgendwie, irgendwo liegen geblieben."

56. "des Kaisers Kontrolle entgangen / ist das Unterfangen."

57. "Doch das Reich, / werden zukünftige Kanzler plädieren, wird neue / deutsche Kolonien / regieren."

58. May Ayim, "Afrodeutsch I," in *Blues in schwarz weiss* (Berlin: Orlanda Verlag, 2005).

59. "Komm mir nicht mit Blechtrommel, dit war vor vielen Monden, Freund . . ."

60. Sarrazin is a former member of the SPD. His book *Deutschland schafft sich ab* (2010) caused an uproar because of his controversial statements accusing Germany's Muslims of an inability to integrate.

61. Yasemin Yildiz, *Beyond the Mother Tongue: The Postmonolingual Condition* (New York: Fordham University Press, 2012), 7.

62. Michelle Wright, *Becoming Black: Creating Identity in the African Diaspora* (Durham, NC: Duke University Press, 2004), 197.

63. "Ja, wir [Afro-Germans] können deutsch sein—aber wir müssen es nicht . . . dieser Bruch [ist] unumgänglich—und es ist ein Befreieungsmoment." Philipp Khabo Köpsell, ed., *Afro-Shop* (epubli, 2014), 5.

64. Mark Dery, "Black to the Future," in *Flame Wars: The Discourse of Cyberculture*, ed. Mark Dery (Durham, NC: Duke University Press, 1994), 179–222.

65. John Akomfrah and Greg Tate, "Panel Discussion Afrofuturism," in *AfroFictional Interventions: Revisiting the BIGSAS Festival of African(-Diasporic) Literatures, Bayreuth 2011–2013*, ed. Susan Arndt and Nadja Ofuatey-Alazard (Münster: Edition Assemblage, 2014), 255.

66. In fact, Daniel Kojo Schrade highlights Lee Perry as having influenced his work.

67. Akomfrah and Tate, *AfroFictional Interventions*, 251.

68. Akomfrah and Tate, *AfroFictional Interventions*, 251.

69. Dery, "Black to the Future," 180.

70. *The Last Angel of History*, dir. John Akomfrah, Black Studio Film Collective, 1996.

71. Michelle Wright, *The Physics of Blackness: Beyond the Middle Passage Epistemology* (Minneapolis: University of Minnesota Press, 2015), 4.

72. Wright, *The Physics of Blackness*, 14.

73. Judy Davies, "The Futures Market: Marinetti and the Fascists of Milan," in *Visions and Blueprints: Avant-Garde Culture and Radical Politics in Early Twentieth-Century Europe* (Manchester: Manchester University Press, 1988), 83.

74. Davies, "The Futures Market," 85.

75. Davies, "The Futures Market," 82.

76. Davies, "The Futures Market," 82–83.

77. The Futurists' slogan was "war—only hygiene of the world." Davies, "The Futures Market," 82.

78. Akomfrah and Tate, *AfroFictional Interventions*.

79. Mark Dery, "Black to the Future," 22.

80. Köpsell, *Afro-Shop*, 68.

81. There are at least two distinct strands of Afropessimist thought: one is solely concerned with the African continent, while the other is strongly anchored in African American studies and influenced by the works of Orlando Patterson, Kara Keeling, Saidiya Hartman, Frank Wilderson, and Jared Sexton, though it also builds on theoretical texts by non-American authors like Frantz Fanon and Sylvia Wynter. Frank Wilderson describes the latter group of Afropessimists as "theorists of Black positionality who share Fanon's insistence that, though Blacks are indeed sentient beings, the structure of the entire world's semantic field—regardless of cultural and national discrepancies— 'leaving' as Fanon would say, 'existence by the wayside,' is sutured by anti-Black solidarity." Frank Wilderson, *Red, White and Black: Cinema and the Structure of U.S. Antagonisms* (Durham, NC: Duke University Press, 2010), 58. In this chapter, however, I am positioning Köpsell's Afrofuturist work against the former strand of Afropessimism, which suggests there is "something wrong with Africans." But even within this very simplistic notion there are many different threads. Nevertheless, whether an Afropessimist blames the African continent's political, economic, and social problems on colonialism, bad governments, or simply Africans more generally, as Boulou Ebanda de B'béri and P. Eric Louw point out, "The heart of this discourse derives from the fact that Africans are failing to live up to a set of criteria generated by Westerners who want it to develop such a way that the continent would mesh neatly into the globalised economy built by Europeans and Americans over the past two centuries." Boulou Ebanda de B'béri and P. Eric Louw, "Afropessimism: A Genealogy of Discourse," *Critical Arts* 25, no. 3 (2011): 337.

82. Karin Andreasson, "G2: Arts: My Best Shot: Cristina de Middel: 'The Leader of Zambia's 1964 Space Programme Wanted a Woman and Two Cats to Be First to Walk on the Moon,'" *Guardian*, June 12, 2014.

83. "*übersetzt aus einem Dialekt mit einsilbigen Klick-Lauten.*"

84. "Ich sehe Dich / Mit deinen drei Jutebeuteln Einkauf von Edeka / Reeboks und Nail Extensions."

85. See the virtual museum of German brands, *Das erste Virtuelle Markenmuseum*, http://www.markenmuseum.de/index.php?id=633. Fatima El-Tayeb also briefly remarks on Edeka's legacy in *Undeutsch: Die Konstruktion des Anderen in der postmigrantischen Gesellschaft* (Bielefeld: transcript, 2016), 223.

86. "Ich hocke stumm zwischen Accra und Addis Abeba / Im Staub auf einer quietschenden Tellermine / Neben dampfendem Gummy und russischen Helikoptern / Fliegen trinken das Salz meiner Tränen."

87. "Dein Afrika. Ich sitze / Zwischen Accra und Addis Abeba. Ich spiele / Mit den Scherben alter Feuerzeuge . . . / Vielleicht bin ich morgen in Joburg / In der East Gate Mall™ / Lasse mich über die Vorteile eines Blackberrys beraten / Vielleicht auch in Lagos/ Bei der Pediküre und trinke Gin Fizz / Jedoch heute / Nur für diesen einen Moment / Kaue ich Spucke / Starre von Deiner blanken Straßenecke herab."

88. Weheliye notes that "throughout the sixties and seventies, the presence of Black German children in the popular media reflected their construction as dilemmas for Ger-

man society and culture, rather than as subjects, or even members of the national community." Weheliye, *Phonographies*, 171.

89. Graf, *Kämpfe für dein Leben*, 13.

90. Kaufmann and Droste, *Der weiße Neger*, 37.

91. Kaufmann and Droste, *Der weiße Neger*, 38.

92. Ballhaus Naunynstrasse, "We Are Tomorrow: Visionen und Erinnerung anlässlich der Berliner Konferenz von 1884," 2014. Published in conjunction with an arts festival running from November 15, 2014 to February 26, 2015 in Berlin. http://www.ballhausnaunynstrasse.de/pdf/BN_B-Konferenz_32s_235-315_ffin.pdf

93. This desire to free his work from any predetermined subject matter is a hope Köpsell has voiced on several occasions. In a recent interview conducted at the Ballhaus Naunynstrasse with several other black "Kulturschaffender" (culture makers), Köpsell complained that people have begun to see his work as purely political and this political expectation has made them undervalue or even challenge his aesthetic choices. Ballhaus Naunynstrasse, "We Are Tomorrow."

CONCLUSION

1. Alicia Roost, "'Remove Your Mask': Character Psychology in Introspective Musical Theater—Sondheim's *Follies*, LaChiusa's *The Wild Party*, and Stew's *Passing Strange*," *Modern Drama* 57, no. 2 (2014): 229–51.

2. See Ta-Nehisi Coates, "My President Was Black," *Atlantic*, January–February 2017.

3. Damani Partridge, "Citizenship and the Obama Moment in Berlin," *Journal of the International Institute* 16, no. 1 (2008): 5.

4. Partridge, "Citizenship," 5.

5. Partridge, "Citizenship," 5.

6. Mely Kiyak, "Kein Obama, nirgends," in *Transit Deutschland: Debatten zu Nation und Migration*, ed. Deniz Göktürk et al. (Paderborn: Konstanz University Press, 2010), 560.

7. While "Ich bin Berliner" means "I'm a Berliner," inserting the indefinite article "ein" suggested Kennedy was referencing the German jelly donut which is nicknamed "Berliner." Hence the infamous quote, "I am a jelly donut."

8. Sabine Broeck, "The Erotics of African American Endurance, Or: On the Right Side of History? White (West)-German Sentiment between Pornotroping and Civil Rights Solidarity," in Greene and Ortlep, *Germans and African Americans*, 126–40.

9. Sieg discusses a similar instance of cross-racial masquerade in a 1988 production of *La Retour au Désert* in Hamburg that "cast white German actors in the roles of a black African and an Arab." Sieg, *Ethnic Drag*, 1.

10. Nele Obermuller, "Does German Theater Have a Race Problem," *Exberliner*, May 30, 2012, http://www.exberliner.com/articles/does-german-theatre-have-a-race-problem

11. Obermuller, "German Theater."

12. "Germany Elects First Ever Black Mayor," *The Local*, June 2, 2012, http://www.thelocal.de/20120602/42903

13. "In order to surpass abolitionist pornotroping as the hegemonic representation of African Americans as well as other black peoples, European intellectual Weltanschauung need[s] to first come to grips with their pervasive denial of slavery's constitutive function for the Enlightenment." Broeck, "Erotics of African American Endurance," 138.

Filmography

1 Berlin Harlem. Dir. Lothar Lambert. Perf. Claudia Barry and Ortrud Beginnen. 1974.

Abschied von Gestern [Yesterday Girl]. Dir. Alexander Kluge. Perf. Alexandra Kluge. Independent Film, 1966.

Blackboard Jungle. Dir. Richard Brooks. Perf. Glenn Ford and Anne Francis. MGM, 1955.

A Chorus Line. Dir. Richard Attenborough. Perf. Michael Blevins and Yamil Borges. Embassy Pictures, 1975.

The Comedian Harmonists. Dir. Joseph Vilsmaier. Perf. Ben Becker and Heino Ferch. Bavaria Film, 1997.

Das Wunder von Bern [Miracle of Bern]. Dir. Sönke Wortmann. Perf. Louis Klamroth and Peter Lohmeyer. Little Shark Entertainment, 2003.

Die Blechtrommel [The Tin Drum]. Dir. Volker Schlöndorff. Perf. Mario Adorf and David Bennent. Argos Films, 1979.

Die Ehe der Maria Braun [The Marriage of Maria Braun]. Dir. Rainer Werner Fassbinder. Perf. Hanna Schygulla and Klaus Löwitsch. Albatross Film Production, 1979.

Die Frühreifen. Dir. Josef von Báky. Perf. Hedi Brühl and Peter Krauss. Central Cinema Company Film (CCC), 1957.

Die Halbstarken [Teenage Wolfpack]. Dir. Georg Tressler. Perf. Horst Buchholz and Karin Baal. Interwest, 1956.

Die neuen Leiden des jungen W. Dir. Eberhard Itzenplitz. Perf. Klaus Hoffmann and Léonie Thelen. Artus-Film, 1976.

Die Sehnsucht der Veronika Voss [The Longing of Veronika Voss]. Dir. Rainer Werner Fassbinder. Perf. Rosel Zech, and Hilmar Thate. Laura Film, 1981.

Dreckfresser [Dirt for Dinner]. Dir. Branwen Okpako. Perf. Sam Meffire. 2000.

Ich bin ein Elefant, Madame. Dir. Peter Zadek. Perf. Heinz Baumann and Wolfgang Schneider. Iduna Film Produktiongesellschaft, 1969.

If. Dir. Lindsay Anderson. Perf. Malcom McDowell. Memorial Enterprises, 1968.

The Jazz Singer. Dir. Alan Crosland. Perf. Al Jolson and May McAvoy. Warner Bros., 1927.

Jud Süss. Dir. Veit Harlan. Perf. Ferdinand Marian and Kristina Söderbaum. Terra-Filmkunst. 1940.

The Last Angel of History. Dir. John Akromfrah. Perf. George Clinton, Kodwo Eshun, and Edward George. Black Studio Film Archive, 1996.

Nico Icon. Dir. Susanne Ofteringer. Perf. Nico and Christian Aaron Boulogne. Bluehorse Films, 1995.

Omulaule heißt schwarz. Dir. Beatrice Möller, Nicola Hens, and Susanne Radelhof. Hens/Möller/Radelhof, 2003.

Otomo. Dir. Frieder Schlaich. Perf. Isaach de Bankolé and Eva Mattes. Filmgalerie 451,

1999.

Rebel without a Cause. Dir. Nicholas Ray. Perf. James Dean and Natalie Wood. Warner Bros., 1955.

Rock Around the Clock. Dir. Fred F. Sears. Perf. Bill Haley and Rudy Pompilli. Clover Productions, 1956.

Schultze Gets the Blues. Dir. Michael Schorr. Perf. Horst Krause and Harald Warmbrunn. Filmkombinat, 2003.

Günter Walraff—Schwarz auf weiss. Dir. Susanne Jäger and Pagonis Pagonakis. Perf. Günther Walraff. Arte, 2009.

Strozeck. Dir. Werner Herzog. Perf. Bruno S., Eva Mattes, and Clemens Scheitz. Skellig Edition, 1977.

Toxi. Dir. Robert A. Stemmle. Perf. Elfie Fiegert, Paul Bildt, and Johanna Hofer. Fono Film, 1952.

The Wild One. Dir. Laslo Benedek. Perf. Marlon Brando, Mary Murphy, and Robert Keith. Stanley Kramer Productions, 1953.

Wild Style. Dir. Charlie Ahearn. Perf. Easy A.D., A.J. and Almighty K.G. Wild Style, 1983.

Bibliography

Adelson, Leslie. *The Turkish Turn in Contemporary German Literature: Toward a New Critical Grammar of Migration*. New York: Palgrave Macmillan, 2005.

Adorno, Theodor. "On Lyric Poetry and Society." In *Notes to Literature*, edited by Rolf Tiedemann and translated by Shierry Weber Nicholsen, 37–54. New York: Columbia University Press, 1991.

Akomfrah, John, and Greg Tate. "Panel Discussion Afrofuturism." In *AfroFictional Interventions: Revisiting the BIGSAS Festival of African(-Diasporic) Literatures, Bayreuth 2011–2013*, edited by Susan Arndt and Nadja Ofuatey-Alazard, 248–58. Münster: Edition Assemblage, 2014.

Albrecht, Monika. *"Europa ist nicht die Welt": (Post)Kolonialismus in der Literatur und Geschichte der westdeutschen Nachkriegszeit*. Bielefeld: Aisthesis Verlag, 2008.

Alfons, Simon. *Maxi, unser Negerbub*. Bremen: Eilers & Schünemann, 1952.

al-Samarai, Nicola Lauré. "Neither Foreigners Nor Aliens: The Interwoven Stories of Sinti and Roma and Black Germans." *Women in German Yearbook* 20, no. 1 (2004): 163–83.

Anderson, Paul Allen. *Deep River: Music and Memory in Harlem Renaissance Thought*. Durham, NC: Duke University Press, 2001.

Andreasson, Karin. "G2: Arts: My Best Shot: Cristina de Middel: 'The Leader of Zambia's 1964 Space Programme Wanted a Woman and Two Cats to Be First to Walk on the Moon.'" *Guardian*, June 12, 2014.

Andrews, R. C. "The German School-Story: Some Observations on Paul Schalluck and Thomas Valentin." *German Life and Letters* 23 (1970): 103–12.

Appadurai, Arjun. "Disjuncture and Difference in the Global Cultural Economy." In *Modernity at Large: Cultural Explorations of Modernization*, 27–47. Minneapolis: University of Minnesota Press, 1998.

Arndt, Susan, ed. *Afrika Bilder: Studien zu Rassismus in Deutschland*. Münster: Unrast, 2011.

Austerlitz, Saul. "DJ Darky's Deutschland Daze." *Village Voice*, July 9, 2008.

Ayim, May. "Afrodeutsch I." In *Blues in schwarz weiss*. Berlin: Orlanda Verlag, 2005.

Ayim, May. "The Year 1990: Homeland and Unity from an Afro-German Perspective." In *Germany in Transit: Nation and Migration, 1955–2005*, edited by Deniz Göktürk, David Gramling, and Anton Kaes, 126–29. Berkeley: University of California Press, 2007.

Ballhaus Naunynstrasse. "We Are Tomorrow: Visionen und Erinnerung anlässlich der Berliner Konferenz von 1884." 2014.

Baraka, Amiri. *Blues People: Negro Music in White America*. New York: Harper Perennial, 2002.

Baudrillard, Jean. *Simulations*. New York: Semiotext(e), 1983.

B'béri, Boulou Ebanda de, and P. Eric Louw. "Afropessimism: A Genealogy of Discourse." *Critical Arts* 25, no. 3 (2011): 335–46.

Bean, Annemarie, James V. Hatch, and Brooks McNamara, eds. *Inside the Minstrel Mask: Readings in Nineteenth-Century Blackface Minstrelsy.* Middletown, CT: Wesleyan University Press, 1996.

Beatty, Paul. *Slumberland.* New York: Bloomsbury, 2008.

Becker-Cantarino, Barbara. "'The Black Witch': Gender, Sexuality, and Violence in the Tin Drum." In *Approaches to Teaching Grass's "The Tin Drum"*, edited by Monika Shafi, 176–84. New York: Modern Language Association of America, 2008.

Belting, Hans. "Interview: 5. Februar 1999 / February 5, 1999." In *Marcel Odenbach: ach, wie gut, daß niemand weiß*, edited by Udo Kittlemann, 52–69. Cologne: Verlag der Buchhalter Walther König, 1999.

Benjamin, Walter. "On the Mimetic Faculty." In *Walter Benjamin: Selected Writings*, vol. 2, pt. 2, edited by Howard Eiland and Michael Jennings, 720–23. Cambridge, MA: Harvard University Press, 1999.

Benthien, Claudia, and Inge Stephan, eds. *Männlichkeit als Maskerade: kulturelle Inszenierungen vom Mittelalter bis zur Gegenwart.* Cologne: Böhlau, 2003.

Bergmann, Ulrich. ". . . und fürchte mich immer noch vor der Schwarzen Köchin." *Matrix* 36, no. 2 (2014): 128–32.

Biess, Frank. "Survivors of Totalitarianism: Returning POWs and the Reconstruction of Masculine Citizenship in West Germany, 1945–1955." In *The Miracle Years: A Cultural History of West Germany, 1959–1968*, edited by Hanna Schissler, 57–82. Princeton, NJ: Princeton University Press, 2001.

Blaustein, George. "Flight to Germany: Paul Beatty, the Color Line, and the Berlin Wall." *Amerikastudien* 55, no. 4 (2010): 725–38.

Bogdal, Klaus. "Hard-Cold-Fast: Imagining Masculinity in the German Academy, Literature, and the Media." In *Conceptions of Postwar Masculinity*, edited by Roy Jerome, 13–42. Albany: State University of New York Press, 2001.

Bohlman, Philip V. "Landscape—Region—Nation—Reich: German Folk Song in the Nexus of National Identity." In *Music and German National Identity*, edited by Celia Applegate and Pamela Potter, 105–27. Chicago: University of Chicago Press, 2002.

Bowersox, Jeff. *Raising Germans in the Age of Empire: Youth and Colonial Culture, 1871–1914.* Oxford: Oxford University Press, 2013.

Brandes, Holger. "Hegemonic Masculinities in East and West Germany (German Democratic Republic and Federal Republic of Germany)." *Men and Masculinities* 10, no. 2 (2007): 178–96.

Brandes, Ute, and Ann Clark Fehn. "Werther's Children: The Experience of the Second Generation in Ulrich Plenzdorf's Die neuen Leiden des jungen W. and Volker Braun's 'Unvollendete Geschichte.'" *German Quarterly* 56, no. 4 (1983): 608–23.

Brodsky, Patricia Pollock. "The Black Cook as Mater Gloriosa: Grass' *Faust* Parodies in *Die Blechtrommel.*" *Colloquia Germanica* 29 (1996): 235–47.

Broeck, Sabine. "The Erotics of African American Endurance, Or: On the Right Side of History? White (West)-German Sentiment between Pornotroping and Civil Rights Solidarity." In *Germans and African Americans: Two Centuries of Exchange*, edited by Larry Greene and Anke Ortlepp, 126–40. Jackson: University Press of Mississippi, 2010.

Brown, Jacqueline Nassy. "Black Liverpool, Black America, and the Gendering of Diasporic Space." *Cultural Anthropology* 13, no. 2 (1998): 291–325.

Broyard, Bliss. *One Drop: My Father's Hidden Life—a Story of Race and Family Secrets.* New York: Little, Brown, 2007.

Budds, Michael J., ed. *Jazz and the Germans: Essays on the Influence of "Hot" American Idioms on 20th-Century German Music.* Hillsdale, NY: Pendragon Press, 2002.

Butler, Judith. *Gender Trouble: Feminism and the Subversion of Identity.* New York: Routledge, 1990.

Campbell, Bruce. "*Kein schöner Land*: The Spielschar Ekkehard and the Struggle to Define German National Identity in the Weimar Republic." In *Music and German National Identity*, edited by Celia Applegate and Pamela Potter, 128–39. Chicago: University of Chicago Press, 2002.

Campt, Tina. *Other Germans: Black Germans and the Politics of Race, Gender, and Memory in the Third Reich*. Ann Arbor: University of Michigan Press, 2004.

Cantanese, Brandi Wilkins. "Remembering Saartjie Baartman." *Atlantic Studies* 7, no. 1 (2010): 47–62.

Certeau, Michel de. *The Practice of Everyday Life*. Translated by Steven Rendall. Berkeley: University of California Press, 1984.

Chin, Rita, and Heide Fehrenbach, eds. *After the Nazi Racial State: Difference and Democracy in Germany and Europe*. Ann Arbor: University of Michigan Press, 2009.

Clare, Jennifer. "Der 'männliche' Weg zur Revolte? Andreas Baader als denkende, fühlende und handelnde Figur in retrospektiver Literatur." In *Literarische Männlichkeiten und Emotionen*, edited by Toni Tholen and Jennifer Clare, 201–23. Heidelberg: Winter, 2013.

Coates, Ta-Nehisi. *Between the World and Me*. New York: Spiegel and Grau, 2015.

Coates, Ta-Nehisi. "My President Was Black." *Atlantic*, January–February, 2017.

Connell, R. W. *Masculinities*. Berkeley: University of California Press, 2005.

Coury, David. "Transformational Considerations in the Filmic Adaptation of Günter Grass' 'Die Blechtrommel.'" *New German Review* 8 (1992): 74–84.

Currie, Barbara. "Diverging Attitudes in Literary Criticism: The 'Plenzdorf Debate' in the Early 1970s in East and West Germany." *Neophilologus* 79, no. 2 (1995): 283–94.

Davies, Judy. "The Futures Market: Marinetti and the Fascists of Milan." In *Visions and Blueprints: Avant-Garde Culture and Radical Politics in Early Twentieth-Century Europe*, edited by Edward Timms and Peter Collier, 82–97. Manchester: Manchester University Press, 1988.

Delaney, Antoinette T. *Metaphors in Grass' Die Blechtrommel*. New York: Peter Lang, 2004.

Delgado, Richard, and Jean Stefancic. *Critical Race Theory: An Introduction*. New York: New York University Press, 2012.

Dennis, Mike, and Norman LaPorte. *State and Minorities in Communist East Germany*. New York: Berghahn, 2011.

DeNora, Tia. *Music in Everyday Life*. Cambridge: Cambridge University Press, 2000.

Dery, Mark. "Black to the Future." In *Flame Wars: The Discourse of Cyberculture*, edited by Mark Dery, 179–222. Durham, NC: Duke University Press, 1994.

DuBois, W. E. B. *The Souls of Black Folk*. Oxford: Oxford University Press, 2007.

Dyer, Richard. *White*. London: Routledge, 1997.

Echols, Alice. *Shaky Ground: The '60s and Its Aftershocks*. New York: Columbia University Press, 2002.

Eckartshausen, Karl von. "Isogin und Celia, eine Geschichte von einem unsrer schwarzen Brüder aus Afrika, von einem Mohren (1787)." In *Die edlen Wilden: die Verklärung von Indianern, Negern und Südseeinsulanern auf dem Hintergrund der kolonialen Greuel: vom 16. bis zum 20. Jahrhundert*, edited by Gerd Stein, 157–70. Frankfurt am Main: Fischer, 1984.

Ege, Moritz. *Schwarz werden: "Afroamerikanophilie" in den 1960er und 1970er Jahren*. Bielefeld: Transcript, 2007.

Eggers, Maureen Maisha, Susan Arndt, Grada Kilomba, and Peggy Piesche, eds. *Mythen, Masken und Subjekte: kritische Weißseinforschung in Deutschland*. Münster: Unrast, 2005.

Ehnert, Günter, ed. *Hit-Bilanz: deutsche Chart Singles 1956–1980*. Norderstedt: Tarus Press, 2000.

Elam, Harry J., Jr., and Kennell Jackson, eds. *Black Cultural Traffic: Crossroads in Global Performance and Popular Culture*. Ann Arbor: University of Michigan Press, 2005.

Ellis, Trey. "The New Black Aesthetic." *Callaloo 38* (1989): 233–43.

El-Tayeb, Fatima. "'If You Can't Pronounce My Name, You Can Just Call Me Pride': Afro-German Activism, Gender and Hip Hop." *Gender History* 15, no. 3 (2003): 460–86.

El-Tayeb, Fatima. *Undeutsch: Die Konstruktion des Anderen in der postmigrantischen Gesellschaft*. Bielefeld: transcript, 2016.

Erhart, Walter. "Das zweite Geschlecht: 'Männlichkeit,' interdisziplinär." *Internationales Archiv für Sozialgeschichte der deutschen Literatur* 30, no. 2 (2005): 156–232.

Erhart, Walter. *Familienmänner: über den literarischen Ursprung moderner Männlichkeit*. Munich: Wilhelm Fink, 2001.

Erikson, Erik H. "The Problem of Ego Identity." *Journal of the American Psychoanalytic Association* 4 (1956): 56–121.

Erikson, Erik H. "Reflections on the Dissent of Contemporary Youth." *International Journal of Psycho-Analysis* 51, no. 11 (1970): 11–22.

Erler, Annette. "Von Spielmannszügen und Bergsängern im Harz: Musikalische Aktivitäten in einer geteilten Region." In *Musikalische Volkskultur als soziale Chance: Laienmusik und Singtradition als sozialintegratives Feld. Tagungsbericht Hildesheim 94 der Kommission für Lied-, Musik- und Tanzforschung in der Deutschen Gesellschaft für Volkskunde*, edited by Günther Noll and Helga Stein, 341–75. Essen: Verlag die blaue Eule, 1996.

Ernst, Gustav. *Sprache im Film*. Vienna: Wespennest, 1994.

Fanon, Frantz. *Black Skin, White Masks*. Translated by Charles Lam Markmann. New York: Grove Press, 1967.

Fehrenbach, Heide. *Race after Hitler: Black Occupation Children in Postwar Germany and America*. Princeton, NJ: Princeton University Press, 2005.

Fenemore, Mark. *Sex, Thugs and Rock 'n' Roll: Teenage Rebels in Cold-War East Germany*. New York: Berghahn, 2009.

Fenner, Angelica. *Race under Reconstruction in German Cinema: Robert Stemmle's "Toxi"*. Toronto; Buffalo: University of Toronto Press, 2011.

Fischer, Eugen. *Die Rehobother Bastards und das Bastardierungsproblem beim Menschen: anthropologische und ethnographische Studien am Rehobother Bastardvolk in Deutsch-Südwest-Afrika*. Jena: Fischer, 1913.

Fischer-Homberger, Esther. "Ich bin ein Elefant, Madame." *Reformatio* 19, no. 2 (1970): 145–46.

"Frau erhält Jobabsage wegen 'Ossi'-Herkunft." *Der Spiegel*, April 8, 2010. http://www.spiegel.de/wirtschaft/soziales/0,1518,687929,00.html

Gabbard, Krin. *Black Magic: White Hollywood and African American Culture*. New Brunswick, NJ: Rutgers University Press, 2004.

Gemünden, Gerd. "Between Karl May and Karl Marx: The DEFA Indianerfilme." In *Germans and Indians: Fantasies, Encounters, Projections*, edited by Gerd Gemünden, Colin G. Calloway, and Susanne Zantop, 243–56. Lincoln: University of Nebraska Press, 2002.

"Germany Elects First Ever Black Mayor." *The Local*, June 2, 2012. http://www.thelocal.de/20120602/42903

Gerund, Katharina. *Transatlantic Cultural Exchange: African American Women's Art and Activism in West Germany*. Bielefeld: Transcript, 2014.

Gilman, Sander. *On Blackness without Blacks: Essays on the Image of the Black in Germany*. Boston: G.K. Hall, 1982.

Gilroy, Paul. *The Black Atlantic: Modernity and Double Consciousness*. Cambridge, MA: Harvard University Press, 1993.

Gilroy, Paul. *Small Acts: Thoughts on the Politics of Black Culture*. Essex: Serpent's Tail, 1993.

Göktürk, Deniz, David Gramling, and Anton Kaes, eds. *Germany in Transit: Nation and Migration, 1955–2005*. Berkeley: University of California Press, 2007.

Göttsche, Dirk. *Remembering Africa: The Rediscovery of Colonialism in Contemporary German Literature*. Rochester, NY: Camden House, 2013.

Göttsche, Dirk. "Self-Assertion, Intervention and Achievement: Black German Writing in Postcolonial Perspective." *Orbis Litterarum* 67, no. 2 (2012): 83–135.

Graf, Charly, and Armin Himmelrath. *Kämpfe für dein Leben: der Boxer und die Kinder vom Waldhof*. Ostfildern: Patmos, 2011.

Grass, Günter. *Die bösen Köche*. In *Theaterstücke*. Neuwied: Luchterhand, 1970.

Grass, Günter. *Peeling the Onion*. Translated by Michael Henry Heim. Orlando, FL: Harcourt, 2007.

Grass, Günter. *The Tin Drum*. Translated by Breon Mitchell. New York: Mariner Books, 2010.

Greif, Mark. "Positions." In *What Was the Hipster? A Sociological Investigation*, edited by Mark Greif, Kathleen Ross, and Dayna Tortorici, 4–13. New York: n+1 Foundation, 2010.

Grimm, Reinhold, and Amadou Booker Sadji, eds. *Dunkle Reflexe: Schwarzafrikaner und Afro-Amerikaner in der deutschen Erzählkunst des 18. und 19. Jahrhunderts*. Bern: Peter Lang, 1992.

Grimmelshausen. *Simplicissimus*. Stuttgart: Reclam, 1996.

Grist, Leighton. "'The Blues Is the Truth': The Blues, Modernity, and the British Blues Boom." In *Cross the Water Blues: African American Music in Europe*, edited by Neil A. Wynn, 202–17. Jackson: University of Mississippi Press, 2007.

Grossmann, Atina. "The 'Big Rape': Sex and Sexual Violence, War, and Occupation in German Post–World War II Memory and Imagination." In *Gender and the Long Postwar: The United States and the Two Germanys, 1945–1989*, edited by Karen Hagemann and Sonya Michel, 31–50. Baltimore: Johns Hopkins University Press, 2014.

Haas, Astrid. "A Raisin in the East: African American Civil Rights Drama in GDR Scholarship and Theater Practice." In *Germans and African Americans: Two Centuries of Exchange*, edited by Larry Greene and Anke Ortlepp, 166–84. Jackson: University Press of Mississippi, 2010.

Hall, Stuart. "What Is This 'Black' in Black Popular Culture?" In *Stuart Hall: Critical Dialogues in Cultural Studies*, edited by David Morley and Kaun-Hsing Chen, 465–75. London: Routledge, 1996.

Harvard, Joe. *The Velvet Underground and Nico*. New York: Continuum, 2004.

Hauze, Emily. "Keyed Fantasies: Music, the Accordion and the American Dream in *Stroszek* and *Schultze Gets the Blues*." *German Life and Letters* 62, no. 1 (2009): 84–95.

Hebdige, Dick. *Subculture: The Meaning of Style*. London: Routledge, 1979.

Heinrichs, Jürgen. "Mixed Media, Mixed Identities: The Universal Aesthetics of Marc Brandenburg." In *From Black to Schwarz: Cultural Crossovers between African America and Germany*, edited by Maria I. Dietrich and Jürgen Heinrichs, 309–32. Berlin: LIT Verlag, 2010.

Heinrichs, Willi. *Gottes zweite Garnitur*. Munich: Berterlsman, 1962.

Herzog, Dagmar. *Sex after Fascism: Memory and Morality in Twentieth Century Germany*. Princeton, NJ: Princeton University Press, 2007.

Heylin, Clinton, ed. *All Yesterdays' Parties: The Velvet Underground in Print, 1966–1971*. Cambridge, MA: Da Capo Press, 2005.

Hildreth, Richard. *The White Slave*. London: C.H. Clarke, 1890.

Höhn, Maria. *GIs and Fräuleins: The American-German Encounter in 1950s West Germany*. Chapel Hill: University of North Carolina Press, 2002.

Höhn, Maria, and Martin Klimke. *A Breath of Freedom: The Civil Rights Struggle, African American GIs and Germany*. New York: Palgrave Macmillan, 2010.

hooks, bell. *Outlaw Culture: Resisting Representations*. New York: Routledge, 2006.

hooks, bell. *Yearning: Race, Gender and Cultural Politics*. New York: Routledge, 2015.

Horak, Greta. *Tiroler Kinderleben in Reim und Spiel: Volksmusik in Tirol.* Innsbruck: Innsbruck Eigenverl. d. Inst. für Tiroler Musikforschung, 1986.

Hunnicutt, Susan E. "'The Werther-Pistol Killed Me!': Understanding Ulrich Plenzdorf's Novel Die neuen Leiden des jungen W. as a Cult Book." *Focus on Literatur: A Journal for German-Language Literature* 5, no. 1 (1998): 13–26.

Husmann-Kastein, Jana. "Schwarz-Weiß. Farb- und Geschlechtssymbolik in den Anfängen der Rassenkonstruktionen." In *Weiß—Weißsein—Whiteness: kritische Studien zu Gender und Rassismus,* edited by Martina Tißberger, Gabriele Dietze, Daniela Hrzán, and Jana Husmann-Kastein, 43–60. Frankfurt am Main: Peter Lang, 2009.

Hutchinson, Peter. "Plenzdorf, *Die neuen Leiden des jungen W.*" In *Landmarks in the German Novel,* edited by Peter Hutchinson and Michael Minden, 61–76. Bern: Peter Lang, 2010.

"Ist die schwarze Köchin da?" *Volksliederarchiv.* 2009, http://www.volksliederarchiv.de/ist-die-schwarze-koechin-da-kreisspiel/

Jackson, Kennell. "Introduction: Travelling While Black." In *Black Cultural Traffic: Crossroads in Global Performance and Popular Culture,* edited by Harry J. Elam Jr. and Kennell Jackson, 1–42. Ann Arbor: University of Michigan Press, 2008.

Jerome, Roy, ed. *Conceptions of Postwar German Masculinity.* Albany: State University of New York Press, 2001.

John, D. G. "Ulrich Plenzdorf's *Die neuen Leiden des jungen W.:* The Death of a Fool." *Modern Drama* 23 (1980): 33–43.

Kabić, Slavija, and Eldi Grubišić Pulišelić. "'Ich Idiot wollte immer der Sieger sein': Der Anti-Held Edgar Wibeau aus Ulrich Plenzdorfs Erzählung 'Die neuen Leiden des jungen W.'" *Zagreber Germanistische Beiträge: Jahrbuch für Literatur- und Sprachwissenschaft* 16 (2007): 49–75.

Kaiser, Georg. "From Morning to Midnight." In *German Expressionist Plays,* edited by Ernst Schürner, 146–97. New York: Continuum, 2002.

Kampmüller, Otto. *Oberösterreichische Kinderspiele.* Linz: Oberösterreichischer Landesverlag in Komission, 1965.

Karremann, Isabel. "Männlichkeitsforschung und Literatur(wissenschaft) in Deutschland." *Jahrbuch für finnisch-deutsche Literaturbeziehungen* 36 (2004): 33–46.

Kater, Michael H. *Different Drummers: Jazz in the Culture of Nazi Germany.* Oxford: Oxford University Press, 1992.

Kaufmann, Günther, and Gabriele Droste. *Der weiße Neger vom Hasenbergl.* Munich: Diana Verlag, 2004.

Ketels, Martin, ed. *Liederbuch.* Ulm: J. Ebner, 1984.

Kiyak, Mely. "Kein Obama, nirgends." In *Transit Deutschland: Debatten zu Nation und Migration,* edited by Deniz Göktürk, David Gramling, Anton Kaes, and Andreas Langenohl, 560–61. Paderborn: Konstanz University Press, 2010.

Klimke, Martin. *The Other Alliance: Student Protest in West Germany and the United States.* Princeton, NJ: Princeton University Press, 2010.

Kohns, Oliver. "An Aesthetics of the Unbearable: The Cult of Masculinity and the Sublime in Ernst Jünger's *Der Kampf als inneres Erlebnis* (Battle as an Inner Experience)." *Image and Narrative* 14, no. 3 (2013): 141–50.

Kolko, Beth, Lisa Nakamura, and Gilbert B. Rodman, eds. *Race in Cyberspace.* New York: Routledge 2000.

Kónya-Jobs, Nathalie. "'Ist die Schwarze Köchin da?': Angst und Raum in Günter Grass' 'Die Blechtrommel.'" *Transcarpathica* 9 (2010): 249–59.

Köpsell, Philipp Khabo, ed. *Afro Shop.* Berlin: epubli, 2014.

Köpsell, Philipp Khabo. *Die Akte James Knopf: Afrodeutsche Wort- und Streitkunst.* Münster: Unrast, 2010.

Köpsell, Philipp Kabo, and Asoka Esuruoso. *Arriving in the Future: Stories of Home and Exile*. Berlin: epubli, 2014.

Kosta, Barbara. "*Väterliteratur*, Masculinity, and History: The Melancholic Texts of the 1980s." In *Conceptions of Postwar German Masculinity*, edited by Roy Jerome, 219–41. Albany: State University of New York Press, 2001.

Kretschmer, Paul. *Wortgeographie der hochdeutschen Umgangsprache*. Göttingen: Vandenhoeck and Ruprecht, 1969.

Krimmer, Elisabeth. "'Ein Volk von Opfern?' Germans as Victims in Günter Grass's Die Blechtrommel and im Krebsgang." *Seminar* 44, no. 2 (208): 272–90.

Krugler, David F. *The Voice of America and the Domestic Propaganda Battles, 1945–1953*. Columbia: University of Missouri Press, 2000.

Kunze, Reiner. *Die wunderbaren Jahre: Lyrik, Prosa, Dokumente*. Edited by Karl Corino. Frankfurt am Main: Büchergilde Gutenberg, 1978.

Lacquer, Thomas. *Auf den Leib geschrieben: die Inszenierung der Geschlechter von der Antike bis Freud*. Frankfurt am Main: Campus, 1992.

Ladson-Billings, Gloria. "Just What Is Critical Race Theory and What Is It Doing in a Nice Field Like Education?" *International Journal of Qualitative Studies in Education* 11, no. 1 (1998): 7–24.

Lamb, Stephen, and Anthony Phelan. "Weimar Culture: The Birth of Modernism." In *German Cultural Studies: An Introduction*, edited by Rob Burns, 53–100. Oxford: Oxford University Press, 1995.

Langston, Richard. "Roll Over Beethoven! Chuck Berry! Mick Jagger! 1960s Rock, the Myth of Progress, and the Burden of National Identity in West Germany." In *Sound Matters: Essays on the Acoustics of Modern German Culture*, edited by Nora M. Alter and Lutz Koepnick, 184–96. New York: Berghahn Books, 2004.

Lennox, Sara. "Claiming Blackness in Germany." In *The Meaning of Culture: German Studies in the 21st Century*, edited by Martin Kagel and Laura Tate Kagel, 177–92. Hannover: Werhahn, 2009.

Lennox, Sara. "Reading Transnationally: The GDR and Black American Writers." *German Monitor* 74 (2011): 111–29.

Lennox, Sara, ed. *Remapping Black Germany: New Perspectives on Afro-German History, Politics and Culture*. Amherst: University of Massachusetts Press, 2016.

Lorde, Audre. Foreword to *Showing Our Colors: Afro-German Women Speak Out*, edited by Katharina Oguntoye, May Opitz, and Dagmar Schultz, vii–xiv. Amherst: University of Massachusetts Press, 1992.

Lorenz, Matthias N. "'von Katz und Maus und mea culpa.'" Über Günter Grass' Waffen-SS-Vergangenheit und 'Die Blechtrommel' als moralische Zäsur. In *Wendejahr 1959*, edited by Matthias N. Lorenz, 281–305. Bielefeld: Aisthesis-Verlag, 2011.

Lott, Eric. *Love and Theft: Blackface Minstrelsy and the American Working Class*. New York: Oxford University Press, 1995.

Lotz, Rainer. *Black People: Entertainers of African Descent in Europe and Germany*. Bonn: Birgit Lotz Verlag, 1997.

Lusane, Clarence. *Hitler's Black Victims: The Historical Experiences of Afro-Germans, European Blacks, Africans, and African Americans in the Nazi Era*. New York: Routledge, 2002.

Lützeler, Paul. *Schriftsteller und "Dritte Welt": Studien zum postkolonialen Blick*. Tübingen: Stauffenberg, 1998.

Maase, Kasper. *BRAVO Amerika. Erkundungen zur Jugendkultur der Bundesrepublik in den fünfziger Jahren*. Hamburg: Junius, 1992.

Maihofer, Andrea, Klaus Theweleit, and Nina Degele. "Das moderne männliche Subjekt im Anschluss an Adorno, Horkheimer und Foucault." *Freiburger GeschlechterStudien* 21 (2007): 329–67.

242   Bibliography

Mailer, Norman. *The White Negro*. San Francisco: City Lights, 1957.

Mallinckrodt, Rebekka von. "There Are No Slaves in Prussia?" In *Slavery Hinterland: Transatlantic Slavery and Continental Europe, 1680–1850*, edited by Felix Brahm and Eve Rosenhaft, 109–32. Woodbridge, Suffolk, UK: Boydell Press, 2016.

Martin, Peter. *Schwarze Teufel, edle Mohren*. Hamburg: Hamburger Edition, 2001.

Massaquoi, Hans-Jürgen. *Destined to Witness: Growing Up Black in Nazi Germany*. New York: Perennial, 1999.

Mbembe, Achille. *On the Postcolony*. Berkeley: University of California Press, 2001.

Mercer, Kobena. "Skin Head Sex Thing: Racial Difference and the Homoerotic Imaginary." In *Masculine Studies Reader*, edited by Rachel Adams and David Savran, 188–200. Malden, MA: Blackwell, 2002.

Mews, Siegfried. *Günter Grass and His Critics: From "The Tin Drum" to "Crabwalk"*. Cambridge: Camden House, 2008.

Michael, Theodor. *Deutsch sein und schwarz dazu: Erinnerungen eines Afro-Deutschen*. Munich: Deutscher Taschenbuchverlag, 2013.

Michelsen, Peter. "Oskar oder das Monstrum: Reflexionen über 'Die Blechtrommel' von Günter Grass." *Neue Rundschau* 84 (1972): 722–40.

Mills, Charles. *Blackness Visible: Essays on Philosophy and Race*. Ithaca, NY: Cornell University Press, 1998.

Mitscherlich, Alexander, and Margarete Mitscherlich. *Die Unfähigkeit zu trauern: Grundlagen kollektiven Handelns*. Munich: Piper, 1967.

Moore, Suzanne. "Getting a Bit of the Other: The Pimps of Postmodernism." In *Male Order: Unwrapping Masculinity*, edited by Rowena Chapman and Jonathan Rutherford, 165–92. London: Lawrence and Wishart, 1988.

Müller-Schwefe, Hans-Ulrich. *Männersachen—Verständigungstexte*. Frankfurt am Main: Suhrkamp, 1979.

Muniz de Faria, Yara-Col Lemke. *Zwischen Fürsorge und Ausgrenzung: afrodeutsche "Besatzungskinder" im Nachkriegsdeutschland*. Berlin: Metropol, 2002.

Nagl, Tobias. *Die unheimliche Maschine: Rasse und Repräsentation im Weimarer Kino*. Munich: Edition Text und Kritik, 2009.

Neal, Mark Anthony. *Soul Babies: Black Popular Culture and the Post-soul Aesthetic*. New York: Routledge, 2002.

Neal, Mark Anthony. *What the Music Said: Black Popular Music and Black Public Culture*. New York: Routledge 1999.

Nitschack, Horst. "Modernisierung als Bedrohung der Männlichkeit bei E. Jünger, J.M. Arguedas, und J.L. Borges." *Brückenschlag* (2002): 232–40.

Obermuller, Nele. "Does German Theater Have a Race Problem?" *Exberliner*, May 30, 2012. http://www.exberliner.com/articles/does-german-theatre-have-a-race-problem

Oji, Chima. *Unter die Deutschen gefallen*. Wuppertal: Peter Hammer Verlag, 1992.

Olster, Stacey. "Inconstant Harmony in 'The Tin Drum.'" *Studies in the Novel* 73, no. 1 (1982): 66–81.

Pakendorf, Gunter. "Die gehäutete Zwiebel oder Dichtung und Wahrheit bei Günter Grass." *Acta Germanica* 35 (2007): 53–66.

Partridge, Damani. "Citizenship and the Obama Moment in Berlin." *Journal of the International Institute* 16, no. 1 (2008): 4–5.

Partridge, Damani. *Hypersexuality and Headscarves: Race, Sex and Citizenship in the New Germany*. Bloomington: Indiana University Press, 2012.

Paul, Heike. "Cultural Mobility between Boston and Berlin: How Germans Have Read and Reread Narratives of American Slavery." In *Cultural Mobility: A Manifesto*, edited by Stephen Greenblatt, 122–71. Cambridge: Cambridge University Press, 2005.

Pezold, Klaus. "Günter Grass' *Blechtrommel* in der Literaturgeschichte." *Germanica Wratislaviensia* 81 (1990): 9–18.

Piesche, Peggy. "Black and German? East German Adolescents before 1989: A Retrospective View of a 'Non-existent Issue' in the GDR." In *The Cultural After-Life of East Germany: New Transnational Perspectives*, edited by Leslie A. Adelson, 37–59. Washington, DC: American Institute for Contemporary German Studies, 2002.

Pirro, Robert. "Tragedy, Surrogation and the Significance of African-American Culture in Postunification Germany: An Interpretation of *Schultze Gets the Blues*." *German Politics and Society* 26, no. 88 (2008): 69–92.

Plenzdorf, Ulrich. *The New Sufferings of Young W.* Translated by Kenneth P. Wilcox. Long Grove, IL: Waveland Press, 1996.

Poiger, Ute G. *Jazz, Rock, and Rebels: Cold War Politics and American Culture in a Divided Germany.* Berkeley: University of California, 2000.

Poikane-Daumke, Aija. *African Diasporas: Afro-German Literature in the Context of the African American Experience.* Berlin: LIT Verlag, 2006.

Prickett, David James. "The Acceleration of the Masculine in Early-Twentieth-Century Berlin." *German Life and Letters* 65, no. 1 (2012): 20–35.

Quinn, Eithne. "'Tryin' to Get Over': *Super Fly*, Black Politics, and Post-Civil Rights Film Enterprise." *Cinema Journal* 49, no. 2 (2010): 86–105.

Rath, Wolfgang. *Not am Mann: zum Bild des Mannes im deutschen Gegenwartsroman.* Heidelberg: C. Winter, 1987.

Rauhut, Michael. "Lass es bluten: Blues-Diskurse in West und Ost." In *Ich hab' den Blues schon etwas länger: Spuren einer Musik in Deutschland*, edited by Michael Rauhut und Reinhart Lorenz, 108–21. Berlin: Christoph Links Verlag, 2008.

Rauhut, Michael, and Thomas Kochan, eds. *Bye Bye, Lübben City: Bluesfreaks, Tramps und Hippies in der DDR.* Berlin: Schwarzkopf and Schwarzkopf, 2004.

Reid-Pharr, Robert. *Once You Go Black: Choice, Desire, and the Black American Intellectual.* New York: New York University Press, 2007.

Rellstab, Daniel. "Jugendsprache verstehen in den 1960er Jahren: Thomas Valentins Schulroman 'Die Unberatenen' (1963)." In *Kannitverstan: Bausteine zu einer nachbabylonischen Herme(neu)tik: Akten einer germanistischen Tagung vom Oktober 2012*, edited by André Schnyder, 397–416. Munich: Iudicium, 2013.

Rickels, Laurence A. "*Die Blechtrommel*: zwischen Shelmen- und Bildungsroman." *Amsterdamer Beiträge zur neueren Germanistik* 20 (1986): 109–32.

Robinson, Amy. "It Takes One to Know One: Passing and Communities of Common Interest." *Critical Inquiry* 20, no. 4 (1994): 715–36.

Rogin, Michael Paul. *Blackface, White Noise: Jewish Immigrants in the Hollywood Melting Pot.* Berkeley: University of California Press, 1996.

Roost, Alicia. "'Remove Your Mask': Character Psychology in Introspective Musical Theater—Sondheim's *Follies*, LaChiusa's *The Wild Party*, and Stew's *Passing Strange*." *Modern Drama* 57, no. 2 (2014): 229–51.

Rosson, Chester. "Some Thoughts on the Survival of German Music in Texas." In *Musikalische Volkskultur als soziale Chance*, edited by Günther Noll, 159–70. Essen: Die blaue Eule, 1996.

Sarrazin, Thilo. *Deutschland schafft sich ab: Wie wir unser Land auf Spiel setzen.* Munich: Deutsche Verlags-Anstalt, 2010.

Schäfer, Frank, ed. *Kultbücher: von "Schatzinsel" bis "Pooh's Corner": eine Auswahl.* Berlin: Schwarzkopf and Schwarzkopf, 2000.

Schlüter, Heinz, ed. *Thomas-Valentin-Lesebuch.* Paderborn: Igel Verlag Literatur, 1997.

Schmidt, Christian. "Dissimulating Blackness: The Degenerative Satires of Paul Beatty and

Percival Everett." In *Post-soul Satire: Black Identity after Civil Rights*, edited by Derek C. Maus and James J. Donahue, 150–61. Jackson: University of Mississippi Press, 2014.

Schroer, Timothy L. *Recasting Race after World War II: Germans and African Americans in American-Occupied Germany*. Boulder: University Press of Colorado, 2007.

Schweinfurth, Elisa. "'They Looked German, Albeit with Even Tighter Pants and Uglier Shoes, but There Was Something Different about Them': The Function of East and West Germany and the Fall of the Berlin Wall in Paul Beatty's *Slumberland*." *COPAS: Current Objectives of Postgraduate American Studies* 11 (2010). http://copas.uni-regensburg.de/article/view/123/147

Scott, Joan W. "'Entre braguette'—Notes on the Translation of Gender." In *Border Crossings: Translation Studies and Other Disciplines*. Edited by Yves Hambier and Luc van Doorslaer. Amsterdam: Philadelphia John Benjamins Publishing, 2016.

Sebald, W. G. *On the Natural History of Destruction*. Translated by Anthea Bell. New York: Random House, 2003.

Seibert, Nils. *Vergessene Proteste: Internationalismus und Antirassismus 1964–1983*. Münster: Unrast, 2008.

Shohat, Ella, and Robert Stam. *Unthinking Eurocentrism: Multiculturalism and the Media*. London: Routledge, 1994.

Short, John Phillip. *Magic Lantern Empire: Colonialism and Society in Germany*. Ithaca, NY: Cornell University Press, 2012.

Sidran, Ben. *Black Talk*. New York: Da Capo Press, 1983.

Sieg, Katrin. *Ethnic Drag: Performing Race, Nation, Sexuality in West Germany*. Ann Arbor: University of Michigan Press, 2002.

Siegfried, Detlef. "Authentisch schwarz: Blues in der Gegenkultur um 1970." In *Ich hab' den Blues schon etwas länger*, edited by Michael Rauhut and Reinhard Lorenz, 216–27. Berlin: Christoph Links Verlag, 2008.

Siegfried, Detlef. *Time Is on My Side: Konsum und Politik in der westdeutschen Jugendkultur der 6oer Jahre*. Göttingen: Wallstein Verlag, 2006.

Slobodian, Quinn. *Foreign Front: Third World Politics in Sixties West Germany*. Durham, NC: Duke University Press, 2012.

Slobodian, Quinn. "Socialist Chromatism: Race, Racism, and the Racial Rainbow in East Germany." In *Comrades of Color: East Germany in the Cold War World*, edited by Quinn Slobodian, 23–42. New York: Berghahn, 2015.

Smith, William Gardner. *The Last of the Conquerors*. Chatham, NJ: Chatham Bookseller, 1973.

Snead, James. "On Repetition in Black Culture." In *Racist Traces and Other Writings: European Pedigrees / African Contagions*, edited by Kara Keeling, Colin MacCabe, and Cornel West, 11–33. New York: Palgrave Macmillan, 2003.

Sollors, Werner. *The Temptation of Despair: Tales of the 1940s*. Cambridge, MA: Harvard University Press, 2014.

Solórzano, Daniel G. "Critical Race Theory, Race and Gender, and the Experience of Chicana and Chicano Scholars." *Qualitative Studies in Education* 11, no. 1 (1998): 121–36.

Stallings, L. H. "Sampling the Sonics of Sex (Funk) in Paul Beatty's *Slumberland*." In *Contemporary African American Literature: The Living Canon*, edited by Lovalerie King and Shirley Moody-Turner, 189–212. Bloomington: Indiana University Press, 2013.

Steinecke, Hartmut. "Nachwort." In *Die Unberatenen*, by Thomas Valentin. Oldenberg: Igel Verlag, 1999.

Stewart, Mark. *Passing Strange: The Complete Book and Lyrics of the Broadway Musical*. New York: Applause Theatre and Cinema Books, 2008.

Stiftung der Geschichte der Bundesrepublik in Deutschland and Bundeszentrale für politische Bildung. *Rock! Jugend und Musik in Deutschland*. Berlin: Ch. Links Verlag, 2005.

Stokes, Martin. "Introduction: Ethnicity, Identity and Music." In *Ethnicity, Identity and Music*, edited by Martin Stokes, 1–27. Oxford: Berg, 1994.

Stratton, Jon. "Jews, Punk and the Holocaust: From the Velvet Underground to the Ramones—the Jewish-American Story." *Popular Music* 24, no. 1 (2005): 79–105.

Taylor, Charles, ed. *Multiculturalism: Examining the Politics of Recognition*. Princeton, NJ: Princeton University Press, 1994.

Theweleit, Klaus. *Male Fantasies*. Translated by Stephen Conway in collaboration with Erica Carter and Chris Turner. 2 vols. Minneapolis: University of Minnesota Press, 1989.

Tholen, Toni. "Perspektiven der Erforschung des Zusammenhangs von literarischen Männlichkeiten und Emotionen." In *Literarische Männlichkeiten und Emotionen*, edited by Toni Tholen and Jennifer Clare, 9–25. Heidelberg: Winter, 2013.

Thurman, Kira. "A History of Black Musicians in Germany and Austria, 1870–1961: Race, Performance, and Reception." PhD diss., University of Rochester, 2013.

Till, Rupert. "The Blues Blueprint: The Blues in the Music of the Beatles, the Rolling Stones, and Led Zepplin." In *Cross the Water Blues: African American Music in Europe*, edited by Neil A. Wynn, 183–201. Jackson: University of Mississippi, 2007.

Timm, Karin, and DuRell Echols. *Schwarze in Deutschland: Protokolle*. Munich: Piper and Co. Verlag, 1973.

Tißberger, Martina, Gabriele Dietze, Daniela Hrzán, and Jana Husmann-Kastein, eds. *Weiß—Weißsein—Whiteness*. Frankfurt am Main: Peter Lang, 2006.

Tisserand, Michael. *The Kingdom of Zydeco*. New York: Arcade Publishing, 1998.

Todd, Loretta. "Notes on Appropriation." *Parallelogramme* 16, no. 1 (1990): 24–33.

Trappe, Heike, Rachel A. Rosenfeld, and Janet C. Gornick. "Gender and Work in Germany: Before and after Reunification." *Annual Review of Sociology* 30 (2004): 103–24.

Unbehauen, Peter. *Daß ihr euch ja nich' schietig macht. 111 Lieder und Spiele von Hamburger Straßen und Höfen*. Hamburg: Dölling and Galitz, 2000.

Valentin, Thomas. *Die Fahndung*. Hamburg: Classen, 1962.

Valentin, Thomas. *Die Unberatenen*. Oldenburg: Igel Verlag, 1999.

Valentin, Thomas. *Hölle für Kinder*. Hamburg: Classen, 1961.

Vilsmaier, Joseph. *Comedian Harmonists: Eine Legende kehrt zurück: Der Film*. Leipzig: Gustav Kiepenheuer Verlag, 1998.

Vlagopoulos, Penny. "Rewriting America: Kerouac's Nation of *Underground Monsters*." In *On the Road: The Original Scroll*, edited by Howard Cunnel, 53–68. New York: Viking, 2007.

von Flotow, Luise, and Joan W. Scott. "'Entre braguette'—Notes on the Translation of Gender." In *Border Corssings: Translation Studies and Other Disciplines*, edited by Yves Hambier and Luc van Doorslaer, 349–74. Amsterdam: Philadelphia John Benjamins Publishing, 2016. 355–56.

Voss, Julia. "Jim Knopf rettet die Evolutionstheorie." *Frankfurter Allgemeine Zeitung*, December 16, 2008. http://www.faz.net/aktuell/wissen/darwin/wirkung/darwin-jahr-2009-jim-knopf-rettet-die-evolutionstheorie-1741253.html

Voss, Thorsten. "Schmerz und seine stoisch-heroische Kompensation als Konstrukt soldatischer Maskulinität bei Alfred de Vigny, Ernst Jünger und Céline." In *Schmerzdifferenzen: physisches Leid und Gender in kultur- und literaturwissenschaftlicher Perspektive*, edited by Iris Hermann and Anne-Rose Meyer, 169–89. Königstein: Ulrike Helmer Verlag, 2006.

Ward, Andrew. *Dark Midnight When I Rise: The Story of the Jubilee Singers, Who Introduced the World to the Music of Black America*. New York: Farrar, Straus and Giroux, 2000.

Weheliye, Alexander. "My Volk to Come: Peoplehood in Recent Diaspora Discourse and Afro-German Popular Music." In *Black Europe and the African Diaspora*, edited by Darlene Hine Clark, Trica Danielle Keaton, and Stephen Small, 161–79. Urbana: University of Illinois Press, 2009.

Weheliye, Alexander. *Phonographies: Grooves in Sonic Afro-modernity.* Durham, NC: Duke University Press, 2005.

Westdickenberg, Michael. "'Es ist zu empfehlen, dem Buch ein Nachwort über die Alternative beizugeben': Veröffentlichungsstrategien und Literaturzensur westdeutscher belleristischer Literatur in der DDR am Beispiel von Thomas Valentins Roman *Die Unberatenen.*" *Internationales Archiv für Sozialgeschichte der deutschen Literatur* 28, no. 1 (2003): 88–110.

Wicke, Peter. "Die Leiden des weißen Mannes: Konstruktionen von Authenzität in der Geschichte des Blues." In *Ich hab' den Blues schon etwas länger: Spuren einer Musik in Deutschland,* edited by Michael Rauhut und Reinhart Lorenz, 243–53. Berlin: Christoph Links Verlag, 2008.

Wicke, Peter. *Rock Music: Culture, Aesthetics and Sociology.* Cambridge: Cambridge University Press, 1987.

Wilderson, Frank. *Red, White and Black: Cinema and the Structure of U.S. Antagonisms.* Durham, NC: Duke University Press, 2010.

Williams, Linda. *Playing the Race Card: Melodramas of Black and White from Uncle Tom to O.J. Simpson.* Princeton, NJ: Princeton University Press, 2001.

Wipplinger, Jonathan. "The Racial Ruse: On Blackness and Blackface Comedy in *Fin-de-Siècle* Germany." *German Quarterly* 84, no. 4 (2011): 457–76.

Witts, Richard. *The Velvet Underground.* Bloomington: Indiana University Press, 2006.

Woolf, Brandon. "Negotiating The 'Negro Problem': Stew's Passing (Made) Strange." *Theater Journal* 62, no. 2 (2010): 197–207.

Wright, Michelle. *Becoming Black: Creating Identity in the African Diaspora.* Durham, NC: Duke University Press, 2004.

Wright, Michelle. "Others-from-Within from Without: Afro-German Subject Formation and the Challenge of a Counter-discourse." *Callaloo* 26, no. 2 (2003): 296–305.

Wright, Michelle. *The Physics of Blackness: Beyond the Middle Passage Epistemology.* Minneapolis: University of Minnesota Press, 2015.

Wynn, Neil A., ed. *Cross the Water Blues: African American Music in Europe.* Jackson: University Press of Mississippi, 2007.

Yildiz, Yasemin. *Beyond the Mother Tongue: The Postmonolingual Condition.* New York: Fordham University Press, 2012.

Young, James O. *Cultural Appropriation and the Arts.* Malden, MA: Blackwell, 2008.

Zadek, Peter. *My Way: eine Autobiographie 1926–1969.* Cologne: Kiepenheuer and Witsch, 1998.

Zak, Albin, and Albin Zak III. *The Velvet Underground Companion: Four Decades of Commentary.* New York: Schirmer Trade Books, 2000.

Zantop, Susanne. *Colonial Fantasies: Conquest, Family, and Nation in Precolonial Germany, 1770–1870.* Durham, NC: Duke University Press, 1997.

Index

Page numbers in italics denote a figure.